FINDING

SERENITY

IN THE

AGE OF

ANXIETY

FINDING
SERENITY
IN THE
AGE OF
ANXIETY

ROBERT GERZON

BANTAM 🐓 BOOKS

NEW YORK   TORONTO   LONDON
SYDNEY   AUCKLAND

This edition contains the complete text
of the original hardcover edition.
NOT ONE WORD HAS BEEN OMITTED.

FINDING SERENITY IN THE AGE OF ANXIETY
A Bantam Book / published by arrangement with Macmillan, Inc.

PUBLISHING HISTORY
Macmillan, Inc. edition published 1997
Bantam trade edition / May 1998

Bantam Books are published by Bantam Books, a division of Bantam
Doubleday Dell Publishing Group, Inc. Its trademark, consisting of
the words "Bantam Books" and the portrayal of a rooster, is Registered
in U.S. Patent and Trademark Office and in other countries.
Marca Registrada. Bantam Books, 1540 Broadway, New York,
New York 10036.

PRINTED IN THE UNITED STATES OF AMERICA
FFG   10   9   8   7   6   5   4   3   2   1

To my father:
Koert Gerzon, Ph.D.

Contents

The problem of anxiety is a nodal point, linking
up all kinds of most important questions; a riddle,
of which the solution must cast a flood of light
upon our whole mental life.

—SIGMUND FREUD

This is an adventure that every human being must go
through—to learn to be anxious in order that he may not
perish . . . Whoever has learned to be anxious in the right
way has learned the ultimate . . . the more profoundly
he is in anxiety, the greater is the man . . . Then anxiety
enters into his soul and searches out everything and anxiously
torments everything finite and petty out of him, and then
it leads him where he wants to go . . . [Thus] the individual
through anxiety is educated into faith.

—SØREN KIERKEGAARD

Fear is an instructor of great sagacity.

—RALPH WALDO EMERSON

Life is suffering.

—BUDDHA

Let one who seeks not stop seeking until one finds.
When one finds, one will become anxious.
When one is anxious, one will be awestruck
and will enter the kingdom.

—JESUS

Introduction

Serenity? In today's Age of Anxiety?

Yes.

True serenity may be both more necessary and more possible in today's anxious and stressful age than at any other time in history. Although anxiety is one of the most profound problems facing human beings, it also presents us with our greatest opportunity. Anxiety keeps us from being the best we can be, yet it is also the source of our greatest gifts and achievements. It can be love's greatest enemy, yet it is also the deeper path to love.

Anxiety is the shadow cast by human consciousness. Because it is a natural—even sacred—part of life, we need to learn how to become anxious about the right things in the right way, one that leads to serenity. Unfortunately, many current therapies are directed primarily toward reducing stress and anxiety. But if anxiety is life being aware of its own aliveness, then the only way to reduce our anxiety is to become less alive, to numb ourselves to life. The problem is not that we are too anxious, it is that we are not anxious enough and that we are not anxious about the right things.

Pollsters tell us that most people are more anxious about public speaking than they are about death. We become more anxious about what to wear than about how to live. We are more anxious about finding a parking place than about finding solutions to social and economic injustice. We worry more about whether our investments are growing than about whether we are growing. Yet we can learn to let anxiety lead us along the path to inner peace, a path that is available to every one of us.

Serenity is not the permanent absence of anxiety but rather an inner confidence derived from the ability to continually transform naturally arising anxiety into deeper trust and faith. The authentic way to master anxiety is transformative—the path of Buddha, the way of Christ, the sacred path of transmutation—changing anxiety into love, transforming anxiety into the "peace that passes understanding." Knowing how to be anxious about the right things in the right way is crucial for personal growth and for the survival of humankind.

As a child, I became aware of the mysterious relationship between *love* and *fear* (or *anxiety* as I prefer to call it here—later we will explore the differences between true fear and anxiety). I first observed these two primal poles of human emotion as they operated in my family and within my own heart. These dual forces are so deeply intertwined that they are almost impossible to separate. In my childhood family I could feel love as a sweet, palpable energy that bound us to each other and that motivated my immigrant parents to work hard and care for their children. Yet I also felt the harsh, corrosive force of anxiety when it divided and estranged us.

As I grew up, I began to see the powerful effect that love and anxiety had upon the world at large. Many years later I learned that, when rightly used, anxiety can also serve as a path to deeper love and inner peace. I have focused this book on anxiety, the darker pole of human consciousness, because it is both the greatest impediment to love and the most direct route to loving more fully.

As a psychotherapist and educator, my greatest joy is to help people liberate themselves from an anxiety-saturated existence—to become free and responsible creators of their own destiny. As I counseled thousands of men, women, and children over the years, I kept searching for the root cause of the problems people brought with them into my office: relationship problems, worry, insomnia, stress, depression, nervousness, lack of confidence, self-sabotaging behavior, physical illnesses, bad habits and addictions, and low self-esteem. Gradually, one factor emerged that was common to all my clients—their problems with anxiety. I began to see that a person's happiness and success in life varied directly with the ability to handle anxiety.

I am referring to anxiety not just in its limited modern psychological sense but in its broadest compass. Simply put, anxiety is the feeling that our well-being is threatened in some way. Anxiety can be provoked by everything from our primitive biological urge for self-preservation to everyday worries about money, health, and relationships to our most profound philosophical and spiritual dilemmas about death and the purpose of life. All human endeavors and inventions, including art, science, technology, government, and religion, can be understood as attempts to deal with our anxiety.

How we respond to the basic feeling of anxiety determines our character and our personality. For example, Aaron is uneasy about making a commitment to Sue because the idea of marriage fills him with anxiety. Phil and Tamara have serious relationship problems because they respond to their own anxiety in ways that exacerbate instead of calm the other person's anxiety. Larry is addicted to alcohol because he uses it to numb his anxiety. Jenny has chronic headaches and Ron has heart problems because internalizing their anxiety has taken a physical toll over the years. Maria is depressed and has low self-esteem as a result of years of dysfunctional responses to anxiety.[1]

Finding Serenity in the Age of Anxiety does not skirt the mundane problems of everyday life or gloss over the harsh realities of existence. True serenity can only develop from a wholehearted acceptance of the human condition. Quite appropriately, this book was written on the front lines of the Age of Anxiety. My wife and I both work, yet we still find it difficult to meet our expenses each month. For the past sixteen years, we—including our five children and stepchildren who range in age from eight to twenty-five—have lived in a postmodern family with constantly shifting boundaries. Our spliced-together lives mean that having a child in day care, another in college, and an ailing parent in the hospital can all tumble together in a single year.

The juggling act of making time for work, family, friends, and community activities becomes ever more demanding; just when it starts to feel manageable, another ball is thrown in. For me, as for most of my clients, friends, and colleagues, the Age of Anxiety is no abstraction—it is scribbled all over our calendars and appointment books.

When I began to look at my own life, I saw that I had been dancing with anxiety since the day I was born, sometimes evading and avoiding it, sometimes attracted to it, but always interacting with it. Over the years, I became more conscious of my own anxiety and learned to use it as a guide and teacher. As a psychotherapist, I specialized in treating anxiety and found that it held the key to psychological change. From anxiety's tangled knot began to emerge three distinct yet related strands.

From medicine and psychology comes the strand first studied by Freud—the unhealthy kind that he called neurotic anxiety and that I term *Toxic Anxiety*. This is the type of anxiety I had experienced during my life as worry, self-doubt, panic, and even hopelessness.

In the realms of popular success literature, the human potential movement, and traditional folk wisdom, I found the healthy strand of anxiety, an emotion that could be mastered and channeled into achievement and personal fulfillment. This second type of anxiety is a normal part of the dangers, challenges, and uncertainties of everyday life, so I refer to it as *Natural Anxiety*. I recognize it in my own life as the realistic fears that protect me and the enlivening kind of anxiety-excitement that accompanies times of growth.

For many years, I have been fascinated with yet a third strand of anxiety that winds through all the world's philosophical and religious traditions—existentialist angst, awe, and the religious fear of God.[2] This is anxiety on a cosmic level, a *Sacred Anxiety* that cannot be medicated away or channeled into material success. It is the spiritual, existential anxiety that I had become aware of as a child and never had a name for. It concerns the ultimates of life—death, life after death, and the meaning and purpose of our lives.

I realized that a lack of clarity regarding these three types was at the root of our difficulty in dealing with anxiety. Fortunately, distinguishing these three strands from each other and relating them to each other enables us to begin unraveling the riddle of anxiety. Understanding that there are actually three distinct types and that each requires a different kind of response is crucial to mastering anxiety and finding serenity. As I used this deceptively simple concept in my own life and taught it to clients and workshop participants, I found that it possessed the power to liberate people from the tyranny of anxiety.

How do we find serenity in this Age of Anxiety? Peace of mind is not a static state, not something we find once and for all. The notion that ideally we should be free of anxiety and experience some kind of permanent peace of mind may cause more anxiety than any other belief.

"Enlightenment," "salvation," and "heaven" imply an abiding serenity, yet this state comes from accepting the human condition, not from trying to transcend it. Serenity, derived from a Latin word meaning clarity, results from seeing life clearly, without our usual filters. Serenity is commonly misunderstood to be a static (even boring!) state rather than a dynamic, evolving process. Both polarities—anxiety and tranquillity, conflict and peace—are essential to growth. Anxiety accompanies the disequilibrium of change, those times when we allow new and unknown possibilities to disturb our old mindsets. Peace of mind comes when we heed anxiety's call and act to successfully integrate new growth into our wholeness. Then, as the wheel of growth continues to turn, we again experience the anxiety of the unknown.

The more we relax with anxiety and the less compulsively we

strive to achieve serenity, the more the line between the two be-gins to blur. When we can welcome anxiety as readily as seren-ity, then we truly begin to experience that deeper peace that "passes understanding." Then an experience of anxiety no longer makes us anxious, but transmutes into deeper faith and greater aliveness.

Finding Serenity in the Age of Anxiety is my way of sharing with you what I have learned about how to become anxious about the right things in the right way—a way that can lead to serenity and an unconditional love of life. I hope this book will shine a welcome light to guide your steps and nourish your spirit.

Part One

FACING

ANXIETY

Chapter One

_____

THE SECRET OF ANXIETY

LIFE IN THE AGE OF ANXIETY

Jim lifted Jason into his child's safety seat and slid the buckle over the latch until it clicked into place. *Pretty soon he won't need this seat. He's getting so big,* Jim thought.

Tossing his briefcase and the small blue backpack into the back seat next to Jason, Jim got behind the wheel. *These mornings when Sally works the early shift are murder. I'm already running late.*

As soon as he started the car, the radio blared: "Last night a 16-year-old boy was killed in a drive-by shooting in Roxbury. The police have . . ." Jim quickly pushed in one of Jason's favorite tapes. *If the traffic's not too bad, I'll be able to make that meeting.*

After he'd made sure that Jason was playing happily at the day-care center, Jim streaked out of the parking lot. "Traffic is backing up at the 128/93 interchange due to a three-car accident . . ." the radio chattered.

As he drove toward the freeway, Jim hoped the accident would be cleared by the time he got there. He mentally reviewed his report for the meeting. He was a marketing representative for a small electronics company. Getting "downsized" out of a big corporation a few years ago had been a real shock, but it was exciting to be part of a new start-up. There was a lot of potential for him to learn and move ahead, but he was expected to put in very long days which made it hard to spend time with his family or have any time for himself.

As he sipped his lukewarm coffee, Jim felt the fatigue in his body. *Sometimes I feel like I'm paying with my life blood just to keep up with the pace at work. And for what, really? Is it worth it?*

On the freeway, traffic was slow but at least it was moving. *You'd think at age 43 things might be getting a little easier. I never imagined I'd have to make another big push to prove myself. It's like I'm a kid and just starting out again. Well, I shouldn't complain—I'm lucky I got this job when I did.*

"And now the latest on yesterday's tragic crash of a TWA 747. Federal investigators say that all passengers are now presumed—"

Jim switched the radio to a music station.

He glanced at the clock on the dashboard. His shoulders tensed even more and the furrows in his brow deepened.

Traffic on the northbound side of the big eight-lane freeway slowed to a crawl as thousands of commuters tried to squeeze into the two open lanes that skirted the accident scene. *Now, I'm going to be late. Bruce will kill me!* Jim felt a surge of anger. *Why the hell does he always have to schedule these meetings first thing in the morning!* He felt his chest tighten and his head begin to throb.

Jim heard the wail of sirens and saw the flashing lights as rescue vehicles and ambulances sped by in the southbound lanes across the divider. Beads of perspiration broke out on his forehead. *My heart's beating a mile a minute.*

This was the third time he had experienced one of these strange "attacks." *I wish I knew what the hell this is. I feel like I could have a heart attack any minute. Sally's right, I really should get a physical. And I need to get to the health club more often. But where am I supposed to find the time? Hey, concentrate on your driving, Jim!*

The last time he'd had these sensations he'd been in a meeting. The room had started to swim and he couldn't concentrate on anything. Fortunately, he'd recovered sufficiently by the time he had to give his presentation and was able to white-knuckle his way through it.

The accident was being cleared and the cars on the inside lane were starting to move more quickly. He maneuvered his way over. *Great, I can still make it!*

At two o'clock Sally's supervisor at the hospital asked her if she could work three more hours because another nurse had called in sick.

"I'm sorry, Andrea," Sally said. "I wish I could, but I have to pick up Jason at three." Andrea grimaced.

Well, what do you want me to do, clone myself? Sally hated the stress caused by trying to combine full-time work with motherhood. *But I can't imagine not working, and we need both our incomes.*

She signed out and walked to the parking lot. *I'm glad to be out of there—they expect us to care for twice as many patients compared with when I first started. I could really use a nap. Oh, we need milk.*

At the day-care center, when Jason jumped into her arms and kissed her, Sally forgot how tired she and decided to take him to the park on the way home. *He's such a great kid! I love him so much.*

As she watched Jason scrambling up the slide, Sally sighed. *I wish I could enjoy him more. Everything's always so rushed.* Her head began to ache.

When she got home, Sally emptied Jason's backpack and washed his lunch box. *I've got to lay down. I'm just too tired. I think I'm getting my period.*

She put Jason in front of the TV and tuned it to a cable channel for kids. *I swore when I had kids I'd never use TV as a babysitter.*

She collapsed on the unmade bed. *I wish Jim and I could spend* more time together. *I'm pretty sure he wants to, we just haven't had any time . . . damn, I forgot the milk!*

She got up to call Jim and saw the pile of bills on her desk. *Those were supposed to go out yesterday, and then I got the phone call from Mom about Dad being in the hospital again.* Sally felt a little dizzy and decided to lie down again. The sign on the treadmill at the health club popped into her mind: "Warning: Use common sense, stop if you feel dizzy or exhausted." *But how do you get off this treadmill?* she wondered.

She felt the queasy sensation in her stomach and her breath came fast. *Maybe it's just hormones.* Her thoughts raced on. *Are we ever going to get ahead financially? I'd like to have another child, a girl would be great, but how can we afford it? I keep getting these weird dizzy spells. Do I have a brain tumor? Probably just stress. I should get a CAT scan—it's just down the hall from my station. But what if they find something? I hope Dad doesn't have another stroke. Why is my heart beating like this when I'm just lying here? Am I losing my mind?*

Sally fell asleep. When she woke up a little while later she felt better. She took two aspirin, called Jim about the milk, and started to think about what to make for dinner. *Oh God, Jason's been watching TV for nearly two hours.*

When Jim came home at 6:30 with the milk, Sally smiled. *He remembered.*

After dinner, when Jason was in bed, Sally sat down on the couch and read her nursing journal. Later, after reviewing some papers for the next day, Jim sat down next to her. He put his arm around her and felt her relax as she snuggled up to him. He sighed, "What a day!" and let some of the stress drain out of his own body.

He glanced at the clock. *Ten-thirty already. I should be in bed. But I'll probably just lie there tossing.* He clicked on the remote control and the blank TV screen sprang to life.

"A terrorist attack in the Mideast has halted the current round of peace talks. . . ."

"Jim, can we talk?" Sally asked.

"Sure, honey." He turned off the TV.

"You know those 'heart things' you've had? Well, I've been having something like that too. We should both get a medical work-up, but you know what I really think it is?"

"No, what?"

"Anxiety."

Sally's diagnosis is correct. Both she and Jim are experiencing a number of clinical anxiety symptoms: worry, negative thinking, self-sabotaging behaviors, unhealthy lifestyle habits, muscular tension, neurohormonal arousal, insomnia, fatigue, inability to concentrate, and even occasional anxiety attacks.

Anxiety is one of the most mysterious and profound aspects of the mind. It has been humanity's most perplexing problem since the dawn of consciousness, yet the medical profession has concentrated its attention almost exclusively on the pathological variety I call Toxic Anxiety.

If Jim and Sally visit their physician they will probably be offered some medication to help reduce their physiological anxiety reaction. They also may receive the customary admonition to try and take it easy and, if they are lucky, they will be referred to a stress management program. It is almost certain that their anxiety will be treated as a negative factor that needs to be reduced or eliminated and not as potentially useful energy or a source of inner guidance.

It would be grossly unfair, however, to simply label Jim and Sally as emotionally dysfunctional, "neurotic," to use the classic Freudian term, or as suffering only from Toxic Anxiety. They are also dealing with very real Natural Anxiety. They are coping with the stress of earning a living in the harshly competitive environment of a swiftly changing global economy. They are trying to raise a child in a fragmented, demanding society that often splinters families apart instead of knitting them together. These and other issues won't go away simply by doing a breathing exercise—they require clear thinking and creative action. And unfortunately, their Toxic Anxiety habits are getting in the way of solving these problems.

Beyond this, Jim and Sally are also dealing with Sacred Anxiety, the underlying anxiety regarding their life purpose and the inevitability of death. Both are experiencing midlife and the need to examine their values and priorities, but so far they have neglected to take the time to honor this potentially life-enhancing opportunity.

When Jim wonders about whether his job is worth the expenditure of his "life blood," he is asking himself about the meaning and purpose of his life. When he hears about a plane crash on the radio and witnesses a highway accident on the way to work, he is forced, at some level of his psyche, to confront the unpredictability of life and the reality of death.

When Sally regards the end of her childbearing years and struggles with her desire for a daughter, she too must face the time-limited nature of human life. Sally is especially aware of this as her father nears the end of his life and her concerns about her own mortality take the form of worries about a possible brain tumor.

This Sacred Anxiety, traditionally referred to by religions as the fear of God, is our most profound anxiety and, rightly used, it can lead us to spiritual growth and a deeper encounter with life. But our society provides us with few opportunities to identify and use Sacred Anxiety in creative ways. It often goes unrecognized and consequently fuels Toxic Anxiety and magnifies Natural Anxiety.

More insidiously than anything else, it is our culturally limited understanding of anxiety that sabotages our attempts to master it. When all three types of anxiety are simply lumped together as generic "anxiety" or "fear," it is impossible to deal with any of them effectively. This undifferentiated anxiety induces escalating tension and confusion because we cannot decide upon the proper response. Should we ignore it or pay attention to it? Should we struggle to overcome it or surrender to it? Our mind spins as we flip back and forth from one possibility to another. But after we untangle the knot of anxiety and separate the three strands, it becomes much easier to deal successfully with each one.

Transforming negative forms of anxiety into positive, growth-promoting ones is a practical method that can be applied effectively to everyday situations. First, we can learn how to reduce and gradually eliminate the destructive force of Toxic Anxiety from our lives. As we probe more deeply we will uncover the healthy Natural Anxiety that can be harnessed to fuel personal growth and achievement. Finally, drawing upon philosophical and spiritual traditions, we will discover the Sacred Anxiety that can guide us to finding our life purpose and true peace.

THE ANXIETY EPIDEMIC

As a culture we lack accurate models and effective methods to help us deal with everyday anxieties, not to mention the overwhelming existential ones. We become habituated to responding to anxiety with self-destructive and dysfunctional behaviors that are passed down from one generation to another. As a result, one out of four Americans (65 million) has experienced the crippling effects of clinical anxiety symptoms.[1] Many millions more suffer each day from the subclinical versions we call tension, worry, stress, low self-esteem, the blues, and the blahs. The economic costs of anxiety disorders are staggering—over $65 billion per year, including $50 billion in lost productivity.[2]

Anxiety and depression are closely related. Mixed anxiety-depression mood disorders are a rapidly growing diagnostic category. One out of five Americans will struggle with the hopelessness of depression during their lifetime, after having lost crucial earlier battles with anxiety. Seeking relief from anxiety and depression is a major reason why over one-quarter of the population at some time in their lives plunge into the hell of substance abuse and addiction. Even those for whom the American way of life is still working complain of living with increasing personal anxiety, higher levels of stress, and deep concerns about their own and their children's futures.

This epidemic of unhappiness and mental dysfunction continues to escalate and affect ever younger segments of the population. The number of school-age children with attention and behavior disorders increases annually. The top three causes of death among young adults—car accidents, homicide, and suicide—are the direct result of a toxic cocktail of anxiety, depression, and substance abuse.

An increasing number of Americans are caught in this tangled web of anxiety, depression, and addiction. The social toll this epidemic takes on relationships, productivity, and health is immense. Anxiety, when left untreated, metastasizes into distrust, alienation, anger, violence, and hopelessness.

Anxiety is a far greater problem in our society than has been generally recognized. Most of us have been socialized to be ashamed of feelings of anxiety and fear—they go against the American myth of rugged independence and can-do optimism. Both men and women suffer from this anxiety taboo, though usually in different ways. Because the macho ideal is usually imposed on boys to a greater extent than it is on girls, it is generally easier for women to admit that they experience anxiety than it is for men. The taboo against acknowledging anxiety means that male anxiety is all too often converted into alcoholism and addiction, workaholism, emotional withdrawal, violence, and health problems such as high blood pressure and heart attacks. For many women, anxiety tends to manifest itself as overt anxiety symptoms, eating disorders, low self-esteem, the "superwoman" syndrome, over-concern for others, emotional dependence, and health problems such as premenstrual syndromes and headaches. The hidden toxin of anxiety has poisoned too many relationships, both intimate and societal, with distrust and destructive conflict.

Far too often, anxiety has been allowed to do its destructive work under the cover of darkness and denial. Until recently even physicians and psychologists frequently failed to properly diagnose and treat cases of anxiety. Anxiety denied or suppressed is like a virus that eats away at our minds and bodies, an infection that is passed on to each new generation. Today the taboo is lifting and people are beginning to talk more openly about anxiety and its many consequences. Anxiety is normal and natural; it is part of being human. By learning how to deal with it effectively we can begin to liberate both individuals and society at large from the tragic consequences resulting from the denial of anxiety and we can begin to resolve some of the most troubling problems of modern society. Mastering anxiety is a required course in the school of life: It has become crucial for personal growth and the survival of humankind into the twenty-first century.

GRIPPED BY ANXIETY

Anxiety can block our growth more effectively than anything else—more than poverty, illness, misfortune, or any environmental factor. Why? Because anxiety affects the way we think. It influences how we perceive the circumstances of our lives. Freud was a pioneer in bringing the attention of the modern world to the crucial importance of anxiety; he understood that it was the riddle that held the key to understanding human behavior and human suffering. But before we can unravel the secret of anxiety, we must clarify its true nature, for it is obscured by widespread misunderstanding.

Those of us who have been tormented by anxiety know that it often feels like a phantom stalking the inner recesses of the mind. Anxiety is difficult to fight because it can change its shape and appearance. It may first approach us in the guise of a concerned friend and then suddenly transform into a relentless, merciless fiend. When anxiety lurks malevolently in the background, we may feel vaguely uneasy, tense, or on edge. When anxiety is in full fire-breathing pursuit, it can induce the most heart-pounding terror we have ever experienced.

All of us know what anxiety feels like, for we have all experienced it in some form. Anxiety is a generalized state of arousal in response to a perceived threat to our well-being. In its milder forms—which we often call stress, tension, and worry—we find ourselves feeling vaguely hassled, irritated, or uptight. Like many people, I have long been familiar with anxiety, and when I forget to practice what I teach it can drain much of the enjoyment out of my day.

During episodes of anxiety, my thoughts are drawn by some mysterious magnetic force toward the negative pole of my mind, and the world appears more hostile. I feel pursued by time, compelled to move faster and get more done. My breathing becomes shallower. My body tenses, shoulders hunch up. My heart beats faster, and my blood pressure rises. My brow furrows, and I feel a vague, disquieting sense that things are not OK the way they are, that *I* am not quite OK. Mild anxiety is the feeling of being attacked, not by a big bear, but by swarms of mosquitoes.

During the day I can usually stay ahead of this anxiety by moving faster or thinking faster, but if I haven't faced it consciously sometime during the day, anxiety will get the upper hand at night. Just when I'm exhausted and ready for sleep my mind suddenly jolts into full alertness, like a soldier snapping to attention. My mental searchlight scans the horizons of my life for possible problems to focus on, dissect, examine, and obsess on. When sheer exhaustion finally offers the surcease of sleep, anxiety invades my dream life and I soon find myself once more in some familiar anxiety dream—in a classroom with a test in front of me, realizing I have neglected to study for the final exam, or in a courtroom facing absurd and serious charges that somehow I cannot disprove.

High anxiety, or panic, is a totally different experience. I will never forget the characteristic feelings of high anxiety—the sinking feeling in my stomach, the churning nausea, the terrifying feelings of impending doom, the pounding heartbeats reverberating in my chest, the sensation of suffocation, the flush of heat and sweat alternating with freezing paralysis, the jumbled thoughts racing through my mind, and the feeling that I am rapidly spinning out of control. In panic, all hell breaks loose, and the subterranean creatures of the unconscious rise up to wreak havoc upon the rational mind's carefully constructed reality. Chaos and pandemonium reign throughout the kingdom of the mind and body. Certain death, insanity, or total annihilation appear imminent. Little wonder that a widely used physician's handbook ranks anxiety attacks as one of "the most painful life experiences."

In these descriptions of Toxic Anxiety, anxiety appears to serve no useful purpose. Yet there are other times that anxiety clearly functions as a vitally important and trustworthy guide in life, and even unhealthy forms of anxiety always have a message for us, if we can learn to listen to them. Many times Natural Anxiety has warned me of real problems and prevented me from making the wrong decision. Every day Natural Anxiety stands ready to remind me if I have forgotten to take my wallet with me or have neglected to prepare for an upcoming workshop. Appropriate and healthy anxiety activates my nervous system to a higher level of alertness whenever I encounter a new situation in which I need to process a large quantity of information—such as skiing an unfamiliar mountain or walking into a conference filled with people whom I've never met before.

At a higher level, Sacred Anxiety may begin as self-doubt, or as deep concerns about social injustice and the future of humanity. This Sacred Anxiety leads me into periods of meditation and contemplation, during which I attend to inner work that needs to be done—perhaps some emotional healing or a deepening of my spiritual life.

In the following chapter, we will return to these three distinct yet related types of anxiety and examine them in greater depth.

ANXIETY AND FEAR

You may be surprised to learn that nearly all of our fears are actually anxiety, and that stress, as the term is commonly used, refers to anxiety as well.

The word "fear" is Anglo-Saxon in origin, but the word "anxiety" comes to us through Latin and is derived from the Indo-European root *angh*, which refers to a feeling of torment and strangulation, the helpless sensation of being trapped and losing control. From the beginning anxiety has referred to a terrifying inner state, rather than an outer danger. The German word *angst* comes from the same root and is the word used by Freud and the existentialist philosophers.

A great deal of confusion exists regarding the difference between anxiety and fear, even in the professional psychological literature. Anxiety and fear are related to each other, but in English "fear" is by far the more commonly used term and has become a catch-all category; we speak of having a fear of flying, a fear of death, and a fear of intimacy. The various phobias also are commonly referred to as fears. Yet all these feelings are much more accurately termed anxieties, and much of the difficulty we experience in dealing with anxiety stems from the confusion about the very language we use to describe it.

The familiar Anglo-Saxon word "fear" originally meant a calamity or disaster. Later it came to mean the emotion triggered by such catastrophic events. Over the centuries, the word "fear" has come to mean almost any negative emotion including anxiety, agitation, apprehension, worry, nervousness, depression, grief, dread, terror, and panic. The fear a hunter feels as a large bear lunges toward him is a very different emotion than the fear of intimacy someone experiences after the painful breakup of a relationship.

Because anxiety thrives on confusion and ambiguity, let's begin by making a clear distinction between anxiety and fear. When used correctly, the word "fear" refers specifically to the feeling of arousal we experience in response to a clear and present danger in our external environment. Fear triggers the primitive fight-or-flight mechanism, releasing a surge of adrenaline to prepare the organism to deal with a physical threat. In the past, such dangers were often wild animals; today they might be a speeding car or a fire. The emotion of fear is our natural biological response to any such tangible threats. The adrenaline is utilized and dissipated by taking physical action, just the way evolution designed it to do.

Pure anxiety, in vivid contrast, refers to a nameless dread, an encounter with the formless and mysterious. *Anxiety is the feeling of arousal we experience when we perceive an abstract or unknown danger, often in the form of a possible threat existing in the future.* The variety of anxiety we call worry often warns us of vague, threatening possibilities, but doesn't tell us what to do with the adrenaline rushing through our arteries at the present moment. If unchecked, this unused adrenaline can quickly push us up the anxiety escalator.

All fears begin as anxiety, even if the anxiety lasts only for a split second. Before we can identify the screeching sound behind us as a car braking, a generalized anxiety alarm signals us that something's wrong and gets our adrenaline flowing. Fear is anxiety that has found a realistic object, a specific threat to which to respond. Fear is an immediate and tangible form of Natural Anxiety.

During the experience of fear, the danger is specific and outside, the sense of self is intact and the mind is fully operational. Anxiety is experienced in relation to an unknown, an abstract "nothingness." The threat, though possibly triggered externally, has become internalized; our sense of self begins to disintegrate and we feel a sense of terror. Our mind becomes our worst enemy; we may feel like we are falling apart or going crazy.

When we use it accurately then, the word "fear" describes

only the emotion we feel when we are actually in danger, such as being confronted by a mugger on a dark street. All other fears—the fear of death, fear of public speaking, and all the phobias such as fear of heights, fear of flying, and claustrophobia—are more accurately termed anxieties, for while they may arise in response to a specific event they represent no clear and present danger.

In the eight centuries since the word "fear" gained common usage, the world we live in has changed radically. While our ancestors dealt primarily with clear and present dangers, we face a far higher proportion of vague and future dangers. The increasing frequency with which the word "anxiety" has been used over the past two centuries illustrates this shifting proportion. "Anxiety" is certainly more descriptive of the mental condition that postmodern humanity experiences daily. If it is true, as Norman Mailer wrote, that "the natural role of twentieth century man is anxiety," this becomes even more true as humanity enters the twenty-first century.

THE TERROR OF PANIC

In human development, anxiety is fundamental and always precedes fear. The newborn infant first exhibits an all-purpose, relatively undifferentiated anxiety reaction to any discomfort. A crying baby senses that something is wrong but lacks the skills to identify the problem. Our ability to focus anxiety into fear of a specific object or condition is a later development. Only through experience do children learn to identify dangers and adjust their level of anxiety to fit the situation. They must learn to tolerate the feeling of anxiety and develop the capacity to delay gratification. The ability to calm oneself and use anxiety effectively needs to be modeled by their caregivers if children are to learn these skills. Most children do not receive the proper training to master anxiety because their parents have never fully come to terms with their own anxiety and consequently, dysfunctional anxiety responses are often passed along from one generation to the next.

Undifferentiated primal anxiety always precedes fear. But if the presenting threats become overwhelming, fear also can escalate into an extreme state of undifferentiated high anxiety, which we know as *panic*. One attacking wolf triggers fear, but at least we know in which direction to run. If an angry, snarling pack of wolves rushes over and surrounds us, our fear suddenly has too many threatening objects to deal with effectively; we no longer can identify where safety lies, and fear erupts into high anxiety and panic. Our behavior loses its focus and becomes disorganized and irrational.

What really terrifies us in any experience of fear is the possibility that a manageable threat in the present could become overwhelming in the future. When we contemplate the ultimate horror of losing our mind or going crazy, subconsciously we dread being thrown back into the helpless, bewildered primal anxiety state of infancy. The French writer Georges Bernanos described the wild, disordered state of anxiety that has gone over the edge as "a savage frenzy." "Of all the insanities of which we are capable, it is surely the most cruel," he wrote. "There is nought to equal its drive, and nought can survive its thrust." We witness the fearsome power of unbridled anxiety in the psychotic's terror-filled delirium and the mass murderer's explosive orgy of bloody violence.

Again, our language tends to disguise the full power of anxiety because the word is so often associated with relatively mild experiences such as nervousness and worry. In reality, anxiety spans the gamut from a healthy surge of alertness to the utmost bone-rattling panic and mind-shattering terror.

ANXIETY, STRESS, AND PAIN

As we have observed, "stress" is another generic term commonly used to describe feelings of being anxious or overwhelmed. In the middle of a hectic day of meetings, phone calls, and deadlines, Jim may say to himself, "Man, am I getting stressed out!" In reality he is experiencing external stressors and responding to them with anxiety about whether he can cope with them all.

When Sally experiences inner conflict regarding her commitments to work and her desire to spend time with her son Jason, she tells herself, "All this stress is getting to me." It would be more accurate (and more helpful) for her to say, "I am experiencing anxiety because I feel pulled in two directions at the same time."

When someone is feeling tired, anxious, tense, and discouraged, it is usually more socially acceptable in our culture to say "I'm stressed out" than to say "I'm feeling anxious." Part of the reason for this is that stress locates the cause of our problem out there somewhere in our environment, while anxiety infers that we may have something to do with how we are feeling and reveals our vulnerability. Stress sounds more macho than anxiety, as if we are hanging tough while fending off the attacking hordes. Yet locating the problem outside ourselves also puts the solution out there and out of reach.

For most of us, daily life means living with high levels of external stressors due to time pressures, financial uncertainties, overwork, and conflicting values and beliefs. Stressors have always been part of life, but the kinds that we encounter in our postmodern society are far more anxiety inducing than the more direct physical challenges our ancestors had to deal with. The good news is that we don't have to get stressed out in response to stress; it is our response to stressful events that determines their effect on us.

Most of us have been conditioned to respond to external stressors with anxiety, often without even being aware of it. It is this internal anxiety reaction that causes us to feel the symptoms of stress: physical tension, fatigue, increased heartbeat and blood pressure, shallow breathing, worry, frustration, and negativity. And it is no accident that these stress symptoms are exactly the same as those of anxiety—because they *are* anxiety. By learning to master anxiety we are automatically learning to deal effectively with stress because we are striking at the root of the problem. Using the term "stress" to refer to both outer events and internal states is confusing and unproductive. We never feel stressed unless a stressor has triggered an internal anxiety reaction. So stress is an internal anxiety reaction that we often attribute to outer events and situations. In this book, you will learn many effective ways to become aware of and change habitual anxiety reactions.

Pain, whether emotional or physical, is one of the greatest challenges to human happiness. Pain triggers anxiety more effectively than almost anything else. Yet responding to pain with anxiety is only useful for a brief moment—enough to get our attention and take appropriate action. Chronic physical pain or emotional pain are only exacerbated by a fight-or-flight anxiety response. As with stress, it is our response to pain that largely determines how painful it feels to us. Learning to notice our habitual anxiety reactions to stress and pain enables us to begin to separate the triggering sensations and events from our response to them and to regain our ability to choose more effective ways of coping.

FOLLOW YOUR ANXIETY AND FIND YOUR SELF

Most people go to work each day, not because they love being there, but to avoid the anxiety of being unproductive, unemployed, and penniless. Most people pay their taxes and obey traffic laws because the thought of getting caught makes them anxious. Even people who do the right thing for moral reasons do so to avoid the anxiety and guilt they would feel if they violated their moral code.

Anxiety is a primary motivating force in human life. Emerson wrote: "We are afraid of truth, afraid of fortune, afraid of death, and afraid of each other."³ He knew that it was only by realistically recognizing anxiety's role in human life that we could cultivate such higher traits as love and altruism.

We human beings have always had a love/hate relationship with anxiety. We say we would like nothing better than to be free of anxiety, yet at the same time we seek it out. If our anxiety level gets too low we call it boredom and seek more anxiety—negatively in the form of emotional crises and addictions, or positively as novel experiences and new challenges. This universal fascination with anxiety is reflected in our novels, movies, TV shows, and games. Entertainment provides an opportunity for us to experience anxiety from the safety of our seats. Some of us crave the heart-stopping anxiety of suspenseful thrillers that keep us on the edge of our seats. Sporting events enable spectators to safely experience the primal anxiety of tribal warfare—the ancient us-versus-them battle for survival. Horror movies aim directly for the gut—the visceral thrill that accompanies sheer fright. Ever since Freud we have known that comedy and humor provide a socially acceptable way to release our common anxieties by laughing at them. Tragedy and drama have long offered catharsis for the ultimate human anxieties about fate and death.

We might as well admit that we are as attracted to the thrills of anxiety as we are to the bliss of serenity. Because anxiety is always there motivating us in some way, how can we use it to guide us?

Amid the cacophony and confusion of our swiftly changing society, many people today are searching for their own true path, thinking, "How can I find the right career, the right mate, the right place, or the right spiritual path?" Joseph Campbell's sage advice was, "Follow your bliss." A vital companion piece of advice is: Follow your anxiety.

To become our true, authentic selves is both our greatest desire and our greatest anxiety. Because of this paradox, if we follow our bliss we will inevitably meet our greatest anxiety along the way, and if we follow our anxiety it will unerringly lead us to our greatest bliss. But most of the time we are not at all certain where to find our bliss, while we have no trouble knowing exactly where our anxiety lies. Because it is usually right there with us, anxiety provides a convenient place to start our journey.

Only when we confront the true source of our anxiety can we find the wellspring of serenity and joy—the full ecstasy of being alive. Anxiety is the call to adventure, a hero's journey into the dark forest. The secret of anxiety is that it is the hidden path to inner peace. Rightly used, it can lead us to where we have always longed to go.

Chapter Two

_____

NATURAL, TOXIC, AND
SACRED ANXIETY

UNRAVELING THE THREE STRANDS OF ANXIETY

It's past 1:00 AM; my teenage daughter hasn't come home yet and I'm feeling anxious. But what kind of anxiety am I experiencing? The internal debate begins: (A) "She's probably just forgotten what time it is, like the last time she was late—you worry too much; just forget about it and go to sleep," and (B) "She might be in real trouble this time—you'd better do something!"

Much of the time, even when we know we're anxious, we're not sure whether the anxiety we're experiencing is a real warning that we should heed or just a negative fantasy. Will the real anxiety please stand up?! In this chapter we will shine some light into anxiety's darkest corners to clarify this confusion.

When we unravel the thread of anxiety that runs through life, we find that it is composed of the three distinct, yet interwoven, strands: Natural, Toxic, and Sacred Anxiety. Examining each of these strands and identifying their distinguishing characteristics enables us to untangle anxiety's knot and free ourselves from its bonds. Natural Anxiety is the most familiar and most basic of the three, and we will see how this healthy type of anxiety can either degrade into Toxic Anxiety or lead us onward to Sacred Anxiety. We will also observe these three types of anxiety in the lives of two individuals. Finally, a series of charts and diagrams will further clarify the relationships between Natural, Toxic, and Sacred Anxiety.

NATURAL ANXIETY: ENERGY FOR PROTECTION AND GROWTH

Natural Anxiety is rooted in the awareness of our status as vulnerable biological organisms whose well-being can be threatened in countless ways: by unseen bacteria and viruses, by hurricanes and earthquakes, by poisonous spiders and rabid dogs, by colliding automobiles on rain-slick highways, by economic and political upheavals, and by other people who may wish to harm us. Natural Anxiety springs from what Shakespeare called "The heartache and the thousand natural shocks/ That flesh is heir to."[1] When the biological instinct for self-preservation collides with the recognition that life comes with absolutely no guarantees, the inevitable consequence is Natural Anxiety. This reality-based form of anxiety is what Freud classified as "objective anxiety" and Rollo May called "normal anxiety." Freud described this as "a very natural and rational thing . . . a reaction to the perception of external danger . . . and an expression of the instinct of self-preservation."[2] In Natural Anxiety the object of the anxiety is usually an external challenge or threat and its temporal focus is in the present.

Natural Anxiety includes the positive, protective kind of anxiety that instantly responds to an immediate danger and is quickly channeled into an effective response. Proportionate and appropriate to the situation, Natural Anxiety disappears as soon as the object of the anxiety has been acknowledged and dealt with. Our capacity to experience Natural Anxiety is hardwired into our nervous system and is related to the biological fight-or-flight reaction that we share with all mammals.

As human beings, however, we also possess the unique capacity for future-oriented thinking that produces a more evolved (and more problematic!) form of Natural Anxiety. This future-oriented anxiety involves the awareness of possible dangers or problems that are yet to come. It includes all the normal human concerns regarding our fundamental inability to guarantee the fulfillment of our needs and desires.

Natural Anxiety gives us the ability to foresee potential problems and to plan for the future constructively. This familiar form of anxiety prompts us to take an umbrella along when rain is in the forecast. It is the healthy form of anxiety that helps us to stop smoking or to pass up a high-fat dessert because of realistic health concerns. Natural Anxiety advises us to save money for retirement. Yet as we shall see, this valuable future-oriented strand of anxiety also makes us vulnerable to that quintessentially human trait, worry.

Natural Anxiety also works in a positive way to alert us to possibilities for growth. Being able to recognize and take advantage of opportunities is just as important for our survival as is the avoidance of dangers, and it too requires a state of heightened alertness. Natural Anxiety accompanies every new experience and produces the focused attention needed for rapid information processing. It is closely related to our capacity for interest and excitement. (In fact, the fight-or-flight mechanism is really the emergency version of our fundamental capacity to notice and become interested in something.) At normal levels Natural Anxiety is not uncomfortable and may even be enlivening and exciting. This is the positive anticipatory arousal that a well-trained athlete or performer experiences before an important event or the sensation we feel before a first date. It is the anxious-excited feeling we experience when we face that moment of truth as a major project nears completion. It accompanies all acts of personal growth as we venture into the unknown.

Natural Anxiety can be symbolized by the Dragon of ancient myth, for the Dragon, especially in the Orient, was considered a powerful natural force that could be harnessed for success. If we learn to ride this Dragon, we can use it to propel us forward toward our goals and dreams.

Nevertheless, Natural Anxiety can become highly uncomfortable if we feel inadequate to the challenge at hand or if we are confronted with a situation where we risk the loss of something we hold essential to our well-being. This is the double-edged sword of Natural Anxiety: Without its protective function we would never survive in the world, yet we dread its tendency to transform into regressive forms of Toxic Anxiety, such as obsessive worry or panic.

The boundaries of Natural Anxiety form crucial territory. At the outer limits we reach the ultimate anxiety of the human organism—the fear of death and the mystery of life that usher us into the spiritual/existential realm of Sacred Anxiety. At the other end we find the deadly swamp of Toxic Anxiety, where the powerful energy of Natural Anxiety is subverted and turned against us.

TOXIC ANXIETY:
A POWERFUL SELF-DESTRUCTIVE FORCE

Toxic Anxiety has often been symbolized in myth and story by the image of a monster. The Monster represents a terrifying antilife entity; it is a vampire that sucks the life energy out of its victims. In traditional religious imagery, it is Satan, the evil force that leads humans into paths of self-destruction and harming others. Imagine the anxiety Monster stalking its prey, then leaping and grabbing the victim with its claws, and finally crushing the poor soul within an inch of his or her life. Then the Monster may hurl its victim into a black and bottomless pit, condemning it to an endless free fall to nowhere. The Monster always stops short of killing its victim, however, because that would all-too-mercifully end the victim's suffering and end the Monster's cruel cat-and-mouse game. Instead, the Monster allows its terrified victim to recover, so that it can begin the game again. The most frightening aspect of this Monster is that we cannot outrun it because the Monster lives within our own mind. The Monster that torments us so mercilessly is our self. The hands that are strangling us are our own.

Toxic Anxiety has been called the "fear of fear itself," or "being anxious about being anxious." Toxic Anxiety develops when we refuse to face our own Natural and Sacred Anxiety. This refusal, whether conscious or not, causes our real anxieties to go underground and then to rise up again in highly destructive forms. Toxic Anxiety's relentless pursuit may eventually push its victims into the realm of the psychotherapist's office, the hospital, and the courtroom. It has its origin in our past: past conditioning, past traumas, and past experiences of unresolved anxiety. The specific forms and habits of Toxic Anxiety are often handed down from one generation to the next.

This is the form of anxiety that Freud called neurotic anxiety, and today's psychologists and psychiatrists may diagnose as an anxiety disorder, mood disorder, substance abuse, or some other category of mental dysfunction. Toxic Anxiety may affect us physically as chronic tension, pain, or illness. Researchers at Duke University exposed people to a variety of mental stressors, such as public speaking or solving a problem under a deadline. Using sophisticated imaging technology, they discovered that those who responded with anxiety actually experienced reduced blood flow to their hearts. So intense were their responses that these anxious subjects were later found to have double and triple the risk for future cardiovascular disease![3] In addition to taking the form of anxiety symptoms, depression, addiction, or other psychological problems, Toxic Anxiety may be expressed as dependent, critical, abusive, or violent behavior toward others.

Toxic Anxiety is antithetical to human happiness and the enemy of life and growth. It is quantitatively toxic because the degree of anxiety is so extreme that it overwhelms one's ability to think clearly and respond effectively. It is qualitatively toxic because the anxiety has been displaced from its true object to a false object, thereby eliminating all possibility of a real solution.

This strand of anxiety is inherently distressing because it is a state of inner conflict: The object of the anxiety is within ourselves. When we fail to consciously recognize our Natural and Sacred Anxiety they reappear wearing bizarre disguises and we fight these phantoms, monsters of our own creation. Yet we usually have no idea that we have done this; our habits of suppression have become so automatic that we are no longer aware of them. Thus we have the strange sensation that we are fighting ourselves, and when we are fleeing from our self, there is nowhere to run and nowhere to hide.

Toxic Anxiety misuses our normal human tendency to want to reduce anxiety. As we know from experience, the nervous tension of anxiety becomes highly uncomfortable when it is chronic or extreme, and we naturally want to diminish it. If we reduce our anxiety by facing it and dealing with it effectively, we grow from the experience. But this takes a combination of conscious awareness, courage, and a special set of learned skills that few of us have had the good fortune to acquire.

Skilled or not, we are still faced with the overriding need to reduce our anxiety to manageable levels so we can continue to function effectively in the world. And because prolonged anxiety is such an uncomfortable state, we will do almost anything to escape from it. The two most popular (and dysfunctional) strategies for getting rid of anxiety are "stuffing it" and "dumping it."

We try to stuff, or suppress, the anxious feelings by pushing them down inside ourselves in the hope that they will disappear after they are out of sight. Unfortunately this drives the anxiety deeper, where it begins to feed on itself and do its work under cover of darkness. We also try to get rid of anxiety by dumping it on others. Anxiety can lead us to criticizing, blaming, controlling, and manipulating other people. These tactics inevitably create an interpersonal system characterized by conflict and the implicit threat of violence, in which anxiety circulates and escalates. When we try to get rid of anxiety by dumping it on others, it eventually results in more anxiety for us when it gets tossed back in our direction.

Denial and distraction are the primary methods we use to avoid anxiety. We begin to disown our own feelings and construct inner walls to insulate ourselves from our own anxiety. In addition to its often being the hidden cause behind overeating, smoking, alcoholism, addictions, and other self-sabotaging behaviors, anxiety sometimes propels people to seek relief from its discomfort in activities such as shopping, gambling, compulsive sex, and watching TV. Any distraction from anxiety is welcomed by the anxiety sufferer for the temporary relief it offers. In our culture, workaholism is probably the most common, socially accepted way of dealing with anxiety. Unfortunately, trying to outrun anxiety by living a hectic life in the fast lane never works; like our own shadow, the faster we run from it, the faster anxiety follows us.

If we suffer from chronic anxiety we become susceptible to mood swings and depression, for anxiety involves a hyperactivation of the nervous system that is often followed by a depleted, low-energy phase. In this latter phase we feel lethargic, hopeless, and depressed. Anxiety insidiously undermines self-confidence, self-esteem, and effectiveness. We may become irritable and overreact to events. Good relationships become more difficult to maintain. Work performance suffers as anxiety affects the ability to concentrate and think clearly.

When we attempt to reduce Natural or Sacred Anxiety by stuffing it (suppressing the thoughts and feelings) or by dumping it (projecting the anxiety onto others), we achieve only a Pyrrhic victory. Yes, we have succeeded in removing anxiety from our awareness. But we have failed to eliminate the anxiety in any real sense; it simply goes underground and becomes Toxic Anxiety.

This suppressed anxiety begins to float around in our unconscious mind. It hovers at the edge of conscious awareness, creating a vague sense of unease that continually threatens to escalate into formless terror. The impulse to find an object for formless, free-floating anxiety is so strong that the human mind constantly fixates amorphous anxiety onto objects in an attempt to turn the terror of anxiety into a manageable fear. Our deepest anxieties about life and death are continually being displaced onto more mundane and manageable terrain such as an upcoming airplane flight, an irritating person, an unrealistic worry about a loved one, or an exaggerated concern about a health problem. Projecting our anxiety onto specific worries or fears may be neurotic, but it gives relief from the more deeply disturbing emotions aroused by vague, formless anxiety.

There is a way to use this natural tendency to seek a focus for anxiety that is not neurotic, but healthy. The key lies in exploring the roots of our anxiety with full awareness instead of allowing our subconscious emotional programming to find the objects for us. Because it is caused by our refusal to deal with the natural, existential anxieties of life, Toxic Anxiety can be reduced and even eliminated by making the courageous choice to become aware of our deeper Natural and Sacred Anxiety.

SACRED ANXIETY:
THE "LIFE-AND-DEATH" DIMENSION OF ANXIETY

Natural Anxiety's ultimate concern is with the indisputable fact that, no matter how successful or charmed our life may be, one day our body will cease to function and we will die. Of all earth's creatures, it is only we human beings who carry this fateful knowledge with us along each step of our life's journey. Alfred Adler wrote that "none but human beings are conscious of the fact that death is in the destiny of life, and this consciousness alone is enough to give mankind a sense of being terribly overpowered by Nature."[4] The awareness of our own death is the gateway from Natural to Sacred Anxiety. While Toxic Anxiety fights phantasms of the past and Natural Anxiety deals with the challenges of the present, Sacred Anxiety confronts the unknown and uncertain future and life's ultimate questions.

We enter Sacred Anxiety's terrain when we confront the reality of death and when we grapple with issues that relate to our most basic values and beliefs: the very meaning and purpose of our life. A divorce, a serious illness, a major decision, the death of a loved one, a serious setback, or a midlife crisis all provoke anxiety at the deepest stratum of our being. Sacred Anxiety is anxiety about the "Big One"—about the dread of death, the mystery of life, and our encounter with the ultimate, or God. As Paul Tillich wrote, "The basic anxiety, the anxiety of a finite being about the threat of nonbeing, cannot be eliminated. It belongs to existence itself."[5] The "object" of Sacred Anxiety is objectless nonbeing, nothingness.

Sacred Anxiety brings us into the realm of ethics, philosophy, and religion. The existentialist philosophers grasped the fundamental importance of this level of anxiety; they called it "ontological anxiety," the anxiety about our very existence (and nonexistence). The existentialists courageously faced anxiety and allowed it to strip away the usual defenses and comforting cultural illusions. They regarded culture and religion as a collective attempt to create a bulwark against the ultimate anxiety of nonexistence. They boldly followed anxiety beyond conventional rationalizations to the farthest edges of alienation and absurdity.

Yet many existentialists overlooked the full importance of the spiritual dimension, the holy terror and divine yearning, contained within ontological anxiety. They stopped at the edge of the irrational, not really trusting anxiety enough to leap into the chasm of nothingness. Others, such as Kierkegaard and Tillich, had the paradoxical wisdom to understand that it is in nothingness that we find our true ground of being. The term Sacred Anxiety connects these two realms of existential dread and spiritual faith and forms a pathway to reunion with our source.

In the language of religion, Sacred Anxiety is often called the fear of God or divine awe. It strikes our very core—our relationship with our creator and our very existence as an individual self. The archetypal Angel provides a symbol for Sacred Anxiety. The Angel is traditionally a source of spiritual wisdom and guidance, yet it may initially appear as a fierce and terrifying adversary, as in the Biblical story of Jacob wrestling with the angel. Like Jacob, we can say to this Angel of Sacred Anxiety, "I will not let thee go, except thou bless me."[6]

Sacred Anxiety has two paradoxical aspects: death anxiety symbolizes our dread of dying and nonexistence, while life anxiety represents our trepidation of living with full, sensual aliveness, authentic self-expression, and passionate commitment to our dreams. Sacred Anxiety is the essence of our humanity; our response to it is the key to our personal and spiritual growth.

Sacred Anxiety is the origin of all our fears and apprehensions; it entered human life the moment we became self-conscious beings and began to feel separate from the rest of the universe. The positive aspect of human consciousness lies in our ability to think intelligently, to create, and to wonder. With the advent of human beings the universe became aware of itself and life became conscious of being alive! Yet in the same instant that the light of awareness dawned within the human mind and illuminated the self, it also cast a shadow. Existential anxiety is the shadow of consciousness. In knowing we are alive, we also know we will die. In becoming self-conscious we also become aware of being separated from our source. This separation gives rise to both the terrifying aloneness of an isolated self adrift in a vast universe and the deep yearning for reunion with our source—the salvation promised by religion and the state of enlightenment spoken of by mystics and spiritual teachers. Both the terror of existential abandonment and the desire for reunion are part of Sacred Anxiety.

Learning to distinguish among the three levels of anxiety is the first step toward mastering anxiety. Instead of allowing it to become fuel for Toxic Anxiety, we can learn to channel the

powerful energy of anxiety into tangible achievements and spiritual growth. Natural and Sacred Anxiety are fundamental to
human life. There is no escaping them. Choosing to face life's
anxieties with full awareness is the most direct path to total freedom, inner peace, and joyful living.

PORTRAITS OF ANXIETY

Every one of us experiences a mixture of the three types of
anxiety. In the clinical vignettes that follow, the various guises of
anxiety will assume human faces. We will observe how easily we
can become entangled in these three strands and how, through
conscious awareness, we can begin to separate them and use
them for healing and growth.

JANET *Janet, 48, graduated from college with a degree as a librarian
and worked at a local library. She consulted me because she wanted to
learn better ways of dealing with the stress and anxiety in her life. An
escalating problem with her 17-year-old daughter, Cathy, had prompted
Janet to seek help. Cathy, who had been staying out late, was using alcohol and marijuana and becoming increasingly uncommunicative.
Janet's concerns about Cathy had intensified her tendency toward excessive worry. She said that the situation was putting her over the edge and
that she was now suffering from insomnia on a nightly basis. In the
morning she awoke feeling tired and depressed, and her performance at
work was being affected. Janet's occasional migraines had also become
more severe. She had gained 15 pounds over the past year. "I just don't
feel very good about myself and I don't know why," she told me, but her
voice betrayed an anguish that went deeper than the concerns she was
describing.*

*Janet was in a quandary about Cathy's behavior and felt that she
was worrying about her all the time. Her older child, Larry, who would
soon be graduating from college, had never behaved this way as a
teenager. Janet and her husband Roger had taken Cathy to a counselor
who specialized in adolescents, but Cathy had stopped going after three*

sessions, saying that they were a waste of time. The counselor had told Janet and Roger that Cathy's behavior seemed to be "within the range of normal experimentation for her peer group." This neither reassured them about Cathy's behavior nor gave them confidence in the counselor.

As Janet and I worked together, I learned more about her background and her current life. She described a normal, mostly happy childhood. Her father was an accountant for a large firm, and she remembered him as good provider, though strict and judgmental. "He expected everything to be done his way—or else." Janet's mother was kind and nurturing, but unassertive. "She was a saint. She never got angry. Maybe she should have sometimes."

I asked about her relationship with her husband. "It's OK, I guess, we don't fight. But we don't talk much, except about the kids and the house and so forth." She said that Roger wasn't much help in resolving the problem with Cathy because he tended to lose his temper with her and just make things worse. She wished he would help out more around the house and wondered what their relationship would be like when Cathy left for college in a year, assuming that Cathy managed to keep her grades up this year so she could go to college.

Like many people suffering from anxiety, Janet was confused and conflicted. Her typical inner dialogues went something like this: "I'm worried about Cathy. I need to get her to change her self-destructive behavior, but nothing I'm doing is working. She just won't listen to me. Roger isn't much help and that irritates me. Well, maybe that counselor was right and I'm just overreacting and being a worrywart. I should just try to stop worrying so much and lose weight and take care of myself for a change." A few hours (or minutes!) later, the same debate would begin again.

Janet's mind went around in circles, leaving her dizzy and confused. Her behavior cycled from frustrated outbursts to trying to ignore the problem to overeating to battling insomnia. I began by helping her clearly identify her Toxic Anxiety symptoms and develop strategies for dealing with them. We both agreed that she needed to learn some vital self-care techniques and to calm her mind before she could resolve the problems she faced.

I trained Janet in several effective relaxation and meditation techniques that she began practicing regularly (these are described in Part 2). Within three weeks she was sleeping more soundly and feeling better in general. She also learned how to deal with worry and negative thinking by using a cognitive technique called positive Inner Talk (described in Chapter 5). Together we began to separate out the strands of anxiety that had become so tangled in her mind.

The toxic level of her anxiety included the insomnia, overeating, and worry. It was rooted in her tendency to stuff her anxiety and blame herself for Cathy's problems or dump her anxiety by blaming Cathy for misbehaving and Roger for being uncooperative. Then she would feel guilty and confused and behave in ineffective ways. To get to the source of her Toxic Anxiety, Janet began to work with Inner Talk and reprogram the negative voice that blamed her and accused her of being a bad mother. She learned to calm herself and, even more important, to stop creating unnecessary anxiety in the first place.

We also identified Janet's Natural Anxieties. It was important for her to know that some of her concerns were realistic. Worrying every night that Cathy was in a car accident was neurotic, but her concern about Cathy's changed behavior was very realistic. Janet had good reason to experience the Natural Anxiety she felt about her daughter, about her own physical and mental condition, and about the lack of intimacy and communication in her marriage. These were real problems that required effective responses, and I helped her develop strategies for communicating with both Cathy and Roger that got their attention. She stopped criticizing and blaming and began to listen more.

She began to address her own anxiety first and blame Cathy less. "I feel like we've opened up the lines of communication some more," she told me. "We still don't see eye to eye on everything, but at least we're able to enjoy each other's company again and agree on some basic ground rules."

Janet became more assertive at home and found that she had a great deal of power that she hadn't been using. "Roger's agreed to go with me to an evening workshop on parenting teenagers that's being offered at Cathy's high school," she told me.

I had taught Janet some effective techniques for entering the meditative state and she had been practicing meditation at home (using a tape I gave her) to relax and enhance her self-awareness. We also used the meditative state during our counseling sessions so she could access the deeper parts of her mind. Janet was genuinely interested in getting to the root causes of her issues.

During meditation she realized for the first time that at the bottom of her various anxieties about Cathy was an extremely negative fantasy: "I imagine that Cathy's going to die in a car accident and I'll feel terribly guilty the rest of my life for being a bad mother who failed to protect her daughter."

Janet realized that to ward off this horrible fate, she tried to control Cathy's behavior as much as possible. I asked her to imagine herself in Cathy's place to understand how this felt to her. For the first time, Janet was able to see the negative feedback cycle that anxiety had set up between them.

As her daughter was growing more independent, Janet was being forced to realize that Cathy's life was beyond Janet's control. She could no longer control Cathy's environment or activities in the way she had when Cathy was younger. Janet needed to let go of what was beyond her control and accept the possibility that Cathy might make choices in her life that were not to Janet's liking. I helped her see how her worry stemmed from her deep love for her daughter and that she could find healthier ways of expressing her caring and affection. She also realized how her father's critical temperament and her mother's passivity had affected her own personality.

Janet began to probe the strand of Sacred Anxiety that ran through her relationship with Cathy. Trying to control what is outside of one's sphere of control is a formula guaranteed to produce worry and anxiety. On a deeper level Janet needed to accept the existential reality and ever-present possibility of death. To accept this Sacred Anxiety of the unknown is a challenge, but when we let go of trying to play God, it leads to acceptance and peace. Using visualization techniques, Janet began to replace her anxiety-producing model of a hostile, dangerous universe with one that is fundamentally safe and loving.

In subsequent meditation sessions Janet faced her image of a harsh, condemning God who would blame her if Cathy died or chose a life that was contrary to Janet's values. In this sense, Janet's Sacred Anxiety had to do with the anxiety that she would have to feel bad about herself forever, a kind of psychological "damnation." She became aware of how guilt-oriented the religious training of her childhood had been and how she could now choose to replace it with a loving and forgiving God who was more in harmony with her own values and beliefs. Taking responsibility for creating our own image of God is one of the most important tasks of adulthood. Until we do so, our childhood programming is still governing our behavior, whether we want it to or not.

In later sessions with me and through her own meditations, Janet was able to listen to her body more clearly. "I notice I'm not censoring myself as much. I'm telling people how I feel about things. And I've begun to lose weight, just by not snacking and nibbling whenever I feel anxious." The frequency and severity of her migraines were also greatly reduced. Cathy and Janet found they shared an interest in art and took a painting class together at a local art center. Both were able to communicate their needs and their bottom lines to each other and managed to reestablish a sense of caring and connection that was far from problem-free, but vastly more satisfying than their previous anger and arguments.

Roger agreed to work with Cathy on her college application process. Janet and Roger began to go out for dinner and movies again and to talk about their relationship and their future plans. At our twelfth and final session Janet told me: "I never realized anxiety could be so interesting. If I hadn't had all that anxiety I would never have taken the time to do this work. Because the Toxic Anxiety is so much less now, I feel I have much healthier ways of dealing with the Natural and Sacred levels. I've actually volunteered to take an active role in our library system's reorganization process—something anxiety would have kept me from doing before."

Understanding the anxiety triad and doing the appropriate work on each level enabled Janet not only to reduce or eliminate many of her anxiety symptoms, but also to resolve the real-life developmental issues that were facing her. Because she was willing to deal constructively with her Natural Anxieties about her daughter's growing independence and the transitional midlife phase of her own life, Janet's psyche no longer needed to divert that anxious energy into psychosomatic symptoms. She went even deeper and began a very useful process of midlife psychological housecleaning by examining her subconscious programming and consciously choosing to face the underlying spiritual and existential anxiety about her own relationship with life, death, and God.

BILL *Bill was 33 and a respected physician at a teaching hospital. He had important responsibilities and told me at our first session that he felt tense and stressed most of the time. He had always liked to party as a way to relieve the stresses of his life, but lately he'd had to admit to himself that his drinking had become a problem. By using his willpower, he was able to stop drinking for two or three weeks, but he invariably started again.*

Two recent incidents disturbed Bill enough to seek counseling. "Last month I misdiagnosed a simple problem and put a patient through a grueling battery of unnecessary and risky tests," he told me with obvious shame. "I know it's because I was doing some heavy drinking." The second incident had occurred the previous week while Bill was driving his girlfriend, Beryl, home. "She asked me to slow down, and I just snapped. I lost my temper totally and nearly had an accident." He was shocked at his own behavior and apologized afterward, but Beryl had told him that she wouldn't go out with him again until he stopped drinking.

Bill knows his problem has gotten out of control, but knowing it just makes him want to have a drink. He has also begun abusing some prescription drugs. "I can't believe that in spite of all my medical knowledge I've managed to become a substance abuser." His confusion and pain were evident.

It was immediately clear to me that Bill was a very caring and sensitive person. His initial reserve vanished quickly and he was relieved to be able to talk about his life. I asked him why he had become a physician. Bill told me that he had grown up in a blue-collar immigrant neighborhood. The family doctor was one of the few professionals with whom he came in contact; Bill worshipped him and was inspired by the goal of learning the art of medicine.

As a child Bill was very bright and took the bus each day to a special school for the gifted in an upper middle-class neighborhood. He had begun to drink in high school to relieve his social anxiety before parties. He was pleased to discover that his self-consciousness disappeared after a few drinks and that he could be the life of the party.

Bill's father, Tony, was a mechanic and a heavy drinker; he would often come home drunk. Bill remembers becoming quite skilled at an early age in diagnosing his father's condition upon arriving home—if Tony had been drinking, Bill would do his best to stay out of sight to avoid becoming the object of his father's volatile temper. Almost anything could trigger an outburst of Tony's rage and result in a beating for Bill. Bill could tell that, instead of being proud of him, Tony felt threatened by his young son's intellect. When Tony wasn't drinking he could be jovial and friendly, joining Bill and his friends in a game of basketball or taking Bill fishing at a nearby lake.

Even though he went on to graduate at the top of his medical class, Bill told me that he secretly feared that he was not as good as the mostly middle- and upper-class people who were his peers: "I feel like I've been fooling everyone for years and that sooner or later I'm going to be exposed for who I really am—a stupid drunk from the wrong side of the tracks."

Every day Bill lived with this anxiety, barely able to keep it below the surface. Earlier in his life this anxiety drove him to excel in school and prove he could be better than the other kids. Now he found that looking at the impressive degrees hanging on his office wall couldn't quiet the tormenting inner voices of self-doubt nearly as well as alcohol could. Bill also had been battling increasingly frequent bouts of depression during the past year. When he drank he felt good about himself—for a while. But the drinking problem had just added to his anxiety. "I know it's only a matter of time before someone at the hospital finds out I'm abusing drugs and alcohol."

Through our counseling work together, Bill began to understand the anxiety/addiction connection in his life. As he learned about the three levels of anxiety, he was able to see that he was drinking to relieve the Toxic Anxiety regarding his basic self-worth, which went back to his childhood. He had been mentally conditioned by his father's example (and the larger culture) to use alcohol as medication to relieve anxiety symptoms. For Bill, as for many men, it was hard to admit to having feelings of anxiety and self-doubt. It was easier, and seemed more manly as a teenager, to drown those feelings in alcohol.

Bill also had been mentally conditioned as a child to maintain a state of hypervigilance to cope with his father's temper. Many children of alcoholics grow up with chronic daily anxiety, never knowing what mood a parent will be in. Children of alcoholics (and other unstable home environments) literally train themselves to be anxious because they soon learn that being extra alert is an effective strategy to avoid painful negative experiences with their parents. Expecting the worst is a reasonable response in such an environment and is often adopted as an effective survival skill.

We also discussed the possibility that Bill may have been genetically predisposed to become addicted to alcohol (Tony's own father had also been a heavy drinker). Bill knew he had been so strongly conditioned to relieve anxiety with alcohol and drugs that his only recourse now was total abstinence. As part of our treatment strategy Bill joined a support group for recovering alcoholics. I admired the fact that he chose to attend a group at the hospital at which he worked.

"I discovered I'm not the only medical professional who has problems with substance abuse," he said. "I've made an agreement with myself that if I start to drink again I'll immediately inform the hospital and request professional supervision for my cases. I've also started to make time nearly every day to play racquetball with some friends. It really helps me burn off the tensions of the day."

Through counseling, Bill was able to learn healthier ways of responding to his feelings of not being good enough. We worked with meditation and positive Inner Talk, and he began to see that he had been repeating many of the negative things his father used to say to him, such as, "You're a worthless good-for-nothing," and "You'll never amount to anything."

Bill observed that the Natural Anxiety in his life centered on two main areas: his profession and his relationship with Beryl. In the past his Natural Anxiety had become tangled up with his Toxic Anxiety. When a patient did not get well, Bill often used it as evidence that he was not good enough. We spent several sessions exploring how Bill could deal with the anxiety inherent in making daily decisions that dramatically affect the health of other human beings.

"I've always second-guessed my decisions—often late into the night, tossing and turning in bed. Now I'm trying to use this anxiety in a positive way. Rather than letting it gnaw away at my self-esteem, I'm starting out with a basic feeling of being a good enough doctor and using my anxiety to sharpen my diagnosis by looking at each patient from several points of view before making a treatment decision."

Now Bill was able to use positive Inner Talk to release the toxic component of his anxiety and use the healthy aspect to be a better doctor.

Bill also had Natural Anxiety about the direction of his relationship with Beryl. "She's interested in getting married and I feel hesitant. I don't know if it has to do with her or just my own issues with intimacy and commitment." Bill spent several sessions working on this problem, detoxifying the relationship anxieties that stemmed from his childhood experiences. He was able to enjoy a more authentic relationship with Beryl and begin a fruitful dialogue about marriage.

Bill was not a conventionally religious person, but he was able to relate to the notion of Sacred Anxiety. The first thing he realized was that he needed to let go of his tendency to play God.

"As a doctor I'm constantly battling disease, and death is my ultimate enemy. When a patient dies, it makes me feel like I've lost the battle. That makes me anxious because I have such a need to be able to control everything," he admitted. "I need to do every possible procedure even when the situation is hopeless. Otherwise I feel guilty that I didn't do enough."

Through our discussions and through specific guided meditations, Bill was able to come to a more realistic acceptance of death and the natural limits of his power as a physician. "Because I can relate to death less as a personal enemy, I find that I'm able to choose more appropriate treatment strategies for terminal patients by talking honestly with them and their families. I don't let my anxiety make me talk them into trying one more heroic intervention if they are ready to go."

Near the end of our work together, Bill said to me, "I realize

	Toxic Anxiety	Natural Anxiety	Sacred Anxiety
Symbol	Monster	Dragon	Angel
Source	Our own suppressed desires, feelings, thoughts, memories. Suppressed Natural and Sacred Anxiety.	The natural uncertainties of life—not knowing "how things will turn out."	The deeper existential unknowns—"Who am I?", death, meaning and purpose of life, the afterlife, God.
Conflict	Self against self.	Self against world.	Self against life.
Message	Activated by false alarms, overreacts to or is paralyzed by real alarms. Sees opportunities as dangers. Vague, unrealistic, unreasonable, ineffective, repetitive "tape."	Responds to real dangers, anxiety is in direct proportion to degree of danger. Notices new opportunities. Specific, realistic, reasonable, helpful.	Ultimate concerns about death and the meaning and purpose of life.
Duration	Chronic, repetitive.	Usually brief.	Continuous, but only rarely comes to conscious awareness.
Tone	Alarming, negative, shaming, guilt-inducing.	Calm, respectful, friendly, confident. Can also be excited and enthusiastic.	Paradoxical, can be divinely terrifying or unconditionally loving.
Control	Concerns are often beyond one's control.	Concerns usually within one's control.	Concerns ultimately beyond the control of the self.
Resulting Behavior	Inaction or counterproductive behavior.	Effective action and change.	Self-reflection and spiritual growth.
Effect	Anxiety escalates, any relief is temporary.	Anxiety is relieved by responsible action.	Anxiety is relieved by deeper awareness, harmony with the universe.
Self-Esteem	Self-esteem decreases, self-doubt, feeling tired, frustrated, hopeless, helpless, negative.	Self-esteem increases, feeling energized, empowered, confident.	Self-esteem evolves into unconditional love and acceptance. Spiritual empowerment.
Positive Purpose	Gets our attention, leads us to unresolved personal issues and inner conflicts.	Warns us of real dangers. Alerts us to opportunities, energizes us for growth.	Calls us to be aware of our spiritual self and the deeper questions of life.
Personal Growth Goal	Gradually reduce and eliminate Toxic Anxiety reactions by resolving inner conflicts.	Accept the Natural Anxiety in life and use it effectively for personal growth.	Be more aware of the sacred dimensions of everyday life.
Skills & Techniques Needed for Mastery	Self-calming, self-awareness, emotional self-management skills.	Life skills, mental clarity, problem-solving strategies, goal-achieving action, interpersonal skills.	Aligning daily behavior with ethical creed and life purpose, meditation, prayer, self-reflection.
Potential Gift	Inner happiness results from healing and self-integration. Better health, greater aliveness, and authentic self-expression.	Success results from surmounting dangers and achieving goals. More dynamic relationships, creativity, passion.	Serenity results from an unconditional love of life. Spiritual growth, oneness, compassion, love, and joy.
Key Phrase	"Become aware."	"Do it."	"Let go."

that my anxiety conditioning as a child has actually helped me to be a better doctor. I notice things about a patient and notice them more quickly than many of the other doctors. I've learned to use my ability to visualize worst case scenarios in a positive way."

Smiling, he added, "When I told one of my racquetball buddies that I had an anxiety problem, he said, 'Well, believe me, I'd rather have a doctor who's an anxious perfectionist than one who's happy-go-lucky.' " I agreed completely.

THE THREE LEVELS OF ANXIETY: A COMPARISON

In these case histories we have seen how the three strands of anxiety weave through people's lives. The table will bring more conceptual clarity to our understanding of the anxiety triad. Don't be fooled by the black lines and neat little boxes—in real life the boundaries between these levels encompass some interesting gray areas! Looking at the three levels of anxiety in terms of life's problems and issues offers us a useful perspective. Dysfunctional or pathological phenomena fall clearly within the Toxic category; realistic concerns about our lives define Natural Anxiety, while exaggerated concerns (worries) fall somewhere in between the two. Ultimate questions of life, death, and meaning are located in the Sacred dimension of anxiety.

The next few diagrams provide a quick review of the dynamic role that anxiety plays in our lives. Natural Anxiety is the pivot point of life. We can use it to evolve swiftly and surely to our full potential as human beings or we can attempt to evade and deny it, resulting in stagnation and decline.

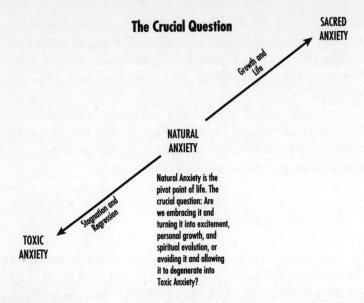

The Crucial Question

SACRED
ANXIETY

Growth and Life

NATURAL
ANXIETY

Natural Anxiety is the
pivot point of life. The
crucial question: Are
we embracing it and
turning it into excitement,
personal growth, and
spiritual evolution, or
avoiding it and allowing
it to degenerate into
Toxic Anxiety?

Stagnation and Regression

TOXIC
ANXIETY

When anxiety is avoided each level backs up and contaminates the previous level, causing an escalation of Toxic Anxiety.

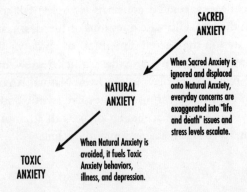

If Ignored, Anxiety
Becomes a Destructive Force

SACRED
ANXIETY

When Sacred Anxiety is
ignored and displaced
onto Natural Anxiety,
everyday concerns are
exaggerated into "life
and death" issues and
stress levels escalate.

NATURAL
ANXIETY

When Natural Anxiety is
avoided, it fuels Toxic
Anxiety behaviors,
illness, and depression.

TOXIC
ANXIETY

The purpose of Natural Anxiety is to move us onward to reach our life goals and to move us upward to our highest spiritual destiny.

Transforming Anxiety into Personal Growth

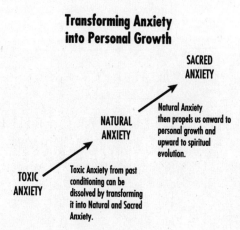

SACRED
ANXIETY

NATURAL
ANXIETY

Natural Anxiety then propels us onward to personal growth and upward to spiritual evolution.

TOXIC
ANXIETY

Toxic Anxiety from past conditioning can be dissolved by transforming it into Natural and Sacred Anxiety.

Sacred Anxiety, when embraced, returns as divine grace, providing love to nourish us and wisdom to guide us in the midst of daily life.

Sacred Anxiety's Gift — Serenity

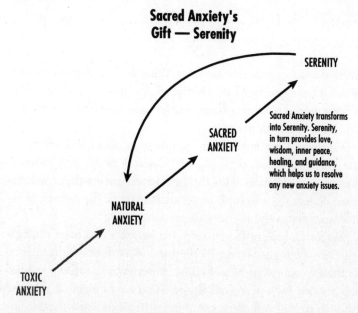

SERENITY

SACRED
ANXIETY

Sacred Anxiety transforms into Serenity. Serenity, in turn provides love, wisdom, inner peace, healing, and guidance, which helps us to resolve any new anxiety issues.

NATURAL
ANXIETY

TOXIC
ANXIETY

In order to fully comprehend anxiety, we need to understand its source. In the following chapter, we will explore the origin of this mysterious and profound human experience.

Chapter Three

THE BITTERSWEET FRUIT
OF CONSCIOUSNESS

THE ORIGINS OF ANXIETY

Why do we experience anxiety? What is its evolutionary purpose? These questions are crucial to finding serenity, for serenity requires mastering anxiety, and to master anxiety we need to understand its origins.

Our search for answers to the questions above will take us to the core of what it means to be human. First we will examine anxiety's connection with the primitive fight-or-flight mechanism. Then we will look to an ancient myth for deeper, spiritual answers to the mystery of anxiety.

Scientists believe that anxiety has its roots in a basic biological fight-or-flight response called the *alarm reaction:* the mental excitation and physical arousal we experience in response to being startled by a perceived danger. The alarm reaction jolts the body into full red alert, pumping adrenaline into the bloodstream and unleashing a cascade of physiological changes. Designed to ensure survival in a world of physical dangers, this primitive alarm system worked well in simpler times. But today it can cause stress and anxiety symptoms.

Imagine for a moment a scene from a more primitive age. Mogwa the caveman is sitting alone by his campfire at night, gazing sleepily at the flickering flames. He hears a loud noise in the forest. Immediately his body and mind galvanize into a highly aware state of anxiety—the alarm reaction. His pupils dilate as his eyes search the darkness for clues. His heart pumps blood to the muscles, preparing them for action. His mind races through an array of possible answers to the life-and-death question, "What made that noise?"

Our ancestors seldom felt anxious for long, and soon Mogwa's anxiety begins to transform into something else. If the noise is followed by a greeting from a fellow clan member, Mogwa's anxiety is released as he laughs and shakes off the cellular residues of his adrenaline rush. However, in this case Mogwa is not so lucky. Through the trees he glimpses a bear crashing toward him and his generalized anxiety focuses into fear. His anxiety has now found a realistic object and its energy can be unleashed into muscular action.

Quickly Mogwa must decide to fight the bear or to flee from it. The bear is not too large, Mogwa has his spear ready and knows the meat will feed his family and increase his status in the clan. He decides to fight. Mogwa is still in great danger but he is no longer suffering from anxiety. He knows what to do and channels the highly aroused energy of his body and mind into action. His eyes narrow as he focuses all his attention on the bear. Hurling his spear with deadly accuracy, Mogwa brings the bear down. He whoops and hollers to celebrate his kill, releasing the remaining adrenaline in his system (in much the same way today's football players do after a touchdown).

Anxiety has just saved Mogwa's life. Not only that, it enabled him to turn a problem into an opportunity. Mogwa's adrenaline-fueled spear thrust has transformed the life-threatening bear into a source of nourishing food and a warm fur coat. Evolutionary anthropologists tell us that the reason we are anxious is because only the anxious survive. Natural selection favors people who are properly attuned to anxiety because it enables them to be more successful in meeting challenges and taking advantage of opportunities. Recent research has shown that the ability to turn anxiety on and off is so vital that it is actually coded into our genes. According to Dr. Una D. McCann, anxiety researcher at the National Institute of Mental Health, "Anxiety . . . is part of our genes because it is protective."[1]

Most of the time, however, our ancestors remained only briefly in the anxious phase of arousal. Faced primarily with physical dangers, they could easily convert their initial anxiety into a specific, focused fear and appropriate action. In doing so, they burned off the adrenaline. After escaping danger, they experienced exhilaration followed by a natural relaxation phase.

Modern life has largely removed us from immediate physical dangers such as wild animals. Instead, we are confronted by a seemingly unlimited array of potential threats and abstract uncertainties that we can do little about at the moment. Today we get anxious about financial insecurity, career issues, relationship problems, carcinogens in the food, airline safety, global warming, unsafe drivers, and the direction of society. We experience many alarm reactions just like the one Mogwa felt at his campfire, but there is no longer a bear to flee or to fight. Instead we may be confronted by a critical, controlling boss who we can neither fight nor flee. Or, while rushing to pick up our child at day care, we may get caught in a traffic jam, with the adrenaline triggering muscular contractions that congeal into tension instead of enabling action.

Time after time the primitive fight-or-flight reaction is activated and we are forced to suppress it. Our body experiences this as the equivalent of driving with one foot on the accelerator and the other on the brake. Our survival mechanism is turned against us and becomes tension, stress, and chronic anxiety. Eventually, this chronic alarm reaction begins to threaten the life of the organism it was designed to protect. Stress and anxiety hormones suppress the immune system and lead to a higher risk of illness both in the short-run (flu, headache, gastrointestinal, and menstrual problems) and in the long-run (heart disease, cancer, and other degenerative illnesses). As the ancients knew, disease is caused by chronic "dis-ease": a lack of physiological relaxation and mental tranquillity.

Nature intended the alarm reaction as a brief phase that led either to action (in case of real danger) or to relief and relaxation (in case of a false alarm). But today this wake-up call has become a continuous, irritating buzz that permeates through far too much of our lives.

For example, Cynthia, who is employed by a mid-sized computer components manufacturer, reads in Tuesday morning's paper that experts predict another round of layoffs in the computer industry. She also finds drug paraphernalia in her daughter's room while looking for a sweater she borrowed. Cynthia quite naturally experiences both of these events as threatening her sense of well-being. The primitive part of her brain triggers the alarm reaction. But she is not sure what, if anything, she should do about either of these problems, and it is time to get in the car for her morning commute anyway.

Cynthia's anxiety "looks for a bear" and, finding none, becomes even more anxious. Toxic Anxiety is fear all dressed up with no place to go. It is as if Mogwa kept hearing noises in the forest but could never identify them, rendering him chronically and impotently anxious. Within Cynthia's body, stress chemicals build up, and the anxiety feeds on itself. At the office, work pressures pile on top of her personal anxieties. She drinks several cups of coffee to help her get through the day. Her mood that day is overshadowed by chronic anxiety, and she gets a tension headache by mid-afternoon. That night Cynthia feels both jittery and depressed and has trouble going to sleep.

Is Anxiety an Evolutionary Mistake?

We quickly sense the stark difference between Mogwa's and Cynthia's experience with the alarm reaction. Mogwa's energy level increased as a result of a threat, the energy was utilized effectively, and a subsequent relaxation phase enabled Mogwa to recuperate. Cynthia, in vivid contrast, became caught in a negative feedback loop.

Could it be that anxiety has outlived its usefulness? Many researchers believe that evolutionary adaptation, which works slowly over the centuries, has not been able to keep up with the rapid technological changes. According to this view, coping mechanisms that worked well in more primitive times have failed to adapt to modern stressors.

While this view is certainly true to some extent, it can be misinterpreted to imply that we are helpless victims of outdated genes. Fortunately, we have a great deal of control over our biological heritage. There are two crucial skills needed to get this primitive alarm reaction working for us instead of against us. The first is awareness. In Cynthia's response sequence, general anxiety precedes the alarm reaction. Then old habit patterns automatically (and inappropriately) trigger her alarm reaction, which she then struggles to suppress. By developing the capacity for greater emotional awareness, she can learn to avoid triggering the alarm reaction unnecessarily. When faced with a problem such as a possible layoff, healthy anxiety is an appropriate response, but there is no bear, and our inner Mogwa does not need to spring into battle mode.

Because we will never be able to prevent all inappropriate alarm reactions we require a second skill, that of self-calming. When our alarm reaction is triggered by an emotional event, it can easily activate our past programming and lead to further escalation. By learning how to defuse false alarms and calm down overreactions to minor alarms, we can recover much more quickly from stressful events.

Nature has not made a mistake—the alarm reaction remains

a vital survival mechanism for dealing with physical attacks from muggers, snarling dogs, and speeding cars. Our task is to learn to use the higher structures of the brain to manage the more primitive "emotional brain" effectively and responsibly. Self-mastery has been the prime focus of philosophers and spiritual teachers throughout the ages and remains one of the greatest challenges for human beings today.

I THINK, THEREFORE I AM ANXIOUS

The explanation of anxiety's origin outlined above is clearly helpful in understanding anxiety, but it does not go far enough to explain our deeper existential anxieties. If anxiety is caused by a threat to our sense of well-being, then why do even those people blessed by material security, good health, a satisfying career, and a loving family still experience anxiety?

The truth is that anxiety is inherent in human consciousness itself. When conscious awareness first shone a bright light upon the self, it cast a shadow that we now experience as existential anxiety—the anxiety intrinsic to an organism that is aware of its own life and death. A slight revision of Descartes's famous dictum describes our human situation quite succinctly: "I think, therefore I am anxious."

To understand this, we must use our imagination to travel back in time to contemplate our own evolutionary origins. Allow yourself to imagine what it must have been like for the first human beings to emerge from Nature's womblike unconscious, to leave behind the animal comfort of an unthinking, instinctual sense of unity with all life. Imagine what it would be like to become aware of being alive, aware of being a separate self!

The familiar story of Adam and Eve, recorded in the book of Genesis, is the creation myth shared by Christians, Jews, and Muslims. However, we will approach this myth, not from a traditional religious point of view as a tale of disobedience and

sin, but instead as a dramatic story of the birth of human consciousness and an illuminating tale about the origins of anxiety.

BITING THE APPLE, SPLITTING THE WORLD

The story of Adam and Eve in the Garden of Eden can be read
as a fascinating allegory about the dawn of consciousness in human beings. Before the development of self-consciousness, according to this myth, we lived in Paradise—a state of blissful
unity and mystical oneness, one with God, whole and innocent.
And, indeed, our body carries a cellular memory of this state, a
dim recollection of floating in a sea of oneness within the paradise of our mother's womb. Various religions suggest that our
soul too carries a memory, from beyond the womb, of a prior
spiritual existence in a transcendent realm.

At birth each of us emerges feeling whole and holy. We
come into the world still united with all of creation, miniature
gods who contain the entire universe within our skin. We are
nude and unashamed; we enjoy being seen, resplendent in our
naked glory. We radiate an inner sense of wholeness that is our
memory of our true identity of spiritual oneness; it is reflected
in the natural innocence and instinctive behavior of the young
child who still inhabits an undivided world, untouched by notions of yours and mine or right and wrong.

Yet this feeling of wholeness soon begins to conflict with our
worldly sense of being an individual, a separate person who has
been set apart from the whole. We all have an intuitive sense of
this process because we have relived it as children during the
process of self-development. Each one of us recapitulates the
entire history of humanity in our own individual life.

In our reinterpretation of the Eden myth, the watershed moment when Adam and Eve partake of the fruit of the Tree of
Knowledge symbolizes the birth of human consciousness. We
can sense the crucial evolutionary drama represented by this
symbolic act: the leap from instinct to intelligence. When Adam

and Eve eat this amazing fruit, which has the power to "make one wise,"[2] they feel a strange and marvelous transformation throughout every cell in their bodies. A divine energy enters the sacrum, snakes up the spine, and bursts forth into the vaulted brain. Like lightning illuminating the darkened sky, the light of conscious awareness sparks across every nerve and synapse. "And the eyes of both of them were opened."[3]

What does this magical fruit bestow upon Adam and Eve? What is the miraculous transformation that occurs at this moment in human history? The bite of the apple is the birth of self-consciousness! The ancient tyranny of instinct is thrown off, and with the bold biting of the apple, freedom and creative possibility enter. For the first time, Adam and Eve become aware of being alive. They marvel and rejoice at the miracle of life. Now they stand outside the oneness and are astonished at the miracle of their own existence.

Their eyes are opened and they can see what before was hidden. Adam and Eve now possess the secret knowledge, the knowledge that they are "as gods."[4] They can now think independently and use the amazing power of their minds to fashion and create their own visions of the world, an ability previously reserved for God alone. They have been initiated into the godlike realm of becoming creators of reality.

Eating the fruit of the Tree of Knowledge is often interpreted as humanity's "original sin" against God, but this is a relatively recent European interpretation of the ancient myth and is not validated by the actual text. Genesis speaks of disobedience but never uses the term sin to describe this event. And certainly, becoming conscious is not a sin; it is a divine gift that has been vital for the development of humanity. We might understand that Adam and Eve disobeyed God in the same innocent way that young children disobey their parents when they try out new skills, experiment, and stretch their limits to grow. But as this creation myth clearly illustrates, there is a heavy price to be paid for the godlike gift of consciousness.

The Primal Moment of Sacred Anxiety— Naked and Shivering

After the initial ecstasy and excitement of becoming as gods, Adam and Eve undergo a shocking experience. They notice that they are naked. This perception conveys the opposite and terrifying aspect of becoming a conscious living organism. About this pivotal moment in the Garden of Eden, Emerson wrote with irony, "It is very unhappy, but too late to be helped, the discovery we have made, that we exist."[5] Previously Adam and Eve had been totally identified with the cosmos. They had no individual identities. Suddenly they become aware of their smallness and vulnerability. Realizing their nakedness shows that they have become aware of being separate, individual biological organisms in a vast cosmos. No longer identified as before with the whole universe, they have shrunk into tiny, skin-encapsulated bits of living matter. Now each of them is a part apart from the whole. Before, God was within them and they were within God; their every thought, their every feeling, and their every movement originated in the mind of God. Now God is suddenly outside, somewhere far away. In becoming gods, they have lost God.

When God calls out to him, Adam says, "I heard thy voice in the garden, and I was afraid because I was naked; and I hid myself."[6] This fear of God is the primal source of all of our fears and anxieties. It symbolizes our deepest fear, the Sacred Anxiety of a mortal self confronting the vast, eternal universe and its own inevitable nonexistence.

As Paul Tillich noted, encountering God, the "naked absolute" (a phrase used by Martin Luther), evokes within us a "naked anxiety."[7] We can imagine Adam and Eve feeling for the first time a chill breeze on their bare skin and shivering the first shiver of separateness. The initial thrill of ecstasy turns into trembling and quaking as they become aware of the full agony of their existential predicament. Within the vastness of infinity, they feel the overwhelming terror of their temporal finiteness.

The shivers symbolize the psychophysical experience of existential anxiety. To shiver is to vibrate with intense aliveness, whether from ecstasy or horror. Sacred Anxiety elicits the deepest shivers, the level at which holy terror merges with divine ecstasy. When we shiver we know that our soul has been touched. Intense spiritual experiences often involve shaking and shivering.

Sacred Anxiety arises inevitably with the formation of individual consciousness. Even the etymology of the word "consciousness" validates the message of this timeless myth, for the word is derived from the ancient Indo-European root *skei*, which means to cut or split off, and describes the individual's sense of being separated from the whole.

The moment we become conscious of being alive, we also confront the shock and horror of our own inevitable death. Sacred Anxiety is separation anxiety on a divine level. After we have become separated from our Creator, we develop an existential anxiety about both life (existing apart from God as a vulnerable, mortal self) and death (losing our existence). This is the ultimate catch-22 of human life, one that we will explore in greater depth in Chapter 15. Our soul carries this awareness of Sacred Anxiety, and our conscious self spends most of its time trying to defend against it.

The essence of consciousness, and the price we pay for becoming independent selves with free will, is this tragic, angst-filled sense of separation from God. Adam and Eve soon discover that the fruit of consciousness is bittersweet indeed. After they become conscious they are on their own. They are exiled from Eden and compelled to take responsibility for themselves, to make their own decisions. As the existentialist philosophers have pointed out, the greater the freedom, the greater the anxiety. Biting the apple was an irreversible act. From that moment forward, human beings were "doomed" to be free.

Eating the fruit of knowledge meant that Adam and Eve had become conscious creators of reality, and that they had tasted death. They were no longer immortal. Although they did not actually die on the day they ate the apple, from that moment onward they knew death, were consciously aware that they could die at any moment. They knew that, no matter how fortunate or blessed their lives, they would inevitably age and die. In the end we lose the battle against Non-Being. Truly the fruit of the Tree of Knowledge was both the sweetest and the bitterest fruit we would ever taste.

EXPELLED FROM EDEN:
ENTERING THE WORLD OF NATURAL ANXIETY

Now Adam and Eve face the consequences of their actions. Because they have eaten the fruit of the Tree of Knowledge, they are expelled from Eden into the outside world. Symbolically this signifies a shift in focus from spiritual anxiety about existence itself to Natural Anxiety about the practical everyday concerns of living in the world. Eve is told that because she ate of the forbidden fruit her suffering will be greatly multiplied—she will experience the pain and heartbreak of childbirth and motherhood, and the bittersweet desire for a husband who will influence and affect her every day of her life.

God tells Adam that his days will now be consumed in a perpetual battle with the earth, "thorns and thistles shall it bring forth to thee . . . In the sweat of thy face shalt thou eat bread, till thou return unto the ground . . . for dust thou art, and unto dust shalt thou return."[8] Here we are given a remarkably stark portrayal of the human condition: the undeniable biological urge to mate and procreate, the daily requirement of providing the material necessities for sustaining life, and, in the end, the inevitability of death.

We see that Adam and Eve found the Sacred Anxiety of Eden far too excruciating for their mortal frames to bear. Yet the Natural Anxiety of life is difficult as well. Meeting the needs of a self in a world of other selves is an anxious enterprise. Even short of death, there is much to be anxious about in life.

Buddha, too, was very aware of Natural Anxiety. The first of his Four Noble Truths was his famous statement, "Life is suffering *(dukkha)*." By suffering Buddha meant the whole gamut of human life which begins with the traumatic separation from our mother at birth; continues through our inevitable sicknesses, injuries, losses, and disappointments; spans the unfulfilled dreams and indignities of old age; and ends at last in death. It is not only the events themselves that constitute our human suffering, but the continual uncertainty of our fate.

One of the most influential contemporary books on psychology and spirituality, M. Scott Peck's *The Road Less Traveled*, begins with a nod to Buddha and the brief sentence, "Life is difficult." This is what Natural Anxiety is concerned with: the inevitability of problems and difficulties in life. I'm certain that none of us would disagree with this rather obvious concept as a philosophical notion, for we see evidence of problems and misfortunes in every edition of our daily newspaper. It is primarily the ones that affect us personally that we have trouble accepting.

CLOTHING OUR NAKEDNESS IN A PERSONALITY

For better or for worse, Adam and Eve have taken form and now need some way of clothing themselves. Although they have been expelled from the Garden of Eden, God has not deserted them. He sees their need for protection in the world and fashions sturdy "coats of skins and clothed them."[9] God knows that Adam and Eve need to build their selfhood, their individual personalities, into strong vessels that can carry their souls into the hard world of form and substance.

Persona is the Latin word from which we derive the English words "person" and "personality." It was the word used for the masks that the Greek and Roman actors wore on stage. The Latin word persona, meaning mask, has come to be used to describe one's self-identity, or ego, because it so accurately describes the phenomenon of creating a symbolic costume with which to clothe the naked soul.

Each of us has learned to cover our naked soul with our personality. We created our self, our identity, to clothe our painful sense of separation. In a sense, the self is the psychological equivalent of the physical body—a vehicle for the embodied soul. When we use it as a channel through which we express our true nature, the self fulfills its purpose. Yet, as the story of Cain and Abel demonstrates, the personality can take on a life of its own. Gradually, human beings began to make their personalities into gods, to make the mask more important than the divine soul behind it. In becoming godlike creators, we gained the ability to use our selfhood for good or for evil.

Because the self is so fragile and so vulnerable in the world, as soon as we develop a self, the need to defend it arises. The personality, this self-constructed symbolic identity, becomes even more real and precious to us than our body or soul and must be defended at all costs because it has become synonymous with our very existence.

Murder represents the extreme in defending the self. Here we perceive the threat to our self-identity coming from another person, and preserving the self becomes equated with the elimination of that person. The object of murder is never the killing of the body but always the annihilation of the other's self and soul.

Most people, of course, stop far short of physical murder. But when it comes to protecting their selfhood, many subscribe to the philosophy that the best defense is a good offense. All too often, human beings try to defend the self by attempting to "murder" other people's personalities through blame, criticism, put-downs, guilt trips, manipulation, insults, and more subtle techniques. This is what the psychiatrist Leonard Shengold has termed "soul murder"—"the deliberate attempt to eradicate or compromise the separate identity of another person."[10]

Self-murder is another tragic extreme in the defense of the personality. In a desperate, last-ditch effort to protect the personality from further attacks and disintegration, we may engage in self-destruction. Though suicide is the most extreme manifestation of this, we often sacrifice our body and soul to our self-image in less dramatic ways such as addiction, self-defeating behaviors, conformity, perfectionism, and overwork. We may take a job that feeds the personality with status and money, while our inner soul starves, or we might choose a relationship with someone who pleases our ego but lacks a true connection with our soul.

CAIN AND ABEL:
THE ORIGIN OF TOXIC ANXIETY AND EVIL

To clarify the origin of Toxic Anxiety and its connection with the defense of the self, we return to the story in Genesis. Sacred Anxiety begins to fade in the face of the Natural Anxiety that Adam and Eve encounter in the daily challenge of surviving. After they recover from their initial shock of being expelled from Paradise, they begin to learn about the world they live in. It contains not only pain and suffering, but also pleasure and joy. It is not only fear of starvation and death that motivates them, it is curiosity and a divine evolutionary impulse for exploration. Adam and Eve regain the spirit of adventure that led to their first bite of the apple. They become godlike creators of life. They create children in their own image just as God created them. They discover how to grow nourishing plants that provide them with delicious food. They begin the fascinating human adventure of mastering the world around them, of using their gift of consciousness to understand the universe in which they find themselves. Leaving Eden is indeed a bittersweet moment; it is a time for weeping but also a time for rejoicing.

Adam and Eve must now engage in the work of becoming full human beings. This journey is one from preconscious wholeness to separate individualism and onward to fully conscious wholeness ("enlightenment" or "salvation"). What makes this project both so interesting and so challenging is that it has a dual nature. We must individualize as a separate self without completely losing our sense of oneness with the whole.

Even though Adam and Eve are now grappling with the Natural Anxiety of everyday survival, they have not forgotten Eden and they have not lost touch with Sacred Anxiety; it continually leads them back to God through prayer and sacrifice. Yet there is now a new generation, and their sons, Cain and Abel, symbolize a further stage in human development. Cain and Abel are the first generation to be born outside of Eden. They, like us, do not have a conscious memory of the Eden-like state of oneness with God. Cain and Abel were born with the capacity for self-consciousness and freedom of choice. And they have developed their own separate personalities.

Chapter 4 of Genesis tells the story of Cain and Abel. The first pivotal event occurs when both brothers offer a sacrifice to God, and God favors Abel's sacrifice and is displeased by Cain's. God's disapproval of Cain's sacrifice is not a capricious response. It signifies that Cain has failed to acknowledge his connection to the whole and is hardening and separating his personality.

The second pivotal event in this story is Cain's murder of Abel. Seeing God's displeasure has made Cain aware that God knows of his intransigence and Cain experiences Sacred Anxiety. Yet he now compounds his initial error by refusing to listen to this healthy anxiety and instead projects his fear of God upon his brother. Cain allows the existence of the other—Abel—to threaten his primitive sense of wholeness. As the firstborn, he was the "one and only" and is not about to surrender to this experience of Sacred Anxiety and use it for spiritual growth. Convinced that Abel is a threat to his own existence as a personality, Cain decides to relieve his anxiety by destroying his brother.

Cain finds Abel and says, "Let us go out in the field together." When they are in the field Cain rises up against his brother and kills him.[11] What a tragic moment in human history this represents, a moment that echoes down through every war, every act of violence, and every uncaring, selfish act that harms another person. Imagine Cain's supreme act of arrogance: to use the strength and intelligence God gave him to destroy one of God's creations solely to defend his self-created personality! All animals must destroy other life to eat; in doing so they serve life, not death. But when humans destroy other life in an attempt to eliminate it from their self's private universe, they serve the powers of death. This first murder, like all subsequent murders throughout history, was done in "self-defense"—in defense of the self-image. When the part attempts to usurp the whole, the natural order is thrown into disharmony.

Here the biblical God uses the word "sin" for the very first time.[12] God never told Adam and Eve that they had sinned, but now he uses this word to describe Cain's destructive intentions. *To sin is to misuse the gift of consciousness.* The essence of evil is using the power of consciousness to create a false version of reality that serves the personality's need to be God. When the personality attempts to usurp God's role and sit on God's throne, we transgress the natural order. When we identify our essence more with our temporary, illusory self-image than with the eternal living God, our powerful psychobiological instinct for self-preservation is mobilized to defend the personality rather than be used for spiritual growth.

The crucial lesson of Genesis is that becoming conscious beings with free will is not a sin. It is the *misuse* of this gift that brings evil into the world.

THE CAIN COMPLEX AND THE ABEL COMPLEX

We have seen that becoming fully human means negotiating the dual challenge of forming an individual self while maintaining our identity with the greater whole. Cain and Abel demonstrate the two ways in which we can fail to meet this challenge.

The Cain complex is the sin of pride, hubris, and megalomania. It is the hubris of the part attempting to become the whole. Cain responded to the excruciating anxiety of being a small, imperfect self in a vast universe by attempting to become the whole through obliterating Abel (the other). He also tried to impose his own reality upon the world by lying to God about what he had done. Cain clearly lacks the sense of healthy shame and healthy guilt that characterizes one who honors Sacred Anxiety. (Freud glimpsed this primal sin through his own personality and saw it as the sexually motivated Oedipal complex, the son's desire to kill the father and marry the mother. But this impulse is not solely or primarily sexual; as we see with Cain, it is existential.)

When we try to impose our reality on others, or on the universe itself, to exclude all other realities, we have overstepped our bounds and have tried to become God. Like Cain, we may feel that, "This town isn't big enough for both of us." When gripped by the Cain complex, we begin to lose the vital perspective that every other person has just as much claim to wholeness as we do. When we attempt to gain our wholeness at the expense of someone else's wholeness, we have transgressed beyond the natural limits of the self.

The Biblical commandment against the creation and deification of "graven images"[13]—self-created images that are worshipped as gods—speaks to this temptation to deify the self. God, the formless and infinite says to us, "Thou shalt have no other gods before me."[14] The most tempting graven image has never been a golden calf; it always has been our own self-image.

At some level Cain remembered his spiritual wholeness, but like others who remain trapped in narcissism and grandiosity, he misapplied it to his transitory personality. The Cain complex appears when we experience Natural or Sacred Anxiety and, instead of allowing it to lead us to spiritual growth, we harden our self and use our personal power to destructively impose our will upon others. Cain cannot find the courage to face his own anxiety and wreaks destruction as he dumps it onto the outside world.

We are free to impose our personal will on the universe, but if we do the universe responds by pushing back and we become locked in a hopeless battle with the infinite. Then we live with the constant anxiety that ultimately we will lose this struggle with the universe. Cain's banishment into exile symbolizes this feeling of living in a hostile universe; the mark that was placed on Cain's forehead is the furrowed brow, the anxiety and alienation that has accompanied Cain and his descendants down through the ages.

The other way we are deterred from becoming fully human is by succumbing to the Abel complex. Whereas Cain projected his anxiety destructively, Abel failed to listen productively to his own anxiety. Abel had witnessed his brother's sullen, angry attitude at the altar and his jealous look. When Cain invited Abel to go out into the field, Abel must have sensed a threat to his existence, but he failed to heed it. Instead of trusting his own truth, disturbing as it might have been, Abel chose to suppress his anxiety. Abel is the prototype of the neurotic, the "nice guy," who turns anxiety against himself, resulting in low self-esteem, self-sabotage, and psychosomatic illness. Whereas Cain was the first murderer, Abel was the first victim. Our sympathies are clearly with Abel, yet by not listening to his anxiety Abel *enables* evil, just as countless others have done throughout history when they failed to listen to their anxiety regarding oppression and injustice in their midst. By clinging to an excessively rosy, naive, and idealistic mindset, Abel failed to honor his Natural Anxiety (also known as "street smarts") sufficiently for self-protection.

The Abel complex symbolizes the failure to bear the anxiety required to develop one's selfhood. It manifests itself whenever we let other people define who we are or what we believe. The existential anxiety of being a separate self is relieved by a premature merging of a partially formed self into a larger whole. When people join groups or adopt belief systems to avoid the responsibility of thinking for themselves, they follow in Abel's footsteps (and often become victimized by power-hungry Cains). Abel fails to find sufficient courage—and it takes great courage—to stand up for his selfhood.

Both Cain and Abel fail to deal with their own anxiety re-

sponsibly and creatively. Both misuse the gift of consciousness
and free will, and this, not consciousness itself, was the true original sin.

FACING ANXIETY OR SUCCUMBING TO EVIL

Why do we so often fail to make the healthy choice and face
our anxiety? This is one of the deepest mysteries of human life
and it takes us to the origin of evil. Evil is the attempt to stop
the flow of life as it courses through us, bringing changes and
challenges. Ironically, "evil" is "live" spelled backward; evil is
misusing free will to turn sacred life energy back against itself.
But why do we choose the lower path over the higher one?

All acts of evil, from the most trivial to the most horrific,
arise from a fundamental unwillingness to face the pain of our
own Natural and Sacred Anxiety. When Cain's sacrifice was re-
jected, he experienced a threat to his self-importance that re-
verberated all the way down to his bones, so deeply that he felt
them rattling with the fear of death. By refusing to face his Sacred Anxiety, Cain descended to the level of Toxic Anxiety and
engaged in a presumptuous effort to enshrine his persona's form
as fixed and eternal. This leads to a hardening of the self, a mind
and body hardening that is the opposite of spiritual growth. M.
Scott Peck called those who succumb to this ancient temptation
"people of the lie."[15] People who have become dominated by
evil have one clear, defining characteristic—a refusal to face
their own anxiety.

Existential evil is the refusal to heed the call to adventure to
which anxiety invites us. This adventure is nothing less than the
adventure of life itself, the adventure of evolution and growth.
When we allow anxiety to work on us in the right way, we begin to evolve spiritually. Every human being possesses freedom
of choice. In some cases, the degree of choice has become tragically limited, yet by making even the smallest decision for
growth and goodness one begins to change one's life course. As

Viktor Frankl observed, ". . . even the helpless victim of a hopeless situation, facing a fate he cannot change, may rise above himself, may grow beyond himself, and by so doing change himself."[16] Then Natural and Sacred Anxiety become the sculptor's chisels that eventually remove everything nonessential from the personality, leaving nothing but the true self.

As human beings, we are all subject to anxiety, so all of us are faced with the same question: How do we deal with our anxiety? This is the most basic question in human life and our answer to it defines our character. Understanding anxiety's role leads to a simple definition of a practical morality: Good is to heed anxiety's call and transform it, often only by enduring personal pain, into spiritual growth. Evil is to refuse to face anxiety; to introject it, killing life inside, or to project it, killing life outside.

This energy that has been cut off from life by an act of human will now becomes an inhuman monster with a life of its own. This is the force of evil (which religions personify as Satan) that circulates through human life and is passed down from one generation to another—a phantasm that feeds on the human habits of aggression and repression. This evil energy can erupt into world-shaking spectacles of horror, such as the Holocaust, but usually it corresponds more closely to W. H. Auden's description in his poem "Herman Melville":

> *Evil is unspectacular and always human.*
> *And shares our bed and eats at our own table.*

That evil is a part of my daily life and yours is a disturbing notion. The insensitive comment, the readiness to blame, the uncharitable thought, the taking advantage of another person's weakness, and the hardening of the heart against a stranger's pain are all part of the continuum of evil. If evil is the unwillingness to face our own anxiety, then we all are touched by evil. In this way, each of us fights our own personal daily battle against the forces of evil. To recognize the reality of evil in our daily life can be greatly empowering for anyone who wishes to fight evil in the world. We need not seek it only in some distant tyrant or great societal injustice; it is here at home with us and can be fought in our daily lives. Recognizing the ubiquity of ordinary evil also prods us to recognize the daily necessity of awareness, repentance, and forgiveness in all our relationships.

It is only when great numbers of ordinary people cease to manage their daily anxieties effectively that demagogues like Hitler can gain popularity with their lethally divisive final solutions. Today, as we see anxiety growing rampantly in virtually every nation of our planet, the fight against evil, on all levels from the personal to the political, is essential to humanity's well-being. Understanding the role of anxiety in human life can provide the tools that are so crucially necessary for combating evil.

The solution to humanity's problems lies not in our ability to acquire knowledge and technology, but in how we use our human powers of consciousness. The Arthurian legend of the grail, like many classic myths, has this dilemma at its core. The great question of the grail is, "Whom do you serve?" It is when the part isolates itself and no longer uses its power to serve the whole that the kingdom falls into disarray.

The more I probe the existential plight I share with other members of my species, the more compassion I have for everyone on this planet. What an anxious and perplexing enterprise it is to be human! We have evolved to become as gods, and yet each of us is destined to be food for worms. We have been given free will but with the understanding that we should use it to do God's will. Furthermore, we are expected to do God's will without having any method of discerning it with certitude. We have developed the capacity for individual selfhood, and yet are expected to sacrifice it for the good of the whole. What makes it all so difficult is finding the balance. We can no longer live the instinct-driven life of an animal, yet neither are we immortal all-knowing gods. As the poets tell us, we are neither beasts nor angels but partake of both. We are the in-between creatures who must constantly balance between heaven and earth.

ACCEPTING ANXIETY

Chapter 4 of Genesis concludes upon a hopeful note for humankind. After Abel's murder and Cain's banishment, Adam and Eve have a third son, Seth. He has heard the stories of his older brothers' fatefully flawed choices and has learned from them. Seth becomes a righteous man and he prospers with God's blessing.

These three sons of the first human family symbolize the archetypal responses to existential anxiety. Cain allowed anxiety to influence him destructively. Abel failed to let anxiety influence him productively. Seth found the balance that eluded them and learned to use anxiety in the right way, for self-development and spiritual growth. From him descended a race of God-fearing people, including Noah who, attuned to Sacred Anxiety, enabled humanity to survive the great flood that covered the earth.

Understanding the origins of anxiety can help us to accept it in our lives. It is not a shameful sign of our imperfection, but an emblem of our spiritual nature. Our task is to embrace our anxiety and elevate it to the highest levels. Ultimately, there are only two things worth getting anxious about: one is life, and how we live it; the other is death, and how we meet it.

This timeless creation myth, this story of Adam and Eve, has suffered greatly from years of misinterpretation. Yet it still contains the hidden wisdom of our ancestors regarding our origins, of which this necessarily brief excavation can only begin to reveal the most immediate layers. This myth tells us that we were created in God's image and that biting the apple of consciousness was the beginning of the greatest adventure in the universe. When we choose to transform our Toxic Anxiety into Natural and Sacred Anxiety, we are doing divine work. The everyday problems and hassles of life, when understood from a higher perspective, become opportunities to further our soul's evolution.

After experiencing the anxiety of consciousness, surely Adam and Eve would have liked to return to Eden. But God blocked their return. First they were compelled to venture forth into the natural world, to till the soil, master the material world, and bear children. After their journey to individuation began, they needed to become engaged with the world to become fully incarnated. Yet we know that as they and the ever-multiplying generations that follow them become entangled in the world and experience the suffering of fleshly existence, they yearn for serenity and begin to search for the path to Paradise. The flaming sword God placed at Eden's gate not only guards the entrance but paradoxically serves as a shining beacon to guide the way to the Tree of Life. This fiery sword symbolizes the light of consciousness, and only through developing our consciousness to the fullest can we find our way back to the garden.

Like Adam and Eve, like Cain, we try to hide from God. Yet God comes looking for us, as God went looking for them. Oneness cannot be denied, yet we fear union with our source as much as we desire it because it reminds us of our smallness and separateness. God calls to us through our Sacred Anxiety, which is inseparable from love. It calls us home to God, to each other, and to this heavenly earth.

Part Two

TRANSFORMING TOXIC ANXIETY

TOXIC ANXIETY

Symbol: The Monster

Toxic Anxiety has been called the "fear of fear itself" and "being anxious about being anxious." It ranges from neurosis, worry, fear, dread, and panic across the gamut of psychological disorders and stress-related illnesses. It is also what impels destructive urges directed at others: disapproval, shaming, manipulation, violence, and abuse.

When we refuse to face our own Natural and Sacred Anxiety, what we suppress turns toxic. Disowned anxieties go underground and then rise up in highly destructive forms. Toxic Anxiety predominates when we habitually suppress our desires, feelings, thoughts, or memories.

The positive purpose of Toxic Anxiety is to get our attention and make us aware of unresolved personal issues and inner conflicts. Conquering the monster of Toxic Anxiety means that we must be willing to do our inner work and to face the Natural and Sacred Anxiety of life on a continuing basis. If we do so, Toxic Anxiety can be reduced and gradually eliminated. The two keys to mastering Toxic Anxiety are self-calming and greater self-awareness (or emotional intelligence). When we learn to listen to Toxic Anxiety in the right way, it can help us achieve greater self-knowledge, mental and physical health, and an integrated, authentic self.

Chapter Four

MASTERING ANXIETY

THE TOLL OF TOXIC ANXIETY

In the story of Cain and Abel we saw how Toxic Anxiety is formed when we refuse an encounter with the Natural and Sacred Anxiety inherent in life. Our refusal blocks the process of growth and turns our own life energy against ourselves. Now toxified, this energy begins to attack the life force. As the Cain complex it launches its assault at others through blame, criticism, abuse, and violence. As the Abel complex it attacks inwardly as illness, psychoemotional problems, low self-esteem, and self-defeating behaviors.

Toxic Anxiety lies at the root of most of our problems. If, like Cain or Abel, we fail to use anxiety for growth, it soon begins to affect the course of our life. Usually the effects are not as sudden or dramatic as Cain's and Abel's, but they are just as certain. When we habitually respond to anxiety in dysfunctional ways, it gradually diminishes our character and diverts the course of our life. Over the years, chronic anxiety can change our posture, etch lines in our face, alter our biochemistry, and even injure the physical structure of our brain and other vital organs. Dysfunctional responses to anxiety are widespread and manifest themselves not only in physical, but in mental and social symptoms as well.

Toxic Anxiety often contributes to developing stress-related physical illnesses—from cardiovascular disease to a common cold. In an experiment by Sheldon Cohen, Ph.D., at Carnegie Mellon University, four hundred people were administered nose drops containing cold viruses. Ninety percent of the people who had previously reported high levels of anxiety-producing stress caught a cold (compared to only seventy-four percent of the less anxious group).[1] Prolactin, a stress-related hormone linked to rheumatoid arthritis, was twice as high in people reporting anxiety-producing interpersonal troubles in a study at Arizona State University.

The stress and anxiety hormones are not just related to the fight-or-flight reaction. They play an important role in maintaining the day to day health of the body. The hypothalamic-pituitary axis, which masterminds our responses to anxiety, also regulates the digestive and cardiovascular systems, sleep and appetite patterns, and virtually every aspect of our biochemistry. So when we become chronically anxious and "stressed-out" every cell in our body knows it, and may be damaged by it.

In the mental sphere, all of us have experienced how anxiety can affect our ability to think clearly. Perhaps most dramatically, when anxiety is too high during important events such as taking an exam or giving a talk, it can interfere with our ability to perform at our best. It can also result in the inattention that causes an accident. In seeking relief from the discomfort of high levels of anxiety-producing chemicals, we may turn to "self-medication" in the form of alcohol, drugs, or food. When we suffer from high levels of anxiety and lack self-calming skills, addictive habits become a way to obtain temporary relief. The inability to handle anxiety productively becomes a continuous and vexing dilemma in life since each day brings with it new anxiety-arousing problems. Overall, chronic Toxic Anxiety can distort our entire way of thinking and lead to delusions, prejudice, paranoia, phobias, and other psychological aberrations.

On the social level, anxiety interferes with human relationships. The process of interpersonal communication is impaired when anxiety-related neurotransmitters create static in the nervous system; we respond to minor slights as if they were major provocations. It becomes harder to listen, harder to empathize, when we are wearing anxiety's armor. (High levels of the anxiety-related hormone ACTH can trigger excess serotonin in the brain, a condition linked to abusive behavior and violence.)

Anxiety not only affects us on the physical, mental, and social spheres of life, but on the spiritual dimension as well. Many of the world's religions have identified "fear" and anxiety as the greatest impediments to moral behavior and spiritual growth.

Clearly, the effects of anxiety are both broad and deep. Since it affects body, mind, and spirit in such interconnected ways, anxiety can best be mastered through a comprehensive, holistic approach.

We are in the midst of a revolution—a revolution in consciousness. The split between mind and body that has characterized Western civilization for centuries is now being replaced by the mindbody connection. Each week brings new reports of scientific research that further erase Descartes' dividing line between mental events (thoughts and emotions) and bodily events (biochemical reactions). Books by holistic physicians such as Deepak Chopra, Larry Dossey, Bernie Siegel, and Andrew Weil are welcomed by readers eager to make the mindbody connection in their own lives. The general public may be ahead of their own doctors in this area—according to the *New England Journal of Medicine*, we spend over $13 billion a year on holistic medicine, most of it out of our own pockets. But physicians are catching up quickly. Dozens of medical schools now offer courses in "alternative medicine." The treatment of stress-related illnesses, anxiety, and depression have brought the mind-body connection onto center stage. Our culture has only just begun to digest the full implications of this dramatic shift in paradigms.

Biological Psychiatry: Rediscovering the Body

For most of this century, psychology neglected the body's important role in mental functioning. During the last two decades we have experienced a massive change in the way mental health problems are treated. Research into the biological aspects of mental dysfunction began to reveal a wide range of potent and sophisticated neurochemicals that could influence psychological functioning. The advent of these powerful and effective medications has ushered in an era of pharmacological psychiatry. Research also led to an array of cognitive and behavioral methods of restoring anxious and depressed people to their former levels of functioning. After many decades of sitting and talking, psychology rediscovered the body and the importance of taking action.

Unfortunately, because our culture remains largely dominated by the split mindbody model, we are still a long way from a holistic synthesis of mental and physical approaches to health care. The medical pendulum seems to swing back and forth between body and mind without genuinely synthesizing them. Not long ago many physicians were advising their anxiety patients that "It's all in your head"; now most tell them that "It's just biological!" In rediscovering the body, psychiatry is now in danger of forgetting the mind, especially its unconscious dimension. One currently popular trend attempts to reduce all difficulties of mental life to problems in biochemistry that will eventually be solved in the laboratory. The long-overdue reemphasis on the physical dimension of mental life is provoking a rush to use pharmaceutical agents rather than a serious appraisal of integrated, holistic approaches to restoring mindbody harmony.

This is unfortunate because the mindbody split is one of the main *causes* of the current anxiety epidemic. Modern life increasingly separates our minds from our bodies. We typically spend the work day in a disembodied cyberspace world of information and computers. We get from one place to the next by sitting in rolling capsules sealed off from the world around us and we relax by sitting on a couch reading or watching TV. Then we try to balance this lopsided mindbody gap by spending a few hours a week interacting with exercise machines at a health club. The resulting alienation from our own bodies—and the emotions that live within them—plays a major role in creating that vague "out of touch with myself" sense of anxiety that pervades our lives.

Do "Biological" Problems Always Need Pharmaceutical Solutions?

Now that psychology has rediscovered the body, we must take care to resist the easy swing to new extremes. Much of the current debate is still couched in dualistic thinking: which is more basic, the mind or the body? The answer is not either/or but both/and. Our thoughts influence our biochemistry and our biochemistry influences our thoughts. When it comes to human suffering, there are always multiple levels of causation: physical, mental, social, and spiritual. One person's anxiety may be caused primarily by genetic and constitutional tendencies; another person's mostly by childhood conditioning; someone else's by economic insecurities or social discrimination; and yet another person's by existential issues of meaning and purpose. The importance of each causative level differs from person to person, but for most of us anxiety is produced by a subtle interaction at all levels of being.

Biological anxiety may also be caused by a wide variety of physical illnesses including cardiovascular problems, digestive illnesses, allergies, hormonal irregularities, and blood sugar conditions. A surprising amount of today's biological anxiety is

caused by medications, including some over-the-counter remedies. Ironically, medications for anxiety and depression frequently caution that anxiety and depression are among the
possible side effects. People who regularly take multiple medications of any kind are particularly likely to suffer from iatro-
genic anxiety (anxiety caused by medical treatment). Persistent,
unexplained anxiety always warrants a thorough physical examination including a review of all medications being taken as well
as a psychological examination.

A large component of every case of anxiety and depression
is biological. But what does that mean? Simply finding a low
level of a certain neurotransmitter in the brain of anxious people does not mean that such a specific deficiency is the cause of
their anxiety. Just because administering a certain drug makes
someone feel less anxious or depressed does not indicate that
this is the best solution.

We need to ask what has caused the body to produce more, or
less, than the optimal amount of a certain neurotransmitter. For
a few people the primary cause may be a genetic glitch of some
kind, in which case supplemental medication would clearly be
the treatment of choice. But for the vast majority, the cause of
biochemical imbalances is far more mundane. Most of the biological aspect of anxiety is caused by ordinary lifestyle habits—
years of drinking too much coffee and caffeinated soft drinks,
not eating properly, not exercising enough, not sleeping well,
never experiencing relief from chronic muscular tension, and
entertaining too many anxiety-producing thoughts throughout
the day. Given this, does it really make sense to take a pill that enables us to continue the same unhealthy lifestyle, or do we need
instead to listen more carefully to the message of the anxiety
epidemic? Are we willing to change our anxiety-producing
lifestyles—and the anxiety-producing society that fosters such
behavior?

YOUR BODY HAS A MIND OF ITS OWN

Experiences change biochemistry. Anxiety-producing experiences, especially in childhood, result in physical changes that predispose people to overreact to stress. According to Seymour Levine, Ph.D., of the University of Delaware, "this sensitization actually alters physical patterns in the brain. That means that once sensitized, the body just does not respond to stress the same way in the future. We may produce too many excitatory chemicals or too few calming ones; either way we are responding inappropriately."

After we have been conditioned to respond to stressors with anxiety, we develop a kind of allergic reaction every time we are exposed to a difficult situation. Just like the hay fever sufferer whose body overreacts, mounting a full-scale attack on itself in response to harmless pollen, the anxious person's body reacts to minor daily hassles as if they were life-threatening emergencies. This continual state of arousal accelerates aging, depletes energy, and weakens the immune system. According to Jean King, Ph.D., of the University of Massachusetts Medical School, chronic anxiety reactions to stress act "like a slow poison" in the body. Toxic Anxiety is aptly named, for it literally creates a toxic biochemical condition in the human body.

A broad-based study by Howard Friedman, Ph.D., of the University of California, found that the presence of chronic negative emotions associated with dysfunctional responses to anxiety *doubled* the susceptibility to a wide variety of illnesses. When we become chronically anxious and stressed-out, every cell in our body knows it—and may be damaged by it.

One research study (reported at the American Psychiatric Association in June 1995) that used magnetic resonance imaging (MRI) to take pictures of the brain made a discovery with potentially far-reaching implications. The researchers found that women with a documented history of sexual abuse had a smaller-than-normal hippocampus (a part of the brain involved in memory and stress reactions) compared with those of women who hadn't suffered abuse. War veterans suffering from posttraumatic stress disorder (PTSD) were also found to have a smaller hippocampus. So experiences, especially chronic or powerful ones, may actually change not only the biochemistry but also the very structure of our brain!

Another recent study at the UCLA School of Medicine showed that effective psychotherapy alone could restore normal brain chemistry in obsessive compulsive patients. Dr. Steven Hyman, director of the National Institute of Mental Health, observes that the latest research shows "that anything—whether a drug, a war experience or a talking therapy—changes the way nerve cells talk to each other. In the brain, hardware as well as software is always changing."[2]

Ironically, the same research that shows how important biological factors are to the life of the mind is also demonstrating how dramatically our biochemistry and our physical bodies are affected by our thoughts and experiences.

This type of research brings the mindbody connection full circle. Mind and body are not only connected, they are one! Just as negative experiences can provoke abnormal biochemical reactions and damage brain structure, positive experiences can restore normal functioning. This understanding can lead to new approaches to treating illness and change the way we choose to live our lives.

Awareness of the mindbody connection forces us to rethink many of our assumptions regarding human behavior. How does chronic poverty affect brain chemistry? How does getting laid-off after twenty-five years at the same company alter one's level of serotonin? How does social discrimination affect the brain? How does an unkind word affect the neurotransmitters in both the speaker and the listener?

Perhaps instead of less therapeutic talk, we need more, much more. What if we could take healing talk beyond the psychotherapist's office and into our homes, beyond workshops and into our workplaces, and beyond clinics and into our streets? What effect would healing talk have on our collective brain chemistry? But we need more than talk; we need healing actions—social action that restores a sense of trust and safety to our culture. If wars, abuse, and muggings can damage brains, then caring communities and healing social rituals can help brains develop and keep them healthy.

MEDICATION OR MEDITATION?

If "listening to Prozac" reminds us that our mind has a body, that is a message worth heeding. By breaking deeply ingrained, self-destructive patterns on the biological level, medications can enable individuals to have a choice regarding their behavior. But a more direct approach might be simply listening to our body. Many new body-oriented psychotherapies provide techniques to do just that. Instead of placing a filter between the inner problem and conscious awareness, these new mindbody therapies use conscious awareness to penetrate and resolve the psychobiological roots of the problem. These methods work at the interface of mind and body and combine counseling skills with hypnosis, meditation, breathwork, bodywork, yoga postures, expressive role play, and other ways of awakening the healing power of the body. In my work with clients and in my personal healing, I have found that the unconscious mind and the body contain an incredible wealth of healing wisdom. We all possess an inner pharmacy that in most cases is fully capable of providing just the prescription we need. Awareness of our inner states can unlock the pharmacy, discard outdated formulas, and mix new remedies.

Meditation is proving to be a potent alternative to medication for many physical problems, such as high blood pressure and chronic pain, as well as for mental problems, such as anxiety and depression. Jon Kabat-Zinn's work at the University of Massachusetts Medical Center provides inspiring data on the efficacy of meditation for both medical and psychological problems.[3]

Many clients I have worked with have experienced substantial, often amazing, psychological benefits from such simple lifestyle changes as getting more sleep (fatigue alone will induce anxiety symptoms), eating a more natural, balanced diet (some people are actually allergic to the very foods they crave), and exercising regularly (without exercise, tension and stress accumulate in the musculature and create biological anxiety).

In my own clinical practice, I both encourage certain clients to explore the benefits of medication and help clients build the skills that enable them to live free of medications. For most of the population, an education/training model that emphasizes skill-building and support in a group setting may in the long run prove to be a more effective and more affordable approach to preventing and treating anxiety and mood disorders than either traditional individual psychotherapy or long-term drug therapy.

We ignore the epidemic of anxiety and despair in our midst only at great peril to society as a whole. Holistic solutions that encompass the biological, psychological, social, and spiritual dimensions provide the most effective response to the challenge anxiety presents to modern civilization. In this book, we explore some of the most effective mindbody approaches to mastering anxiety on the personal level, yet without losing sight of the larger societal and spiritual dimensions.[4]

ANXIETY AND EMOTIONAL INTELLIGENCE

The mindbody revolution offers great hope for solving the problem of anxiety. As a society we are waking up to the price we pay for the mindbody split that has alienated modern humanity from itself. Our emotional life has long occupied a no-man's land between mind and body and suffered from official neglect. We train the intellect in the classroom and the body in the gym, but there is no place in our society for emotional training. A fast-paced materialistic society that does not teach basic skills in emotional self-management to its young is bound to produce increasing numbers of people with mental and behavioral disorders and stress-related illnesses.

Our emotions are the bridge connecting mind and body. They lie somewhere between purely mental intellectualizing and purely physical sensations such as heat and cold. Emotions partake of both worlds. Anxiety, joy, and sadness are bodily as well as mental experiences. (This physical dimension is reflected throughout our language. We describe our emotions as heart-warming, gut-wrenching, spine-tingling, etc.) Emotional intelligence is the ability to bring conscious awareness to the inner world of the emotions, to connect the mental and physical realms of experience.[5] People who suffer from anxiety, mood disorders, or behavioral problems invariably lack proficiency in this skill. As Daniel Goleman has observed, "our culture encourages us to be emotional illiterates, living at the mercy of emotional storms."[6]

Emotional intelligence consists of two interdependent components, which were identified by Howard Gardner of Harvard University in his groundbreaking book, *Frames of Mind: The Theory of Multiple Intelligences.*[7] The first and most basic is *intrapersonal intelligence*—the ability to know how we are really feeling and to manage our emotions in healthy ways. The second, *interpersonal intelligence*, develops along with the first and represents the ability to understand and empathize with other people and to communicate effectively with them.

The most basic element of emotional intelligence is the ability to recognize and utilize anxiety effectively. Every emotion—fear, sadness, anger, even happiness—is closely related to anxiety and often originates as a response to anxiety. For example, anger is an active, self-protective response to the anxiety triggered by a threat or conflict. Grief, sadness, and crying are healthy ways of releasing the anxiety caused by loss and disappointment. Happiness and joy are made possible by the mastery of anxiety and its alleviation. The joy and exhilaration we experience when we succeed at achieving a challenging personal goal are directly proportional to our prior anxiety about its outcome. And, when a loved one finally comes through the gate at the airport, our joy reflects the sudden relief we feel with their safe arrival.

When our basic response to anxiety becomes disordered or confused, every emotion is adversely affected. Becoming emotionally intelligent regarding anxiety involves being able to recognize the feeling of anxiety in oneself and others, to precisely identify the source of the perceived threat that triggered the anxiety, and to devise an effective emotional and behavioral response.

ACQUIRING EMOTIONAL INTELLIGENCE

We learn—or are deprived of the opportunity to learn—these emotional skills as children. Almost all of our emotional responses are programmed into our subconscious mind during our first years of life. Enduring emotional habits are imprinted either through a few highly charged traumatic events or, more frequently, through everyday interactions that are repeated hundreds of times. In the following examples of healthy and unhealthy emotional learning, I have simplified this complex process into a single incident.

If Andy falls off his bicycle and starts to cry, an effective parent will help Andy sort out his anxiety—the fear of being hurt, his sadness about the damage to his bike, etc. His initial undifferentiated anxiety is released through crying, grieving, and talking things over with an empathetic listener. Andy's parent may offer useful information to help him understand why he fell and how to ride more safely. As a result, next time Andy will be able to understand what's happening and comfort himself more skillfully. He feels confident getting back on his bike, knowing that even if he falls off he can calm himself and recover.

But what if Andy's parent had become angry at the damage

to the new bike ("I guess you don't appreciate it enough to be careful!") or had become hysterical ("My God! What happened? Are you OK? What's the matter? I shouldn't have let you ride that thing—bikes are so dangerous!"). Now Andy not only has to deal with his own inner feelings but with the confusing barrage of messages and emotions cascading down on him from the person he looks to for nurturing.

Andy can't learn healthy self-calming in this situation. His anxiety escalates and also becomes mixed with shame and guilt at having done something "wrong" and with unconscious anger about being dumped on instead of helped. His confusing feelings remain unprocessed, and he learns to just stuff them inside and put himself back together as well as possible. Andy has just learned that anxiety is unmanageable and confusing and is best pushed aside as soon as possible. He is now even more anxious about falling off his bike because he doesn't know how to cope with the consequences.

Here is another example involving anger:

Roberta is playing happily with her favorite toy when her younger sister Elana comes over and takes it from her. Roberta experiences anxiety, triggered by this sudden loss of a valued object. She perceives the loss as unfair and estimates her chances of regaining her toy from her little sister as quite high. As a result, her initial anxiety quickly turns into anger-fueled action and she grabs her toy back. Little Elana starts to cry.

Their mother overhears the conflict and asks the girls, "What's the problem here?" Roberta and Elana both tell their sides of the story. Mom helps the girls understand each other's feelings and also helps them work out a solution that pleases both of them: Roberta can continue to play with her toy, but agrees to let Elana have a turn later.

Even more important than the solution was the learning process. Roberta learned that it was normal to feel angry, but that using force to get her way was not the best behavior. She found that she could talk about her feelings and her needs, and both Mom and Elana listened. She also learned the importance of taking into account the other person's feelings and needs.

Roberta just received some important training in assertiveness and conflict resolution. The next time she has a conflict with her sister or a friend she has a successful model she can use to deal with it. She learned that she could change her anxiety about a threat into self-protective anger that she could express through healthy assertive behavior.

Let's look at how the same situation can turn out to have a negative outcome for all concerned when effective anxiety management techniques are not used: Roberta's mother enters the situation and tells her, "Don't be so selfish, Roberta. Be a good girl and share your toy with Elana." When Roberta, still angry and wanting her toy, keeps trying to pry it out of Elana's hands, her mother yanks Roberta up, saying, "If you're going to be a naughty girl then go to your room."

Roberta goes to her room feeling angry about the toy, feeling angry at her mother for being unfair, and feeling guilty about being a bad girl who is selfish and hates her mom. Hurt and alone, she starts to cry and her mother comes and comforts her.

Roberta has now learned that it doesn't work to turn this type of anxiety into anger; turning it into sadness works better. The next time Roberta is faced with an infringement of her rights, instead of becoming angry and channeling that healthy protective energy into assertive behavior, she automatically converts it to sadness and hurt. Years later as an adult she never gets angry, but she suffers from migraine headaches.

When children are conditioned to experience conflict between what they actually feel and what they have learned they should feel, they have been placed in a double bind. They are unfairly forced to choose between two vital needs—the need to be authentically themselves and the need for love and approval. This double bind in many ways symbolizes the core conundrum of Toxic Anxiety, one we will examine later in more detail.

Self-Awareness Is the First Step
Toward Change

An understanding of the central role anxiety plays in human life can help us in two fundamental ways: First, it can help us devise solutions to the many natural and inevitable problems that are part of life, because our ability to deal effectively with such problems is directly proportional to our skill in employing the anxiety which they arouse. Second, since many, if not most, of the problems we experience today are actually caused directly or indirectly by dysfunctional responses to anxiety, even small changes in our relationship to anxiety can prevent and eliminate much of our distress.

Since all of us have been programmed with at least some ineffective anxiety responses earlier in our lives, we can benefit greatly by becoming more aware of our Toxic Anxiety patterns and changing them into healthier responses. The following questionnaire will help you to explore some of your own habitual anxiety responses and discover how to use your natural tendencies in more positive ways.

ANXIETY PERSONALITY-TYPE QUESTIONNAIRE

In the following anxiety personality-type questionnaire you will have an opportunity to identify some of the anxiety response tendencies you have acquired over the years. This questionnaire is designed to help you identify your predominant anxiety reaction tendencies. It is not intended as a diagnostic instrument or as a replacement for therapy. Following the questionnaire, you will learn about the six basic anxiety personality types and how to maximize your ability to respond to anxiety in productive ways.

There are no right or wrong answers to this questionnaire. Each response simply describes a common reaction to a potentially anxiety-producing situation. You will need about 15 minutes to answer the questionnaire and another 10 minutes to tabulate the results on the scoring guide that follows.

Instructions: Each item describes a hypothetical situation. Imagine how you would respond in that situation. Then write a number from 6 to 1 in each blank: 6 represents your most likely response to the situation de-

scribed, 5 represents your next most likely reaction, all the way down to 1, representing your least likely response. Use each number only once and be sure to place a number in each blank.

Here are a few tips on how to have the most fun and get the most accurate feedback from this questionnaire: Read through the entire range of responses (a–f) for each situation and then quickly jot the appropriate number in each blank starting with your most likely response (6) and ending with your least likely response (1). Don't take a long time trying to figure it out; your first impression is probably the most accurate. Make sure you fill in each blank with a different number. Get into the spirit of these hypothetical situations rather than taking them too literally. If you find it difficult to relate to a particular situation, use your imagination to picture what you might do if you found yourself in that (or a similar) situation and only had those six responses available. Questionnaires like this tend to exaggerate behaviors to provide more vivid contrast among the various responses.

Have fun with the questionnaire and be as honest with yourself as possible so that the results you get will be the most meaningful and helpful to you. You may also want to make copies of this questionnaire so you can compare your response profile with those of family members, friends, or co-workers. Knowing how other people react to anxiety can help reduce conflicts and enhance mutual understanding.

1. You overhear two people you care about having a loud argument in the next room.

___6___ a. You feel nervous and wonder if you should do something about it or just leave them alone.

___5___ b. You just shut it out of your mind and concentrate on what you are already doing.

___4___ c. You feel anxious and get a sinking feeling in your stomach.

___1___ d. You feel irritated and yell at them to quiet down.

___3___ e. You tell them to drop it for now and then try to talk about it later.

___2___ f. You offer to sit down with them and try to help

them come up with a solution that will make both of them happy.

2. You feel angry about something your partner or a close friend did.

   _5_ a. You try to talk about it, but back off when it's clear the other person doesn't want to.

   _2_ b. You just pretend it didn't happen.

   _1_ c. You get angry and "give 'em hell."

   _6_ d. You wonder why they did what they did and go back and forth about what to do.

   _3_ e. You are a little upset about it, but you don't say anything because you don't want to get more upset or make things worse.

   _4_ f. You feel they did something wrong so you criticize the other person's behavior.

3. You get a notice from the bank saying that you have overdrawn your account.

   _4_ a. You feel guilty, wondering if you forgot to record a check.

   _3_ b. You worry that several checks you have written recently will bounce and people will think you are irresponsible.

   _1_ c. You are angry at the bank for hassling you—they're probably the ones who made a mistake.

   _6_ d. You go down to the bank the next day and ask to speak with an account representative so you can resolve the problem.

   _5_ e. You review your checkbook and most recent statement and discover a minor error you made. You reprimand yourself for making such a stupid mistake and correct it immediately.

   _2_ f. After glancing at the notice you put the envelope in a drawer telling yourself you'll deal with it some other time.

4. You notice a minor but persistent pain that might be the sign of a health problem.

___4___ a. You feel irritated by it—you don't need any more hassles.

___6___ b. You act like nothing's wrong because you don't want anyone else to worry about you.

___3___ c. You panic at the thought that this may be the first sign of a serious illness. You know you should see your doctor but dread making an appointment.

___2___ d. You know you'll worry about it constantly so you make an appointment with your doctor. He says it's nothing serious, but later you worry that he might have missed something.

___5___ e. You figure it's probably nothing serious and forget about it.

___1___ f. You don't let it stop you because you've got a lot to do. But when you see your doctor, you insist on getting more tests to rule out all possibilities.

5. You have to give a 10-minute presentation at work regarding your portion of a major project.

___5___ a. You know that a friend of yours at work is also nervous about giving her presentation. You spend so much time giving her pep talks and helping her with her presentation that you barely have time to get your own organized.

___6___ b. You want to give a first-rate presentation; it's important that people see you as well-organized and competent. You spend more time than you can really afford getting your talk written out and practicing in front of a mirror.

___4___ c. You are irritated at having to give these "stupid" presentations—they ought to realize by now that you know your stuff.

___1___ d. You are petrified at the thought of giving a presentation. After tossing and turning for several sleepless nights, you start to worry that you might get sick. It turns out you are not feeling well the day of the presentation and call in sick.

_2_ e. You are not sure what you are going to say, but you figure you'll come up with something. It's not worth worrying about.

_3_ f. You dislike speaking in front of groups and lose sleep over it for days. You worry that your mind will race and your face will get red and everyone will know how nervous you are.

6. You win the lottery.

_6_ a. You immediately call a financial planner to get advice regarding taxes, investments, etc.

_1_ b. You feel overwhelmed by your change of fortune and your mood swings from elation to panic to depression.

_3_ c. You worry about how all this money will affect you and your relationships and how you can manage this huge sum of money responsibly.

_4_ d. You think about the vacations you can finally take and how great life is going to be.

_5_ e. You think about how much pleasure it will give you to be able to help your friends and family and your favorite causes.

_2_ f. You're glad you won but still get irritated at how much of your winnings the government takes in taxes.

7. You are at an informal cocktail party following a one-day conference you attended. You feel uncomfortable because you hardly know anyone there.

_6_ a. You feel nervous about not knowing what to say and move around the room checking to see if there is anyone there you know.

_1_ b. You head straight for the refreshment table, knowing that a drink or two will loosen you up and you'll have a good time.

_2_ c. You feel tongue-tied and a little panicky, not knowing what to do. You don't want to get more anxious so you decide to leave the party.

_4_ d. You join a group of people who are talking and try to tell them your opinion of the speakers.

_3_ e. You find the people who organized the conference and tell them that you have some ideas for next year's conference and would like to get involved in planning for it.

_6_ f. You notice someone who is standing alone and looking a little uncomfortable. You go over, smile, and say, "Hi, how did you like the conference?"

8. You are in line at the supermarket with a full shopping cart and someone holding a carton of milk and loaf of bread cuts in front of you, saying, "I'll just be a minute!"

_4_ a. You roll your eyes and pick up one of the magazines from the rack at the checkout counter.

_1_ b. You get angry and exclaim, "Wait a minute, I was here first!"

_6_ c. You smile and say "No problem," assuming they must be in a rush to pick up their child.

_3_ d. You tell the person, "You should wait in line like everyone else."

_5_ e. You're irritated but don't say anything because you don't want to appear unreasonable. Afterward you wonder if you were too much of a pushover.

_2_ f. You hate having to wait in lines and now you have to wait even longer. You wonder why these things always happen to you and you notice your heart is beating faster.

9. You have a disagreement with a friend about something you are planning to do together.

_1_ a. You know you're right and get in an argument with your friend about it.

___2___ b. You worry that if you get your way you might turn out to be wrong, but if you give in your friend might think you're a pushover.

___4___ c. You ignore the problem and hope it will resolve itself.

___6___ d. You see your friend's point of view and decide to do it their way this time, assuming they will return the favor in the future.

___5___ e. You hate conflicts because they make you anxious and give you headaches.

___3___ f. You marshal various facts and reasons to support your view and try to convince your friend to do it your way.

10. You belong to a club and meetings rotate between members' homes. It's your turn this week.

___1___ a. You dread having meetings at your house; it's just overwhelming. You ask a friend who's in the club to help you plan it because you're just not feeling up to it.

___6___ b. You prefer to have the meetings at your home because it's the only way you can be sure everything will be well-organized and the meeting will be productive.

___5___ c. You like hosting the meetings. You know how to make people feel welcome and always take care that everyone is included in the discussion.

___2___ d. You run the meetings your way because you know it's the best way. If other people don't like it that's too bad because it's your turn.

___34___ e. You enjoy having people over. People seemed to have fun last time even though the meeting was not too productive. The main thing is to have a good time.

___45___ f. You like getting together with people but you always feel a little anxious about everything going well. When the members thank you at the end of the evening, you wonder if they really had a good time or were just being polite.

11. When a problem comes up your motto is:
    ___4___ a. I'll worry about it.
    ___3___ b. I'll just forget about it.
    ___1___ c. I can't handle it.
    ___2___ d. I'll do it my way.
    ___5___ e. I can work to fix it.
    ___6___ f. I can help make it better.

12. When things get stressful . . .
    ___4___ a. you try harder and work more.
    ___3___ b. you rely more on "stress crutches," indulging in bad habits, watching TV, or just forgetting about it all.
    ___1___ c. you get irritated and lose your temper.
    ___2___ d. you get sick or give up temporarily, figuring someone else will deal with it.
    ___6___ e. you like to keep your lines of communication open and make sure you're getting along well with everyone.
    ___5___ f. you get anxious and worried.

SCORING INSTRUCTIONS

Write the numbers from your quiz in the appropriate boxes. For example, write your answer to question 1a in row 1, box a; write your answer to question 2c in row 2, box c. Look carefully; the letters are in different positions in each row.

When you have filled in all the boxes with numbers, add each column and write down the total. Then rank each column: your highest score is 1, your next highest score is 2, your lowest score is 6. Copy the results (Worrier, Controller, etc.) to the ranking below. If two or more types are the same or very close in their totals, you may want to indicate that they are tied or nearly equal.

	Worrier	Distracter	Internalizer	Externalizer	Controller	Helper
1	a 6	b 5	c 4	d 1	e 3	f 2
2	d 5	b 2	e 1	c 6	f 3	a 4
3	b 4	f 3	a 1	c 6	e 5	d 2
4	b 4	e 6	c 3	a 2	f 5	b 1
5	f 5	e 6	d 4	c 1	b 2	a 3
6	c 6	d 3	b 1	f 4	a 5	e 2
7	a 5	b 1	c 2	d 4	e 3	f 6
8	e 4	a 1	f 6	b 3	d 5	c 2
9	b 1	c 2	e 4	a 6	f 5	d 3
10	f 1	e 6	a 5	d 2	b 3	c 4
11	a 4	b 3	c 1	d 2	e 5	f 6
12	f 4	b 3	d 1	c 2	a 6	e 5
Total	49	41	33	39	50	40
Rank	2	3	6	5	1	4
	Worrier	Distracter	Internalizer	Externalizer	Controller	Helper

MY ANXIETY PERSONALITY-TYPE PROFILE

1. controller
2. worrier
3. Distracter
4. Helper
5. Externalizer
6. Internalizer.

THE SIX ANXIETY PERSONALITY TYPES

Now you have identified your predominant anxiety personality types. Here is a brief profile of the six different types to help you understand the characteristics of each. Most of us are a combination of various types and, for example, may respond as one type in a work situation and another type in a home situation.

THE WORRIER

Motto: "I'll worry about it."
Worriers respond to anxiety with intense, sometimes obsessive mental activity of a negative nature. They visualize bad things happening to them; worriers have active imaginations and torture themselves by visualizing worst-case scenarios. They often go back and forth with on-the-one-hand/on-the-other-hand thinking, producing more self-doubt and indecision. The worrying that Worriers do seldom leads to resolution; the same worrisome thoughts recycle endlessly. Worriers are overly concerned with how they appear to others and what other people think. They are very concerned with doing the right thing but are seldom clear what the right thing is. They often suffer from insomnia, digestive, or hormonal problems.

If you are a Worrier . . .

Worriers have a very powerful skill—an active mind—and they need to learn to use it to their advantage. Worriers are thinkers who have developed ineffective ways of using their minds. They can train themselves to visualize positive outcomes and to turn the worry habit into a proactive capacity to plan and develop strategies. Worriers also are good at introspection. Instead of using this ability to foster self-doubt and uncertainty, they can learn self-awareness skills like meditation, which help channel introspection in growth-producing directions. Worriers are skilled at recognizing that problems exist and bad things can happen, but they need to turn their anxiety into action. Instead of sitting around worrying endlessly about "what if's," Worriers need to choose a strategy and try it out. Only through actual experience can they learn and move forward.

THE DISTRACTER

Motto: "I'll just forget about it."

Distracters are a diverse group. Some like to go shopping or go out on the town, some like to stay home and watch TV, some love reading novels, some are alcoholics, some are workaholics, some overeat, some are religious, some are sports fans, some have affairs, some procrastinate, some are perennial optimists, and some appear to have no anxiety at all. What they all have in common is that they have developed ways of distracting themselves from their anxiety. Distracters use denial as their main defense against anxiety. (I once had a client who described how she dealt with a problem when one occurred: "I just disappear it.") In contrast to Worriers, who think too much about problems, Distracters don't think enough about them.

Distracters all need to be busy doing something, even if it's just daydreaming, to take their minds off the underlying anxiety. The challenge for Distracters is that problems don't magically disappear and the problems they are so good at ignoring eventually hit them unexpectedly and forcefully. Then sometimes their health crumbles under their bad habits, their spouses file for divorce, or they get fired from their jobs.

If you are a Distracter . . .
Distracters have a very positive trait—their positive outlook. They are often born optimists. They assume that things will work out; they know that many potential problems never develop and some simply solve themselves over time. Distracters have a happy-go-lucky attitude that Worriers would love to possess. They insist on enjoying life and not allowing difficulties to dominate their existence. Distracters are often popular people because of their life-is-fun outlook.

Distracters need to learn to use their positive attitude in a healthy, balanced way, instead of abusing it by ignoring real hazards and problems. These consummate escape artists need to ask themselves what they are trying to escape from. Learning to sit quietly with themselves in meditation will prove very useful. They can challenge themselves to go beyond merely having great dreams and fantasies and begin to manifest them through reality-based thinking and hard work. Distracters can learn to face anxiety and to use their enviable ability to forget about problems only after they have dealt with them responsibly. Distracters can benefit from recognizing the role their anxiety-relieving habits play in keeping them trapped in their comfort zone. Generally more active people than Worriers, Distracters need to turn their action into behaviors that are growth achieving, not merely anxiety relieving.

THE INTERNALIZER

Motto: "I can't handle it."
Internalizers take their anxiety and turn it against themselves. They often suffer from depression as well as anxiety; they have a strong tendency to develop physical symptoms because they

stuff and often ignore their anxiety. Internalizers may suffer from panic attacks, depression, phobias, eating disorders, and a myriad of physical symptoms and health problems. They may even find themselves in a hospital emergency room as a result of severe anxiety symptoms like rapid heartbeat, dizziness, and breathlessness.

Internalizers tend to avoid anxiety-producing situations, each time unintentionally decreasing their confidence. They may become numb, paralyzed, or hysterical when faced with problems because they feel helpless and hopeless. Internalizers usually suffer from low self-esteem and guilt. They often are unaware of how they really are feeling, having spent decades suppressing their emotions, especially anger and sadness. Internalizers often develop dependent personalities and see other people as stronger and more competent.

If you are an Internalizer . . .
Internalizers are wonderful examples of the mindbody connection; they can turn mental anxiety into physical symptoms (and vice versa) instantly! They need to recognize this as a valuable ability that can be used in very positive ways. Internalizers can learn to use visualization, self-hypnosis, and other mindbody techniques to talk to their body in health-enhancing and self-calming ways. They often benefit from engaging in a mindbody type of therapy that helps them learn to become more aware of their true feelings, needs, and desires.

Internalizers have a special wisdom uniquely their own among the six types: They have the ability to recognize that some things in life are beyond our control. They are aware of the limitations inherent in human life, including the ultimate limitation death places on our lives. Internalizers know about the dark side of life, often through having experienced traumatic events. They need to use this wisdom in positive ways instead of allowing it to lead them into hopelessness and self-destruction. Internalizers need to look beyond the shadows and see the light that casts the shadows. With a more balanced perspective, they can affirm their own self-worth and take a more active role in shaping their own life.

THE EXTERNALIZER

Motto: "I'll do it my way."

Externalizers and the two types that follow (Controllers and Helpers) differ from the types described earlier in a basic way: While Worriers, Distracters, and Internalizers tend to deal with anxiety internally, the next three types attempt to relieve anxiety by making changes in the outer world.

Externalizers have a strong tendency to dump their anxiety onto the world around them. They project their inner conflicts onto the external environment and often blame others—their spouse, their kids, their bosses, or the government—for any problems. They believe they are always right. Externalizers have trouble tolerating uncertainty and ambiguity and tend to see things in black and white.

While many other personality types seek to avoid anxiety-producing conflicts, Externalizers actually may thrive on them, for they attempt to relieve their anxiety by repeatedly challenging anxiety.

Externalizers are continually blowing off steam and losing their tempers. This makes it difficult for them to have close friends and emotionally intimate relationships. Often known as Type A personalities, they attempt to master their ever-present anxiety by acquiring power over the external world: by dominating people, being in positions of authority and power, and making money.

At the more extreme end, Externalizers may go beyond simply doing things "their way" to becoming overtly abusive; they may bully others and resort to violence to get their way. Externalizers deal with anxiety by denying it and by a compulsive, overcompensating drive to acquire power over others.

If you are an Externalizer . . .

Externalizers have an active, can-do approach to life. They are able to act decisively and take charge of situations. Externalizers know that the environment plays a big role in what happens in life. Externalizers may become overzealous at defending their boundaries in relationships and need to learn to give greater consideration to other peoples' needs and feelings. Externalizers need to restrain their compulsive drive for action and stop to think, to reflect on their values, and to look at the whole picture before taking action.

THE CONTROLLER

Motto: "I can work to fix it."

Controllers are similar to Externalizers in that they attempt to relieve their anxiety by achieving control over the external world. However, Controllers have more self-control and care more about what other people think of them. They seldom lose their tempers or act impulsively. They are ambitious over-achievers and perfectionists; they are often motivated by the need for approval. Controllers are well-organized, or at least try to be and often enjoy using the latest technology to increase efficiency. Employers love them because they are usually workaholics, always busy and always very responsible. The Controller type is very common in modern society and is probably the most admired and rewarded of all the anxiety personality types because it epitomizes modern civilization's thrust to master anxiety by controlling nature.

Controllers try to overcome their anxiety by planning for all contingencies. They have bottled water, candles, and a battery-operated radio ready in case of a power outage; they carry first-aid kits in the trunks of their cars; they are well-insured and try to save regularly for retirement.

Controllers tend to be overly controlled emotionally which makes it hard for them to relax. They often appear cold and businesslike to other people. Controller parents try to run their children's lives; they may overprotect them or push them too hard, or both. They have specific expectations about how things should be and they can become excessively critical and judgmental. Controllers may suffer nervous breakdowns as the result of unexpected disappointments or tragedies, which threaten their inflexible need to feel in control of their lives. They often suffer from tension and stress-related illnesses such as headaches, gastrointestinal problems, and hormonal imbalances.

If you are a Controller . . .
Controllers are very good at solving problems. They are often highly rational, intelligent people who believe that, given sufficient information and adequate resources, problems can be solved. The greatest liability for Controllers may be that they don't realize how dysfunctional their anxiety pattern is because it works so well in a society that consistently rewards Controller behavior. For many Controllers, the first indication that their *modus operandi* is not ideal may be a stress-related illness.

Controllers possess a productive attitude toward anxiety in their belief that the rational mind has the power to overcome primitive emotions like fear and anger, but they need to learn the difference between healthy emotional self-control and unhealthy emotional suppression. They need to learn which problems are within their sphere of responsibility and which are beyond their control—like other people's behavior, for example. Controllers need to learn the difference between external, technical problems that their direct, logical approach often can deal with successfully and emotional issues that cannot be fixed in the same way. They especially need to recognize when their concerns are in the realm of Sacred Anxiety, which requires the ability to trust and let go.

THE HELPER

Motto: "I can help make it better."
Helpers deal with anxiety by trying to reduce conflict and suffering and are attracted to service-oriented professions. They like to make other people feel good; Helpers think of other people's needs and are very empathetic. They always are willing to talk things over and work things out. They like to see the best in other people and wish that everyone would just be nice to each other. Like other types that suppress their emotions, Helpers may suffer from physical problems, such as overeating, overweight, headaches, depression, mood swings, and allergies.

At the extreme, Helpers become too accommodating and lack the ability to assert their own needs. They can become codependent in relationships because they neglect their own inner life and focus too much on making someone else happy. They make "great moms," "wonderful wives," and "fantastic assistants" in the traditional self-sacrificing mode.

Helpers may become enablers who cover up for other people (for example, a Helper spouse who continues to be too understanding of their mate's alcoholism). Their spouses, friends, and children may end up resenting Helpers for smothering them or making them feel guilty and unworthy of such saintlike sacrifice. Helpers often suffer from disappointment when their helping doesn't produce the results they were expecting. They may feel unappreciated, depressed, and anxious as their children grow up or other circumstances leave them with no one to help.

If you are a Helper . . .
Helpers are wonderful people who truly care about others. They have a genuine sense of empathy for other people. They need to use this capacity out of strength, not weakness. Helpers run the danger of becoming empty shells because they give so much and ask so little in return. Most of all, they neglect their own inner life and their own needs and desires.

Helpers need to learn to recognize when their helping is truly helpful to another's growth and when it weakens them. They avoid their own anxiety by denying it and projecting it onto others; they need to recognize when their desire to help comes from the need to relieve their own anxiety. Taking responsibility for their own anxiety can enable Helpers to reestablish a sense of themselves as individuals with their own needs and their own lives. In relationships, Helpers need to learn to set boundaries and stand their ground. They can benefit tremendously from taking the time to rediscover their personal interests and goals.

THE IDEAL ANXIETY PERSONALITY TYPE IS . . . ALL OF THE ABOVE

Clearly, all six types have their strengths and weaknesses. A healthy anxiety personality draws upon the positive characteristics of each type without getting trapped by the negative aspects. Ideally one would have the Worrier's self-awareness, the Distracter's ability to enjoy life, the Internalizer's mindbody connection and awareness of limits, the Externalizer's ability to take independent action and pursue personal goals, the Controller's cool-headed ability to solve problems rationally, and the Helper's altruistic, empathic awareness of others' needs.

As a result of the increased knowledge and awareness gained from doing the anxiety personality-type quiz, you can become far more conscious of your responses to anxiety and more aware of the range of options available to you in various situations. As you review the anxiety personality characteristics you scored high in, consider which situations they work well in and which they don't. Try to cultivate the positive dimensions of your strongest patterns, while reducing their negative aspects. You can broaden your repertoire of anxiety responses by using more frequently those anxiety personality types you scored lowest in.

As a carpenter once observed, "If all you've got is a hammer, then everything looks like a nail." It is far better, of course, to have a well-stocked tool chest and be able to pull out the right tool for each task. Being limited to only one or two main anxiety personality types restricts our ability to respond appropriately to anxiety in the wide gamut of experiences life presents us with. Consider each of the anxiety personality types as reliable tools that work well when matched with the appropriate situation. Having a wide variety of possible responses in our repertoire enables us to respond to anxiety with maximum effectiveness.

Most anxiety reaction styles are the result of biological tendencies combined with cultural and gender-based social conditioning. Boys in all major cultures are expected to be macho. Generally this translates into suppression of the "soft" emotions such as tenderness, empathy, sadness, and fear, and over-reliance on the "hard" emotions of anger, stoicism, and aggression. Women, in marked contrast, are socialized to suppress the hard or active emotions, especially anger, assertiveness, and taking action. Consequently, it is more likely that an Externalizer/Controller would be a male and that an Internalizer/Helper would be a female.

Most interpersonal problems result from clashing responses to anxiety. For example, when Don, a Distracter/Externalizer, feels anxious about his relationship with Jenny, he wants to do something fun together, like go to a ball game. Jenny, a Worrier/Helper, feeling the same anxiety, wants to have a reassuring heart-to-heart talk with Don. Don views Jenny as too serious and wanting to talk all the time. Jenny feels that Don really doesn't care about her because he just wants to go out and do stuff and never wants to talk about their relationship.

Each of us contains at least some of each anxiety personality type and none of us has a perfect balance. Awareness of the various styles of responding to anxiety can help us to avoid taking it personally when someone does something inappropriate. This person's behavior, which we previously viewed as bewildering, inexcusable, or just plain wrong, can now be recognized as his or her reaction to anxiety.

If we can see the other person's underlying anxiety, we will be less likely to counterattack and more inclined to compassion. In all our relationships, with our parents, our children, our co-workers, and our intimate partners, it helps to be aware that, when it comes to anxiety, we all respond differently—and we all can learn from each other.

Chapter Five

THE POWER OF
INNER TALK

A TOOL FOR AWARENESS

A key theme running throughout this book is that we can choose to meet anxiety, not with dread, but with awareness. As we saw in the story of anxiety's origins, it is our very self-awareness that created our existential anxiety. When we suppress this awareness of our own aliveness (and with it our emotions, dreams, and desires), then our healthy anxiety turns toxic. Chronic Toxic Anxiety habits are the most pernicious block to conscious growth. Thus, it is only through greater self-awareness that we can transform anxiety back into a powerful force that can lead us to peace and love. In his existentialist approach to mastering anxiety Rollo May recognized the necessity of choosing awareness when we are confronted by anxiety:

> . . . just as anxiety destroys our self-awareness, so awareness of ourselves can destroy anxiety. That is to say, the stronger our consciousness of ourselves, the more we can take a stand and overcome anxiety.[1]

For most of us, achieving and maintaining healthy self-awareness is the greatest challenge in life. We need effective tools to help us become more conscious of what is usually unconscious and habitual. In this chapter, you will become familiar with the role your inner mind plays in fostering unnecessary anxiety—and how you can use it to experience greater serenity. You will learn how to use Inner Talk, one of the most effective ways to become aware of and change emotional and cognitive programming.

CONSTRUCTING OUR WORLD WITH INNER TALK

We have seen how early childhood experiences condition us to respond to anxiety in ways that are either effective or dysfunctional. But three crucial questions have yet to be answered: How do these past experiences continue to affect our behavior in the present? Why do we keep repeating behavior patterns that don't work? How can we change dysfunctional emotions and behaviors into effective ones?

The answers to these questions are actually quite simple: past experiences influence us today because they have become stored in our subconscious as mental programming. Ineffective programs are repeated because we are not fully aware of their existence; they operate below the level of our conscious awareness in the unconscious mind ("you can't stop doing what you're doing until you know what you're doing"). By bringing these old habits and mindsets to awareness and learning techniques that enable us to reprogram the subconscious, we can change our behavior.

Learning how to use Inner Talk will help you to change anxiety habits that date back even to early childhood. This is a method that can be learned by almost everyone and, when used correctly, is remarkably powerful. Inner Talk refers to the mental chatter that goes on continuously in our heads. Some people occasionally talk to themselves out loud, but everyone talks to themselves silently—at the astonishing rate of up to 400 words per minute!

This Inner Talk voice is our personal in-house commentator. Just like a TV sports announcer, this voice in our head gives us a continuous play-by-play commentary on our lives. I am constantly amazed at how my experience of the world is filtered through my Inner Talk. It is both daunting and liberating to realize that as adults we no longer experience events directly—we give events the meaning they have for us through the Inner Talk they trigger.

For example, two people receive promotions at work on the same day. The first person generates the following Inner Talk: "Wow, what a great opportunity! I'll be making more money and have a chance to get more management experience." The second person engages in this Inner Talk: "I don't know if I can handle this. It means a lot more pressure. What if I blow it?" Their Inner Talk not only influences the way these two individuals experience their promotions, it continues to affect their subsequent performance.

We are continually constructing the world we live in through our Inner Talk. We like to think that our Inner Talk corresponds to reality, but it actually corresponds more to our prior conditioning than it does to present reality. In Carlos Castenda's *A Separate Reality*, the shaman Don Juan says to the author:

> You talk to yourself too much. You're not unique at that. Every one of us does. . . . We talk about our world. In fact we maintain our world with our internal talk. . . . A warrior is aware that the world will change as soon as he stops talking to himself. . . . If we stop telling ourselves that the world is so-and-so, the world will stop being so-and-so . . .

Sometimes we may be very aware of the content of our Inner Talk (for example, when we say to ourselves, "What a dumb mistake!" after we make an error). At other times its content remains largely unconscious, something like the way a radio playing in the background or the Muzak in a store subtly influences our mood without our conscious awareness. Inner Talk may occur as either "I" statements or "you" statements:

"Watch it! You almost ran into that car."

"Boy, are you behind schedule today!"

"I finally got that done—I really did a great job."

"I can't believe I said that to her. I'm an idiot!"

"What if things don't work out?"

"I wonder if I'm doing this right . . ."

Most of it sounds pretty negative, doesn't it? In fact, most of us engage in a tremendous amount of negative Inner Talk throughout the day, and it often continues through the night in our dreams. Not surprisingly, all that negativity has a considerable effect on us, and clearly it is in our own best interest to become more aware of it. Here is a simple exercise that you can use to tune in to your Inner Talk:

LISTENING TO YOUR INNER TALK

Stop reading and close your eyes. Just sit there and listen to the mental chatter in your head for 60 seconds.

Notice how you felt while doing this exercise. How does the way you feel correspond to your Inner Talk?

Just imagine the effect of listening all day long to some of the negative Inner Talk tapes stored in your subconscious mind. Did you ever have a day when everything was just too much to handle and you could barely drag yourself through the day? What kind of Inner Talk do you think you were listening to on such days? And what about the days when your anxiety level made you feel as if your nervous system was wired so tightly that something was going to snap? Could it have been the result of the Inner Talk messages that were traveling through your nerves?

The body, via the subconscious mind, is constantly listening to our Inner Talk and being affected by it. Every thought is a biochemical event. Negative Inner Talk has an instantaneous effect on every cell in the body and can drain us of vital energy. Negative thoughts produce biochemical states of anxiety, depression, and fatigue; positive thoughts and emotions produce neurochemical reactions that create feelings of health and well-being. There is a continuous feedback loop: thoughts affect the body's biochemistry, which in turn influences thoughts, which again affect biochemistry, and so on. This feedback mechanism between mind and body explains how anxiety escalates. Anxiety-producing trains of thought and stressful physical reactions feed on each other and further fuel the anxiety escalator.

Inner Talk is one of the main bridges connecting the mind and body. Psychological change happens when problem-producing Inner Talk changes to solution-producing Inner Talk. Cognitive therapy's most effective tool is self-talk, a type of Inner Talk. Behavioral therapy focuses on changing actions and behaviors, which in turn change Inner Talk—for example, it's highly unlikely that a person will keep saying, "I can't get into elevators," after having done it successfully several times. Medications such as Prozac alter the neurotransmitter mix in the brain's synapses, a biochemical change that can result in a dramatic transformation of one's Inner Talk. Traditional talk therapy transforms Inner Talk as the client gradually internalizes the therapeutic dialogue. Because successful change always involves a shift toward more effective Inner Talk, it makes good sense to go directly to the source.

MEETING YOUR UNCONSCIOUS MIND

Many people realize that their basic Inner Talk software was installed during childhood, but often feel powerless when it comes to changing it. Our emotional programming mystifies us because it is stored in the subconscious part of the mind. The subconscious (or unconscious) is the part of the mind that contains feelings or thoughts that are partially or completely beyond our conscious awareness; "subconscious" literally means below conscious awareness. Certain subconscious thoughts are so deeply buried that their retrieval is virtually impossible without skilled professional help. Other subconscious thoughts are just below the surface and frequently pop into our awareness on their own.

Properly used, the unconscious mind can be an amazing resource. It has been tapped by poets, actors, inventors, and scientists as a source of creative intelligence. It often knows the answer to a problem before our conscious mind has become aware of it.

One of the most fascinating questions about consciousness has not been answered by neuropsychologists yet: Where is the unconscious mind located in the brain? It is unlikely that we will ever find one specific part of the brain that corresponds exactly to the concept of the unconscious. But current research suggests that the emotional brain—such areas as the limbic system, the hypothalamic-pituitary axis, and the amygdala—contains memories and emotional behavior patterns that are often beyond the awareness of the conscious cerebral cortex.

Because these patterns are stored in the subconscious, two problems arise: First, we may not be aware of the outdated or self-sabotaging programs that are running our mental computer. Second, even if we become aware of the negative programming we may not know how to change it.

A quick example: Jessie keeps getting into relationships with men who leave her. She probably will continue to have the same experiences until she becomes aware that her behavior is being determined by unconscious programming about love and men.

Jessie's mindset—Mr. Right is handsome, exciting, and never there when I need him—was formed by her experience as a young girl whose father was seldom at home and who left the family when she was eight years old. If she becomes aware of this connection, it may help her understand her experiences more deeply. But understanding alone seldom changes behavior. To attract and develop a healthy relationship, Jessie needs to learn how to reprogram the emotional software that runs her automatic, unconscious relationship behaviors.

Becoming more aware of the mental programs stored in the subconscious is the first step to personal freedom. The second step is evaluating those programs to see if they are in harmony with our goals and values and if they are effective in achieving those goals. The final step is to change the ineffective programs to effective ones and to practice the new behaviors.

To quickly grasp the vital implications of the subconscious mind and the power of subconscious programming, try this simple exercise:

MEET YOUR SUBCONSCIOUS MIND

As you read the following sentence (written in capital letters) count the number of times the letter "F" appears in the sentence.

FINDING SERENITY IN THE AGE OF ANXIETY
HAPPENS WHEN THE CONFLICTING
FORCES OF THE MIND ALL FOLLOW
THE GUIDANCE OF THE TRUE SELF.

Now write your answer here _____.

Be sure to do the exercise before reading any further.

Most people miss one, two, or even three of the F's in the sentence. And, believe it or not, they miss them because of their subconscious programming. There are actually eight F's in all. If you counted fewer than eight, see if you can find the missing ones.

You will probably discover that the F's you missed were those in the word "of." How can you miss the F in "of"? There are only two letters in the whole word, and it is printed in big, bold letters. What's going on here?

Your subconscious mind is literally making those F's disappear. Your attempt to find all the F's was taken over by a simple little program that goes like this: To pronounce the word "of" correctly, change the F into a V. The subconscious was conditioned with this basic reading program decades ago when we were in first grade. (The few people who do find all the F's find them because instead of reading the sentence as instructed, they examine each letter individually, thereby disabling their reading program.)

Think of the implications that follow from this exercise: we don't realize that we have been operating under this subconscious program for most of our life and we have absolutely no conscious recollection of learning this lesson. How many other lessons have we learned that we don't remember learning—especially lessons about the nature of life, and who we are as individuals? Nearly everything we "just know" about life and about our self has been learned. What we know is only as accurate as the cultural and familial instruction we received. As Will Rogers observed, "It's not the things we don't know that hurt us. It's the things we know that ain't so."

We are not responsible for what got programmed into our subconscious; all the important software was loaded into our brains during our first few years of life. But, as adults, we are responsible for whether or not we keep it there. A major task of adulthood is to take responsibility for choosing our own thoughts in the present.

"THE" WAY TO THINK

Inner Talk happens at the boundary of the conscious and the unconscious. Freud called dreams the "royal road" to the unconscious, but Inner Talk is a far more accessible avenue to the unconscious mind. Its great advantage is that it occurs while we are awake instead of asleep, which makes it far easier to observe and change.

By paying more attention to our Inner Talk, we actually can begin to see inside the vault of our subconscious mind. We can examine our beliefs, habits, and attitudes and decide what works and what doesn't. The goal is not what is commonly thought of as positive thinking, which is often a reflexive attempt to be hopeful and optimistic, to look on the bright side of things. Many people who try to be more positive find that, while it may help sometimes, they usually become stuck in a battle between their positive and negative inner voices. Thus, when I use the shorthand term "positive Inner Talk," I am not referring to cultivating a Pollyanna attitude that is forever doomed to battle the inner cynic.

Instead, our primary goal is to replace negative, self-destructive Inner Talk with creative, life-affirming Inner Talk—Inner Talk that embraces reality but also shapes it in a way that promotes personal and spiritual growth. This means Inner Talk that cultivates **THE** Way to Think—thinking that is:

True

Happy

Effective

True affirms that our Inner Talk reflects our highest understanding about the truth of any situation. This first principle ensures that our Inner Talk is as accurate as possible. Telling the truth (and not simply basing our Inner Talk on old programming) can accelerate our growth faster than almost anything else. Telling the truth helps us avoid being either a Pollyanna or a cynic. All we need to do is ask ourselves, "What's the truth about this?"

Happy signifies that, after our Inner Talk passes the truth test, we are free to talk to ourselves in a way that is emotionally healing and supportive, that reflects and enhances a high degree of self-acceptance and self-esteem. This second principle helps us replace critical, self-sabotaging dialogues with Inner Talk that enables us to meet life with vibrant energy, enthusiasm, and joy. When we ask ourselves, "What do I need to hear right now?" we are training our emotional intelligence.

Effective refers to Inner Talk that works, helps us cope, and assists us in getting the job done. Negative Inner Talk is based on the faulty belief that the best way to motivate ourselves is through fear, shame, and threats. This approach is widespread in our culture, yet it doesn't work nearly as well as being motivated by inspiration and positive reinforcement. This third principle encourages us to be very pragmatic and to ask ourselves, "What kind of Inner Talk would be most effective in helping me to meet my goals right now?"

Our second goal for Inner Talk is to cultivate the ability to temporarily suspend all Inner Talk. The complete cessation of all mental chatter provides perhaps the deepest possible experience of complete serenity. Imagine how relaxing it would be to stop thinking, judging, and figuring things out for a while and simply experience life directly with simple awareness. Later we will find out how meditation offers us a unique opportunity to free ourselves from the limitations of our habitual Inner Talk. So our goals with Inner Talk are twofold: being able to replace old Inner Talk habits with true/happy/effective ones and being able to suspend all Inner Talk and experience the world directly with a beginner's mind.

Inner Talk awareness doesn't require any special equipment and it doesn't cost anything. All that's required is the willingness to stop and listen with more awareness to our mental chatter.

After we are aware of what we are saying to ourselves, we can begin to learn a lot about the sources of our anxiety. Then we can learn to take care of the scared and anxious parts of our psyche in effective, calming ways.

Because our old Inner Talk doesn't represent reality, but only our past conditioning about reality, changing it to be more true, happy, and effective can only be beneficial. In fact, one of our goals can be to get out of touch with reality as we know it because it is that version of reality that has been keeping us from experiencing serenity.

Another positive aspect of Inner Talk is that we can use it no matter how busy we are because it can be done in our spare time. We're always talking to ourselves anyway, so all we have to do is become more conscious of our Inner Talk and change those aspects of it that don't serve us well. Inner Talk is one of the most powerful tools for emotional self-management; it is a form of active, in-the-world meditation.

THE ANATOMY OF INNER TALK

The most obvious component of Inner Talk is the actual words we are listening to, such as: "There you go, making another mistake!" But notice that this inner voice not only says different things, it uses various tones of voice. As in any conversation, the tone of voice makes a big difference. You can imagine that someone saying, "Wow, that was great!" could have an entirely different effect on you depending on the tone of voice used. An inner voice that is sarcastic, nervous, judgmental, guilt-inducing, doubting, confused, hopeless, worried, or otherwise negative will have an anxiety-producing effect on your body and your emotions. One that is calm, accepting, encouraging, clear, and realistic will reduce anxiety and build self-confidence.

In addition to the words and the tone of voice, Inner Talk

contains other sensory ingredients. Most people find that Inner Talk comes to them as mental pictures and physical sensations as well as words. For example, someone with a fear of public speaking who is worrying about giving a report in a meeting might have an experience something like the following:

Inner Voice (in a nervous, anxious tone): "I'm going to get so anxious when it's my turn that I'll totally forget what I want to say."

Inner Vision: Seeing myself totally speechless and red in the face, with everyone just sitting there staring at me.

Inner Feeling: Butterflies in my stomach, my heart pounding, and feeling lightheaded and dizzy.

This example illustrates that Inner Talk is really "inner communication" and can come to us through any of the senses: auditory, visual, kinesthetic, and even taste and smell. We're focusing here on the auditory messages because they are easiest for most people to work with, but be aware of the other dimensions as well. If you find that your mental pictures or physical feelings seem to be more dominant than the words, then change to the sensory modality that has the most intense effect on you. The same principles and techniques for changing Inner Talk apply to changing inner pictures and feelings.

Learning to Distinguish Between the Voices of Toxic and Natural Anxiety

I have found it very helpful to personify and name the voice of Toxic Anxiety because this makes it much easier to deal with it effectively. I call mine the Anxious Chatterbox. You can give yours any name that feels right to you, such as the Inner Critic or the Voice of Doom. (One workshop participant asked me jokingly, "Is it OK to call mine 'Mom'?") The Anxious Chatterbox is that annoying voice that chatters away in the background saying things like "Something bad is going to happen," "I don't think you can handle this," and "You should have done better." This anxious, critical voice often tries to sound reasonable, as if it's a responsible adult looking after your best interests. Fortunately, the Anxious Chatterbox has a readily identifiable *modus operandi*. And after you know its M.O., the Anxious Chatterbox can no longer fool you into thinking that it is your good friend, Natural Anxiety.

Natural Anxiety, in vivid contrast, is supportive and honest. I call the voice of Natural Anxiety the Inner Guide. (Again, choose any name you like, such as Higher Self or Inner Coach.) Natural Anxiety is a realistic early-warning signal that will alert you to potential dangers. It is an essential part of our survival equipment. Natural Anxiety may start as a generalized sense of danger, but—unlike Toxic Anxiety—it quickly becomes specific and realistic.

Natural Anxiety also alerts us to potential opportunities—good stuff we don't want to miss out on. Often it's like a sixth sense that says, "Pay attention!" It wakes us up anytime we need to be extra alert, to take advantage of an opportunity, or to deal effectively with any new experience.

Unlike the Anxious Chatterbox, who is always anxious, the Inner Guide can raise the red flag of anxiety when it needs to, but it can be excited and enthusiastic as well as calming and reassuring. Whereas the Anxious Chatterbox interferes with being functional, the Inner Guide is your personal coach—100 percent on your side, helping you function at your peak level of performance.

COMPARING THE VOICES OF TOXIC ANXIETY AND NATURAL ANXIETY

	Toxic Anxiety "Anxious Chatterbox"	Natural Anxiety "Inner Guide"
Message	Activated by false alarms, overreacts to or is paralyzed by real alarms. Vague, unrealistic, unreasonable, ineffective, repetitive "tape." Perceives opportunities as dangers.	Responds to real alarms, anxiety is in direct proportion to degree of danger. Notices new opportunities. Specific, realistic, reasonable, helpful.
Duration	Chronic, repetitive.	Usually brief.
Tone	Anxious, alarming, negative, shaming, guilt-inducing.	Calm, respectful, friendly, confident. Can also be excited and enthusiastic.
Control	Concerns are often beyond one's control.	Concerns are often within one's control.
Result	Inaction or counterproductive behavior.	Effective action and change.
Effect	Anxiety escalates, any relief is temporary. Self-esteem decreases, producing self-doubt, tiredness, frustration, hopelessness, helplessness, negativity.	Anxiety is relieved by responsible action. Self-esteem increases, producing feelings of energy, empowerment, confidence.

The main difference between the two voices, and perhaps the best way to tell them apart, is how they make you feel. The Anxious Chatterbox acts as if it has your best interests in mind, but ends up making you feel nervous, insecure, and bad about yourself. The Inner Guide uses anxiety only to get your attention, not to torment you.

It can be very empowering to realize that you don't have to

keep listening to the Anxious Chatterbox anymore. This voice
has no useful information for you, except to make you aware of
your negative programming. It does not protect you from any
real danger; it is only there to hassle and distract you. Practicing
positive Inner Talk strengthens your connection with your Inner Guide and gradually eliminates the Anxious Chatterbox
from your life.

It might take a while to become accustomed to your new-
found independence. Your mind has been conditioned to see
the Anxious Chatterbox as your source of security, and when
you stop paying attention to it, the Anxious Chatterbox may
respond, "You'd better not ignore me. I've kept you alive all
these years, haven't I?" The truth is that it is your Inner Guide
who has been protecting you, while your Anxious Chatterbox
actually has been undermining your self-confidence and draining your energy. As you build a stronger relationship with your
Inner Guide, the old Anxious Chatterbox will begin to fade
away.

FIRE THE ANXIOUS CHATTERBOX AND HIRE AN INNER GUIDE

Write a termination letter to your Anxious Chatterbox, letting it know that you no longer require its services. You can
make the letter humorous, angry, or friendly. The important
thing is to have fun with this exercise and enjoy liberating
yourself from the Anxious Chatterbox's tyranny. Let the
Anxious Chatterbox know the effect it has had on you over
the years and why you are terminating it.

Next you can write an advertisement for a new advisor, one
that meets your current needs. Your ad for your Inner Guide
can list the desired qualifications, personal qualities, and the
job description. Remember, you can pay a top salary and hire
the best Inner Guide in the world.

THREE STEPS TO POSITIVE INNER TALK

Step 1. Observe your Inner Talk Actively pay attention to your mental chatter. What is it saying? Identify any mental pictures or physical feelings that are present. If all you can find is a vague feeling, imagine what the Inner Talk behind it might be.
Key questions: "What am I listening to?" or "What am I saying to myself?"

Step 2. Evaluate your Inner Talk Are you listening to your Anxious Chatterbox or your Inner Guide? If you find that you are tuned into your Inner Guide, congratulate yourself and enjoy it. But if you've been listening to your Anxious Chatterbox, go to Step 3.
Key question: "How is it making me feel?"

Step 3. Change your negative Inner Talk into positive Inner Talk If you don't like the effect it is having on you, change your Inner Talk. Then keep repeating your new positive Inner Talk until you feel a change. Remember, when it comes to your subconscious mind, saying is believing.
Key question: "What would I rather be hearing right now?"

You already have learned a powerful technique that can be applied to constructing growth-promoting Inner Talk. Use "THE Way to Think" to insure that your Inner Talk is true, happy, and effective. Here are two more practical techniques for changing Inner Talk:

THE 180° TECHNIQUE

The 180° Technique simply takes the negative Inner Talk and turns it around 180 degrees. For example, Ray's company has been downsizing and now he always has more work to do than he can manage properly. He observes his negative Inner Talk: "You're way behind schedule. You should be able to get more done." Ray notices that this Inner Talk makes him feel anxious, lowers his self-esteem, and saps his motivation. Using the 180° Technique, he quickly turns it around: "You're right on schedule and doing fine. Enjoy your work and do your best today."

Because there's always more to do than can be done, the Anxious Chatterbox can make us feel behind schedule all day every day. Without ignoring external time frames, we can take back our power to define what being on schedule means. By repeating his new Inner Talk to himself throughout the workday, Ray can turn his Toxic Anxiety into the healthy Natural Anxiety that aids him in working energetically and efficiently.

If Ray noticed he was manufacturing a negative mental picture—his desk becoming piled higher and higher with overdue work, for example—he could change that to seeing the pile on his desk becoming constantly smaller. If he noticed an anxious feeling in his chest, he could calm it down by using a physical relaxation technique, such as the anxiety center calming technique described in Chapter 8.

The 180° Technique is quick, easy, and effective. At first you may find that you resist letting yourself feel good. You may subconsciously believe that the only way to motivate yourself is the Anxious Chatterbox's way, by instilling fear and guilt. But by practicing positive Inner Talk, you begin to develop trust in a new approach—allowing your Inner Guide to motivate you with a good feeling of self-confidence and faith.

Another Inner Talk-changing technique, called the Million Dollar Questions, takes a little more mental effort but it is remarkably effective and works on a deeper level.

THE MILLION DOLLAR QUESTIONS

After you notice your negative Inner Talk, ask yourself the Million Dollar Questions:

"What would I rather be hearing right now?"

"What is the positive intention behind my anxious voice?"

You will soon discover that these are called the Million Dollar Questions because they can make you feel "like a million dollars." This method is based on two concepts: (1) there is a part of us that intuitively knows the perfect Inner Talk for every situation; and (2) even the most negative anxious voice originally had a positive intention behind it. The Million Dollar Questions help us to change the Anxious Chatterbox into an Inner Guide.

Let's apply the Million Dollar Questions to the same example we used earlier, Ray's anxious Inner Talk that chattered, "You're way behind schedule."

Ray examines the first part of the Million Dollar Question: "What would I rather be hearing right now?" He realizes that he needs to hear something supportive and constructive. He turns to his Inner Guide and hears the following Million Dollar Inner Talk: "They are expecting you to do the work two people used to do. Of course there will be times when you can't do it all. You're doing a great job keeping up with a bigger work load. I can't believe how much more productive you've become!" You'll notice that now Ray is telling himself the truth about his situation, instead of simply replaying old low self-esteem tapes. He also is making himself feel happy with praise and encouragement. Ray's new Inner Talk automatically makes him more energetic and effective.

Next, Ray uses the second Million Dollar Question to discover the positive intention behind the negative statement. When he takes a moment to think about it, he realizes that he is afraid that if he doesn't keep up with his work his boss will think he can't handle his job and may be angry or even fire him. Ray's Anxious Chatterbox is trying to scare him into working

harder so he won't lose his job. He realizes that the positive intention behind his Inner Talk is to help him do his best and
keep his job. The problem is that saying, "You're way behind
schedule" to himself doesn't help him work more effectively. In
fact, the anxiety and stress it creates interfere with Ray's ability
to think clearly and concentrate on his work, so he falls even
farther behind.

When Ray gets home after work he continues to use Inner
Talk. He spends some time brainstorming with his Inner Guide
about various strategies he could use to deal with his stressful
work situation—which might range from talking to his boss
about reassigning some of his tasks to looking for another position.

You don't have to believe your new, positive Inner Talk at
first. If you are like most people, you won't for a while. It just
feels too unfamiliar, too strange, to believe it in the beginning
no matter how much you might want to. But Inner Talk has an
effect whether you believe what you are saying or not, so don't
worry if you don't believe it at first. Just say it! And say it often!

And don't get discouraged if at first positive Inner Talk
brings even deeper negative mental programming to the surface.
This is a common experience, and you might think of it as soap
bringing the dirt to the surface where it can be washed off. The
Anxious Chatterbox will try to tell you that your Inner Talk
isn't working, but actually it's working perfectly. Most of us have
some subconscious programming that tells us we don't deserve
to be truly happy or don't deserve to be deeply loved. Ask that
negative voice, "Why not?" And keep changing the negatives to
positives.

If you find that after a few minutes you've slipped back into
negative Inner Talk, don't become discouraged. This, too, is normal. Despite years of practice with Inner Talk, stressful events or
disappointments still can trigger old habits of negative Inner
Talk in my mind. Who cares? It is how I respond in the present
that determines how I feel. When you notice you've slipped
back into negative Inner Talk, simply run through steps 1–3

again. And again. And again—until you begin to rely less on your Anxious Chatterbox and more on your Inner Guide. Eventually you'll find that you have developed a new habit called positive Inner Talk.

USING INNER TALK TO RESOLVE CONFLICT AND DOUBLE BINDS

One of Toxic Anxiety's characteristics is the persistence of a chronic inner conflict that never really gets resolved. For example, when faced with the need to make a decision, we may experience a conflict between what our heart wants to do and what our head tells us we should do. Our conflicts between "should" and "want" may take the form of a parent-like authority figure and a pleasure-oriented child figure. These warring parts can easily raise our anxiety level if we let them fight it out inside our head.

Many of our chronic inner conflicts are double binds, those soul-wrenching phenomena that occur when contradictory demands are imposed on us so that no matter which action we take, we violate one or more of the directives. We feel threatened from two sides at once and can neither fight nor flee. If we allow the Anxious Chatterbox to tie us up in a double bind, we become paralyzed, hold our breath, and our anxiety may escalate uncontrollably.

Anthropologist Gregory Bateson and psychiatrist R. D. Laing considered the double bind to be the essence of anxiety. Rollo May described anxiety as "the experience of being in a dilemma in which [one is] threatened from both sides at once."[2] The double bind is anxiety producing because it always places us in a no-win situation: you're damned if you do and damned if you don't. Sometimes you just can't win, but if you're in a double bind you always can't win.

Mastering anxiety means taking steps to uncover the double binds under whose tyranny we live. One of the Anxious Chatterbox's favorite tricks is to split into two and then "double bind" us. For example, if you have to work late, Anxious Chatterbox #1 criticizes you because you are not spending time with your mate or your kids or working out at the health club. But if you leave work a little early, Anxious Chatterbox #2 accuses you of slacking off and implies that you now will be the first to get downsized. In another classic double bind, we might feel stalemated and frustrated by a power struggle between an inner critical parent figure and an emotional part that feels like a rebellious child. By bringing such double binds to conscious awareness, we can begin to see how toxic they are. Then we can choose to set up win/win systems in our minds instead of the double bind's chronic lose/lose system.

Here's a practical method you can use to untie double binds and resolve inner conflicts that cause anxiety: Identify the conflicting parts and mediate a win/win agreement between them. Use Inner Talk to find out what they are saying. Then enlist your Inner Guide to help you moderate a dialogue to resolve the issue. The more toxic the inner conflict, the more you need to get the inner combatants to tone down the rhetoric and listen to each other's point of view. It often helps to get the debate out of your head, where all it can do is just run around in circles, and write down the dialogue on a piece of paper. You also can use a role-playing technique that uses three chairs; the two chairs facing each other are for the conflicted parts of you and the third chair, off to the side, is for your Inner Guide. You, of course, get to play all three parts! Becoming more aware of these hidden conflicts and developing your skill at resolving them can reduce much of the Toxic Anxiety of everyday life.

PRACTICING THE INNER TALK CHECK-UP

In the past, negative, anxiety-producing Inner Talk may have sent your anxiety level zooming up without your awareness or permission. Now, however, you know how to use Inner Talk to stop it from escalating and even how to prevent unhealthy anxiety in the first place.

Inner communication, just like interpersonal communication, is a dynamic balance between listening and talking. As important as it is to talk to your subconscious in positive ways, this method should never be misused to cover up or avoid unpleasant feelings. The ability to genuinely listen to anxiety, to listen to the subconscious, and to listen to the body is vitally important for effective inner communication. Before you try to talk to your subconscious, be sure to listen to it first.

Rather than waiting for Toxic Anxiety to get your attention, try doing preventive maintenance with your Inner Talk. Negative patterns, like weeds, can sprout up again and again, especially if their roots have not been pulled up. Do an Inner Talk check-up regularly and notice whether your Inner Talk is positive and affirming. If not, change it. Use everyday pauses, such as stopping at a red light, to notice your mental chatter. Take brief mental awareness breaks at work to tune in to your Inner Talk. When you find yourself sliding into a negative emotional state, stop and play back the mental tapes you have been listening to. You will invariably find that the Anxious Chatterbox has taken over again and you can use your Inner Talk skills to restore your mental well-being.

Remember that you are not attempting to eradicate negative Inner Talk once and for all. Negativity has been programmed into almost everyone on a very deep level. It surrounds us in the hundreds of messages that bombard us daily from other anxious people and from the media. (Advertising is based on creating a feeling of anxiety in the consumer and then providing a product to relieve it.) I find that it requires continual awareness and regular Inner Talk check-ups to keep me from falling into old habits of negativity. The goal is not eradication but awareness: to become more conscious of our Inner Talk and to exercise our ability to choose more positive, life-affirming messages in the present moment.

Consider Inner Talk awareness as the mental equivalent of

daily chores like washing, brushing our teeth, or other acts of self-care. We don't expect to do these chores once or even a hundred times and then be done with them forever; we expect to perform them daily. Negativity is psychic dirt, and we need to cleanse it from our system daily or it starts to cloud our awareness. The Zen Buddhists have a wonderful image of the mind as a mirror that needs to be polished daily to stay bright and clear. Most of us were never trained as children to perform this basic mental self-care. Now that we know how, we can brush our hair and check our Inner Talk each day. In fact we can brush up our Inner Talk while we're brushing our hair! It makes sense for us to spend at least as much time taking care of what's inside our head as we do taking care of what's on the outside.

By becoming more aware of our Inner Talk, we can develop greater emotional self-management skills and begin to experience the tremendous benefits that come from living more consciously.

Chapter Six

TRAPPED IN
THE COMFORT ZONE

THE COMFORT ZONE

Have you ever . . .

. . . worked very diligently on a big project, only to do something dumb right at the end?

. . . impulsively made a comment that hurt someone with whom you had been building a good relationship?

. . . felt that you might have a fear of failure *and* a fear of success?

. . . let a long-awaited opportunity slip by because you got nervous at the last minute?

. . . started to relax and feel good and then become inexplicably anxious?

. . . experienced times when you felt as if you were your own worst enemy?

. . . accomplished something challenging and significant but afterward found yourself feeling unexpectedly let down?

All of these incidents illustrate the hidden workings of a psychophysical mechanism called the comfort zone. Here is an example of what it is like to get trapped in one:

Adele likes her work as a sales rep for a medical supply company, but she believes that her performance over the past two years deserves a promotion and a pay increase. Sometimes Adele feels frustrated because her boss hasn't rewarded her for her hard work. Feeling optimistic and confident one day, she resolves to talk to her boss, Sylvia, about this. (Adele begins to move out of her comfort zone.)

Later, when Adele thinks about going into Sylvia's office and asking for what she wants, she becomes nervous. She starts to worry that her anxiety might prevent her from communicating effectively and that she will blow it. So she lets a perfect opportunity to talk to Sylvia pass by. (Adele's Toxic Anxiety blocks her movement forward.)

Afterward Adele begins to criticize herself. "I should have talked to her. But maybe I'm not doing as well as I think; otherwise Sylvia probably would have said something by now. What if I ask her and she turns me down? I'd feel just terrible." Adele starts to feel bad about herself, engages in negative Inner Talk habits, and may even begin an old pattern of overeating at home and snacking on candy bars at work. (Adele slides back into her comfort zone without having addressed her goal.)

Adele becomes depressed, feels sluggish, and loses her enthusiasm for making calls. Her weight increases while her sales performance goes into a slump. (Adele slides down to the depression end of her comfort zone.)

After a few weeks Adele becomes concerned that she may lose her job, so she gets back on track and her performance improves. She works up to her potential and once more reaches the point where she feels she is worth more than she is getting paid.

(Adele's still-unfulfilled desire reemerges, and she begins to move through the comfort zone toward the growth zone.)

Yes, you guessed it. Adele is unaware that she is playing a no-win board game called "Trapped in the Comfort Zone." As she draws another one of those cards that says "Return to Go," she has to start this comfort zone cycle (or some variation of it) all over again.

Adele is trapped in her comfort zone, which despite its cozy-sounding name, can become a living hell if we can't move beyond it. We all have a comfort zone. In fact, we have many comfort zones that regulate different areas of our life. Some control how much money we make, how much love we get, how good we let ourselves feel, and how much we weigh. Most of us have experienced the frustration of gaining and losing the same five pounds over and over again as we cycle back and forth within our comfort zone. We also may have experienced accumulating credit card debt and gradually paying it off, only to begin the same cycle all over again.

Toxic Anxiety does not exist in isolation from the rest of our life. It is part of a well-orchestrated system that serves to keep us trapped in our comfort zone. Many people live nearly their entire lives in their comfort zone. It functions as an emotional thermostat, one that was programmed early in life and restricts us to certain ranges of feelings and behaviors. When the emotional temperature rises higher or drops lower than the thermostat settings, the comfort zone system is activated to bring us back into normal range. If we begin to feel worse than the low setting on our thermostat, our comfort zone system initiates changes to make us feel better. Similarly, if we begin to feel better than the high setting, our comfort zone system activates mechanisms to bring us down.

Every week in my counseling practice, I see the painful consequences that result when anxiety-induced self-sabotage keeps people trapped in their comfort zones for too long. I feel tremendous compassion for the suffering I see because I have struggled with it myself. Before I understood the role of anxiety in my own life, I experienced many painful cycles during which I would try valiantly to reach a goal, only to subconsciously sabotage myself before I could reach it.

By now we have developed some clear photographs of anxiety taken from three different perspectives: Toxic, Natural, and Sacred. In this chapter, we will animate these photos, transforming them into moving pictures to reveal the dynamic role anxiety plays in shaping the course of human life.

We have seen that anxiety is inherent in life itself, that anxiety is the shadow cast by human consciousness. The more creative we become, the more passionately we attempt to express our true nature, the more anxiety we evoke within our psyches. It is our deepest desires that can arouse our greatest apprehension—for what if we should try, really try with all our heart, and fail? We are afraid that failure will then cast us into a bottomless pit of despair. Yet in reality the greater and far more common despair comes not from trying and failing but from failing to try. It is our anxiety about failing (and, as we will discuss later, our anxiety about succeeding) that sabotages the process of growth and keeps us trapped in our comfort zone. As Shakespeare observed, "Our doubts are traitors, and make us lose the good we oft might win by fearing to attempt."

A BRIEF HISTORY OF THE COMFORT ZONE

The comfort zone's physiological basis lies in our body's need to maintain *homeostasis*, a certain range of conditions that allow for optimal functioning. A prime example is our need to maintain a temperature within a few degrees of 98.6°F. The dimensions of our emotional comfort zone are set during childhood. From our childhood experiences we develop an emotional comfort zone that represents the range of feelings it was safe to have in our home. The feedback from parents (and other authority figures) may convince us that it is not safe to become too happy and exuberant—or too sad and quiet.

Children do need to learn how to maintain healthy comfort zones that help them regulate their behavior. Unfortunately, along with all the valid and practical information that becomes encoded into comfort zones, much that is inaccurate and counterproductive also gets embedded there. Then comfort zones can become potential traps that can hamper growth. For example, we may learn to equate any new situation with danger. We may learn that "being myself" results in a withdrawal of love and should be carefully avoided. We may find that expressing anger means getting spanked, so we learn to suppress our angry feelings. We may experience being sent to our room whenever we speak our mind, so we begin to censor ourselves. Being told we're "no good" at math or sports may push learning arithmetic or enjoying basketball beyond our comfort zone. Being raised in an unsupportive atmosphere means that we become more "comfortable" with continual tension and self-suppression than with growth, pleasure, and success.

The secret of the comfort zone is that the more wisely we challenge it, the better it functions. Staying inside a temperature-controlled environment all winter is unhealthy because it weakens our body's ability to regulate itself and adapt to diverse conditions. Taking daily walks or going cross-country skiing, for example, challenges our body and strengthens its healthy temperature-regulating functions. We need a home base, but we also need to be able to leave home and venture forth into the world. Having a comfort zone is healthy; being imprisoned in one is not.

THE COMFORT ZONE CYCLE

When we become programmed so that our Natural Anxiety triggers a Toxic Anxiety reaction, we can no longer focus on achieving the goal we set out to accomplish. Instead of anticipating the excitement of the goal, we hear Toxic Anxiety's voice saying, "Watch out! Danger ahead! You can't handle it. Turn back before it's too late!" Relieving the mounting feelings of anxiety suddenly becomes more important than pursuing our goal.

It is possible to reassure ourselves simply and naturally by self-calming talk ("It's OK. I can relax now."), breathing in a more relaxed fashion or directing our attention to a pleasant activity. Yet most of us, as children, did not receive adequate training in healthy emotional self-management. Instead we learned other, far less healthy ways to relieve anxiety, such as stuffing it and dumping it: eating sweets, pretending it never happened, picking on someone smaller, breaking something by accident, self-numbing, being busy all the time, trying to be perfect, or moping morosely.

When we become adults these anxiety-relieving behaviors may take the form of addictive habits that arise automatically and unconsciously in response to anxiety we may not even be aware of. These include all of the compulsive behaviors and characteristics noted in our previous discussion of Toxic Anxiety: alcohol abuse, gambling, violence, procrastination, compulsive sex, anxiety and depression symptoms, overeating, workaholism, compulsive shopping, watching TV, and so on.

The following diagram illustrates how we become trapped in the comfort zone, which represents our habitual behavior patterns. To the right of the comfort zone lies our growth zone, where our goals and our potential for greater power and awareness are located. To the left is the rejuvenation zone, symbolizing healthy relaxation and self-renewal.

The Comfort Zone Cycle

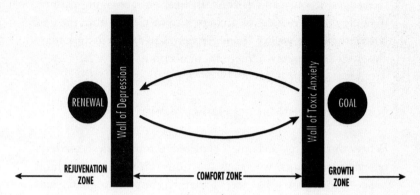

The lower arrow shows that our desires and our energies are always moving toward self-realization, usually in the form of a goal located in our growth zone. Whenever we attempt to grow, problems and obstacles arise that arouse our Natural Anxiety. But if we have been conditioned to overreact, Natural Anxiety and even healthy excitement can automatically trigger a Toxic Anxiety reaction. For example, while anyone would experience some anxiety in asking their boss for a raise, in Adele's case her anxiety immediately escalated to toxic levels. A "wall" of Toxic Anxiety prevented her from moving into her growth zone and pursuing her goal. Her priority shifted from achieving the goal to relieving her anxiety—by any means possible.

As we see in the upper arrow of the diagram, the positive energy of growth is deflected by Toxic Anxiety. It turns into bad habits, addictions, and other dysfunctional behaviors which use up the energy that was diverted from our original goal. These anxiety-relieving behaviors are attractive to us because, no matter how painful they may be, they are familiar. They bring us back to our comfort zone. We know how to do them; we've done them dozens, hundreds, probably thousands of times. These dead-end detours enable us to have the illusion of going somewhere while we avoid having to face the far greater anxi-

ety of venturing into the dreaded unknown represented by the
challenges of our growth zone. In this self-sabotaging pattern,
the only way to reduce the anxiety is to turn away from the goal
when we hit the wall of Toxic Anxiety. Later we will look more
closely at the anxiety-addiction connection.

THE ANXIETY-DEPRESSION CYCLE

When our energy becomes depleted through these anxiety-
relieving behaviors, we reach the other limit of our comfort
zone—depression. We feel lethargic, hopeless, guilty, un-
motivated, and swamped by negative feelings about ourselves.
Anxiety and depression can be viewed dynamically as the
twin poles of the comfort zone cycle. Anxiety is a high-energy
state associated with agitation and hyperarousal; it is the hopeful, goal-seeking phase of this cycle. Depression is a low-energy
state associated with hopelessness, lethargy, and withdrawal
from activity. One follows the other in this toxic cycle as night
follows day. Physiologically, the depressive phase arises as a
protective reaction to Toxic Anxiety's overstimulation of the
nervous system and the self-abusive behavior that follows
it. Psychologically, the depression and guilt emerge from
our awareness that we have squandered our energy once again
in a self-sabotaging manner. On some level we know that we
have let anxiety block our path and divert us again from our
goal.

Depression blocks us from experiencing the healthy self-
renewal of relaxation and rejuvenation. People who become
trapped in the comfort zone not only fear the tingly feelings of
aliveness (the activating shivers of Natural Anxiety), they also
dread the involuntary, relaxing shivers of the "relaxation anxiety" that accompanies the transition into the rejuvenation zone.

Even if we are unable to relax, we still require some physiological downtime to compensate for periods of high anxiety.
And depression, though it is a poor substitute for rejuvenation,

is better than continuing anxiety, for at least some recuperation can occur. After energy becomes restored, the cycle cranks up for another self-defeating round as hope and desire emerge once more and compel us to try again. Lacking any greater self-awareness, our renewed attempts, governed by old habits, will simply follow the old pathway. When we complain about being "stuck in a rut," we are referring to this well-worn route through the comfort zone.

If you stop and reflect on your own experience, you will probably find, as I did, that anxiety and depression often alternate with each other. In the comfort zone system, we tend to cycle between these two poles—the highs and lows of our emotional experiences. As we respond to the stressors in our lives, some of us are biologically predisposed to manifest more depressive symptoms while others are prone to experience more anxiety symptoms. This biological cycle is based on a combination of genetic predisposition, hormone levels, lifestyle habits, and thought patterns.

An extreme stimulation/sedation cycle has almost become the norm in our fast-paced society. Most people jump-start their engines with caffeine in the morning, push themselves to the limit during the day to cope with ever-increasing responsibilities, and then crash or veg out at night with TV, food, and alcohol.

Anxiety and depression often alternate, but they also can be present simultaneously: We can feel depressed, hopeless, and lethargic while experiencing insomnia, anxiety, and excessive worry. If left untreated, the anxiety-depression cycle follows two basic courses over a person's lifetime. The swings between anxiety and depression become more extreme and/or the depression begins to predominate over the anxiety as the person becomes more physically depleted and mentally hopeless with each negative cycle.

If you find that you have times of anxiety and periods of depression, you can use your understanding of the comfort zone to gradually reduce the extremes and come to a more balanced state. As one of my clients put it, "If I'm not anxious, I'm depressed. I'd like more than two choices."

THE ANXIETY-ADDICTION CONNECTION

When we deprive ourselves of the natural exhilaration of growth, we crave artificial excitement, such as that provided by movies, compulsive sex, spectator sports, or emotional crises. When we do not allow ourselves authentic self-renewal, we gravitate toward the pseudo-rejuvenation of self-indulgence, addictive "treats," or emotional numbness.

Unresolved anxiety becomes the fuel behind addictive behaviors. I am using "addiction" in its broadest sense here to include any dysfunctional automatic behavior that we have difficulty stopping despite its negative consequences. Addictive habits are dysfunctional anxiety-relieving behaviors that have become rigid through repetition; the mental groove we have created has become a deep rut, and our energy flows into it automatically.

Although we may have a biological predisposition to become addicted to certain substances or behaviors, whether we act on that tendency depends on other factors, including our mental conditioning. Inherited genes may predispose us to certain problems, but biology is not destiny, only tendency. Reclaiming our ability to be aware and make conscious choices is the essence of human freedom.

Addictive behaviors are so widespread and so difficult to eradicate because they appear to work so well. After we understand the role of addictive behaviors in the comfort zone system it is easy to see why we use them. The most uncomfortable place to be in this whole cycle is the point at which our energy meets the Toxic Anxiety reaction. If we keep pouring our energy into Toxic Anxiety, we know from experience that it will push our anxiety sky-high. At that moment we are in desperate need of a new route for our energy. Addictive behaviors provide that route.

In the short run, addictive behaviors work; we experience definite relief. But in the long run, of course, these quick fixes can destroy our health, wreck relationships, hamper our performance, and drag us seriously off course in life. The obvious solution is to direct our energy where we wanted it to go in the first place—to personal growth and success in meeting our goals.

As we saw earlier, the first step to harnessing anxiety is awareness. Awareness enables us to observe our own behavior and become conscious of what were previously automatic and unconscious behaviors. We can use awareness to change bad habits and addictive behaviors without having to struggle against our urges or rely solely on willpower.

Here's a way you can change a bad habit or addictive behavior by using awareness:

CHANGING ADDICTIVE BEHAVIORS WITH AWARENESS

1. Target a specific habit you would like to change or have more control over. Pick one that is relatively easy to start with. As you gain confidence, you can tackle the more challenging ones. Some examples: Instead of heading for a junk food snack the minute you walk in the door after work, wait a while, and do something else instead. Choose an alternative behavior that might appeal to you, such as preparing a healthy meal or snack or taking a relaxing bath. Or, instead of turning on the radio as soon as you get in the car, first take some time to enjoy your drive in peace and quiet.

2. Practice awareness. Plan ahead so that as soon as you are in the situation that triggers the old habit, you will choose to stop and practice awareness. For example, when you get home and feel the urge to snack even though you are not hungry, instead of acting on it you sit quietly and notice what you are feeling. You may find it useful to sit and take a

---

few deep breaths (see Chapter 8) for a few minutes to quiet your mind. Your purpose in doing this is to learn to relax into the feelings that are there, to relax with the urges.

3. Pay attention. Notice where you feel these urges in your body and see if you can relax that part of your body by breathing relaxation into it. Listen for any inner voices you may hear urging you to act on the old habit or ones that criticize you for having a bad habit in the first place. Here you are gathering information about where the energy for this addictive behavior comes from. You may want to write down what you are feeling. The more you let yourself relax with the feelings, the deeper you can penetrate to the subconscious source of the behavior.

4. Ask yourself, "What would make me feel the best right now?" Imagine acting on your old habit: how do you feel before, during, and after doing it? Do you want to repeat that cycle again? Imagine other pathways your energy could take. How would these alternatives make you feel before, during, and after doing them?

5. Make a choice. Remember that it is perfectly OK to do your old habit again if you want to. This exercise is not about using willpower or getting it right. It is about becoming more aware of whatever you are doing. You have already succeeded with this exercise simply by not acting automatically. If you choose to do your old habit, do it more consciously and really pay attention to how you feel throughout the process. What is it about this habit that works for you? What doesn't? If you feel like making a choice for a new behavior, that's great. Try it out. Notice how it feels. Congratulate yourself. Even if you still go back and do your old habit afterward, you have succeeded in poking some holes in it.

6. Review. Review what you learned from this and how you feel as a result of your choices.

You'll find that this method of changing habits is very different from the old style of browbeating yourself or shaming yourself into changing. The old method may work temporarily, but as you probably know, the unresolved anxiety and resistance soon take advantage of a weak moment or a stressful time to reestablish the old habit. This new approach is very powerful because it doesn't fight the old habit; it uses awareness to give you choices and to dissolve the root cause of the Toxic Anxiety reaction. Give it time and it will work for you.

People are often amazed at the powerful experiences they have when they practice awareness at the very moment their anxiety is trying to compel them to do something self-destructive. I have found that working on little everyday habits as well as heavy-duty addictive behaviors is one of the most practical ways to face anxiety. The key to success is to keep the focus off the bad habit and on your ability to choose freely what *you* want.

THE TRAGEDY OF SELF-SABOTAGE

The main problem with getting trapped within the artificial limits of the comfort zone is that it hampers growth. Ideally our comfort zone is always expanding into our growth zone. Comfort zones are never static. If we are not expanding our comfort zone it begins to contract. We start to lose sight of our true goals, which now lie behind the wall of Toxic Anxiety. In my work with clients, I find that people who have been trapped in their comfort zones for many years have lost the vital ability to know what they really want in life or how they really feel about anything. For years, being drawn into repetitive self-created crises has substituted for real growth. The comfort zone can become a place of living death inhabited by zombies who sleepwalk through life. Theodore Roosevelt's description of "poor spirits who neither enjoy nor suffer much, because they live in the gray twilight that knows neither victory nor defeat," certainly applies to people trapped in their comfort zones.

We've observed how bad habits like procrastination and addictive behaviors, such as watching too much TV, are common ways that we sabotage ourselves, but some of us engage in even more sophisticated methods that keep us trapped in our comfort zone. One client of mine, a bright and likable man named Gary, had sabotaged himself during his life by consistently overshooting the mark when he aimed for a goal. He did this by becoming overconfident and underestimating the difficulties involved in accomplishing his goal. Of course he felt wonderful while he was envisioning his great success ("I'm going to hit the jackpot with this one") during the early phase as he traveled though his comfort zone and avoided thinking about the anxiety-producing challenges ahead. But as soon as the first problem arose, Gary would lose faith and his bubble would burst. Of course, after years of this he had begun to view himself as a loser, and suffered from painfully low self-esteem. When he acquired an understanding of the comfort zone, Gary was able to confront his anxiety earlier and convert it to proactive goal-achieving strategies. Gradually he began to experience the satisfaction of genuine growth.

Another way we sabotage ourselves is by setting goals within our comfort zones. This is a favorite strategy for many people (I must confess that I have used all of these myself in the past). Setting goals inside our comfort zone enables us to have the illusion of growth without having to face the anxiety of true growth.

For example, Edie was the classic perennial student, still preparing for life at 34. I'm a firm believer in lifelong education, but Edie had adopted taking classes as a way of avoiding the anxiety of choosing a career. Her wealthy parents were generous in their support of her educational endeavors, so she didn't have the financial pressure that impels most of us to get a job. Every few years Edie would choose another degree program; some she finished, some she didn't. Edie was good at writing papers and being a student, so these goals were well within her comfort zone. The problem was that her personal development had stalled and she never felt any real satisfaction when she received a degree—even though she had worked hard for it, her response would inevitably be, "Big deal. Another degree. Now what am I going to do with it?"

Finally, by working on the underlying anxiety issues, Edie was able to break her comfort zone cycle. She realized she was perpetually postponing growing up because she was afraid that she would never live up to her parents' expectations. By facing this anxiety, long-buried in her unconscious, Edie was able to liberate the energy she needed to live her life in the present and develop authentic, growth-promoting goals.

TRAPPED IN THE COMFORT ZONE

Learning new skills and mastering new challenges is what makes life interesting and exciting. In studies of the elderly, researchers found that those who frequently challenged themselves with tasks that stretched their abilities actually lived longer than those who did not. To paraphrase Bob Dylan, if we're not busy being born, we're busy dying. The following diagram shows what happens when we have been trapped too long in the comfort zone:

The Comfort Zone Narrows

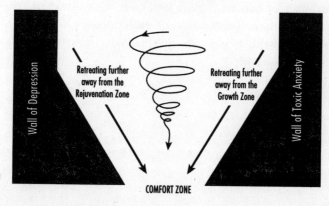

Here we see how the comfort zone contracts and we spiral downward into an increasingly narrow experience of life. Growth fails to occur and our life becomes stagnant. For example, after a painful end to a serious relationship, twenty-three-year-old Luke numbed his emotional life and avoided becoming involved with anyone. Eight years later, when he came to see me for the first time, Luke's social skills and self-confidence had deteriorated to the point that his life had been reduced to going to work and watching TV at home.

Loretta, another client of mine, experienced a panic attack at a party during a stressful time in her life. Because she feared the possibility of having another attack, she occasionally avoided going to social functions. After a while she began having panic attacks in the supermarket and at the mall; she increasingly avoided going out on her own. When she came to see me for help, Loretta had suffered from agoraphobia for seventeen years. This anxiety disorder often progresses to the point where individuals are unable to leave their homes without experiencing an anxiety attack. It is a vivid illustration of the comfort zone becoming a prison with all the "comforts of home."

Fortunately, this comfort zone cycle is not natural; it is a socially conditioned behavior and it can be unlearned. In the following chapters, we will examine ways to transform comfort zone cycles back into the growth cycles they were originally meant to be and learn to rediscover the enlivening goals and passions that may have been lost. Later we will explore the sacred dimension of this model of evolutionary growth, revealing the behind-the-scenes role that Sacred Anxiety plays in our everyday behavior.

Chapter Seven

THE A⁺ FORMULA: TURNING ANXIETY INTO AWARENESS AND ACTION

THE A+ FORMULA FOR MASTERING ANXIETY

The A+ Formula is our ticket out of the comfort zone. Its purpose is to transform Toxic Anxiety into productive energy and personal growth. We can use this formula to handle an episode of anxiety or depression or to deal with a problem we are facing. In fact, all the other techniques we are learning can be used within the overall framework of the A+ Formula—our master plan for converting anxiety into positive energy.

When we become anxious, the first casualty is mental clarity. Toxic Anxiety's primary weapon is confusion, which weakens the will and impairs the ability to think and plan. The following formula, which has been used successfully by many graduates of my Mastering Anxiety program, helps restore calmness and mental clarity. It is easy to understand and remember, but practicing it takes courage and perseverance.

The five-step A+ Formula is versatile. You can use it simply and quickly to deal with daily anxieties, running through the five steps within a few minutes. You can also use it to address major problems and opportunities, in which case the formula becomes the basis of an ongoing strategy. Later in this chapter, we will explore how a woman named Carla applies the formula to a high-anxiety situation—being laid off from her job.

THE A+ FORMULA

1. Acceptance
2. Awareness
3. Analysis
4. Action
5. Appreciation

1. Acceptance
Accept the anxiety—or the problem—as an opportunity to learn and grow.

2. Awareness
Practice active awareness. Relax with the anxiety and bring attention to breathing with awareness (see Chapter 8). Step back and gain more self-awareness by compassionately observing your physical sensations, emotions, and thoughts. Detach from your habitual reactions and imagine new options.

3. Analysis
Tell yourself the highest truth about the situation. Untangle and separate the strands of Toxic, Natural, and Sacred Anxiety. Develop a clear picture of your situation. Decide on a "next-step" strategy to deal with it, one that is goal-achieving as well as anxiety-relieving.

4. Action
Do it! Put your awareness into action and take your next step. Becoming aware of the type of anxiety and its causes leads to action, such as using an anxiety-mastering technique, ex-

ploring inner emotional healing, taking an action step toward
a goal, or letting go to your Higher Power. Channeling the
energy of anxiety appropriately leads to an accomplishment
such as feeling calmer, learning something about yourself, or
achieving a goal.

5. *Appreciation*
Review what you have learned and accomplished. Appreciate who you are and what you have done. Choose an attitude
of gratitude as you notice all the blessings in your life.

Now let's look at the A+ Formula in more detail:

Using the A+ Formula for Mastering Anxiety

1. *Acceptance*
Actively accept that anxiety is paying you a visit. Decide to
turn around and face anxiety instead of running from it.
Welcome your current situation as an opportunity to master
anxiety, strengthen your self-confidence, and deepen your
spiritual life. Accept yourself as an imperfect human being
with human problems. Lighten up and find some humor in
the situation (try laughing at anxiety!).

Accept that anxiety is part of life. Learn how to get it to
work for you instead of against you. Imagine that anxiety is
a tennis ball coming over the net toward you. Are you going
to ignore it and let it hit you? Are you going to run from it?
Or are you going to actively connect with it and hit it where
you want it to go? As with any other skill, mastering anxiety
takes practice, and fortunately life gives us plenty of opportunities to practice. Welcoming anxiety puts you in charge.

DON'T

Don't ignore anxiety or use denial and distraction.

Don't try to fight anxiety. Fighting it just feeds it and makes it escalate.

Don't give in and let anxiety defeat you.

Don't obsess on anxiety or try to figure it out.

Don't criticize yourself for experiencing anxiety or get sidetracked by guilt and shame.

DO

Decide to accept anxiety and face it.

Welcome anxiety as an opportunity to learn and grow.

Laugh at anxiety and try to find the humor in the situation.

Accept anxiety as a call to adventure.

2. Awareness

Anxiety tries to take control by either paralyzing us or provoking us into compulsive, and usually self-defeating, action. We take back control by practicing active awareness, a relaxed-yet-alert, tuned-in state of mind. Decide to relax with the anxiety and become aware of what's going on in your mind and in your body. Just sit with your anxiety, practice self-calming, and breathe with awareness. If you feel like moving, that's fine too; listen to your body and what it needs. Bring your awareness into the present moment. When you are feeling very anxious, it often helps to ground yourself by paying attention to your immediate physical environment or talking to someone. Notice that you are safe. This stage of awareness is not about trying to figure things out in your head. It is about accepting the anxiety and observing it. Notice that, although you may have anxiety, you are not your anxiety. You can step back and observe your anxious thoughts and feelings. Become aware of your Inner Talk.

During active awareness you can practice two main skills: *observation* and *compassion*. Observation refers to the art of stepping outside yourself and simply noticing what you are experiencing—thoughts, mental images, inner voices, physical sensations, your environment, etc. Exercising compassion means refraining from judging your observations. Compassion means accepting yourself and loving yourself just as you are in the present moment. Stay with active awareness until you feel calmer. Ask your Inner Guide to help you. Listen to your inner voice as it leads you into healing action.

> **Transforming questions:** What is the Anxious Chatterbox saying to me? How am I really feeling emotionally? Where is the anxiety in my body? What is it doing? Which thoughts are making me anxious? What does my Inner Guide have to say about this?

3. Analysis

After you have calmed yourself and gathered more information through self-awareness, you can use your ability to think rationally and logically. If possible, try to identify what triggered your anxiety. Now begin the process of untangling the three levels of anxiety. Which part of your anxiety is Toxic and can be released? Which part is Natural and represents a real life problem that needs to be addressed? Which part is Sacred and requires deeper self-reflection and letting go? Begin planning your action step.

Transforming questions: What triggered this episode of anxiety? What am I perceiving as a threat right now? Which part of me (a self-image or role) is feeling threatened, and why? Have I been suppressing an emotion, such as anger, sadness, or excitement? Does this anxiety have a message for me? What do I need to do right now to turn this anxiety into positive energy?

4. Action

You can turn the energy of anxiety into action and accomplishment. Don't become paralyzed or panicked by the anxiety or get sidetracked by old habits. Change your Inner Talk. Ask yourself, "What do I need to do next?" Let awareness and analysis lead you to your next step. You don't have to have all the answers; just channel your energy into taking the next step and do it now.

Your immediate accomplishment might be achieving a concrete goal, experiencing personal growth, or simply surviving an anxiety attack. Viewed from a larger perspective, the action phase represents channeling your energy with consistency and perseverance toward short- and long-term goals based on your deepest values and beliefs. To do this you need to take the time to evaluate your present goals and create new ones if necessary. You can develop step-by-step strategies that lead in the directions of your dreams. Then, when anxiety arises, you can channel its energy into productive action. You may benefit by getting help and new perspectives from a trusted friend, relative, colleague, or counselor.

The key to achieving goals lies in learning to use the energy of anxiety constructively. Ask yourself: Is what I am doing merely anxiety-relieving (a compulsive habit) or is it goal-achieving (part of a strategy to move me beyond my comfort zone into personal growth)?

Action for Toxic Anxiety: The first priority is self-calming. Remember that it's OK to leave an anxiety-produc-

ing situation to calm yourself. Stop negative fantasizing about
the future and tune in to the present moment. Notice your
here-and-now surroundings. Use positive Inner Talk to calm
the anxious part of you; let it know that everything is OK,
that you are safe right now.

Use the 180° Technique or the Million Dollar Questions.
Allow your healthy adult self to comfort the scared, child-
like part of you. Release the excessive anxiety by breathing
it out and breathing in relaxation, using a technique such as
the Ultimate Relaxation Breath in Chapter 8. Do something
physical to release the build-up of anxious adrenaline. Take a
walk. Express—safely and appropriately—any suppressed
emotions, such as anger and frustration, that may be fueling
your anxiety. Pound a pillow, talk, or shout out loud.

> **Transforming questions:** What can I do to prevent this
> same anxiety from happening again? Am I suppressing my
> true feelings about a person or situation? Is there an
> unresolved issue from my childhood or my past that is
> being restimulated by the current situation? Am I
> subconsciously using anxiety symptoms to distract me
> from dealing with a larger problem in my life? What
> might my anxiety symptoms symbolize on a deeper level?

Action for Natural Anxiety: Through awareness and
analysis you have identified an actual problem in your life that
is causing you distress. Now the challenge is to see the opportunity in the problem and turn the anxiety into energy,
excitement, and productive action. You may need to get help,
get more information, or utilize other outside resources to
develop an action strategy. Talk to someone, express your
feelings. Imagine the worst that can happen and then affirm
to yourself that you can deal with it. Use positive Inner Talk.

> **Transforming questions:** Even though I am dealing
> with a real problem, is my anxiety response to it

exaggerated? Has my feeling of self-worth and my
identity become attached to a circumstance (do I feel
"my life will be over" if I lose this job or that "I'll die" if
my spouse leaves me)? Is my real anxiety my belief that I
won't be able to love and accept myself or feel good
about life if this dreaded event happens? Am I feeling
anxious because I am unwilling to accept the natural
uncertainties of life and looking for a guarantee that
things will work out my way? Am I trying to control
another person's behavior? Is this situation beyond my
control—do I need to let go?

Action for Sacred Anxiety: Allow everyday anxieties to
lead you to higher levels of anxiety. Question everything, especially your own limiting beliefs. Observe what sort of
model of the universe you are operating within, and if it
isn't working for you, change it! Be willing to let go of a
limiting self-identity; expand your sense of self to include
the universe. Bring an "attitude of gratitude" to your life.
Have a conversation with God or with whatever source
brings you spiritual comfort. Step back and see your situation from a higher perspective. The appropriate action for
Sacred Anxiety is often non-action, or letting go. Be willing
to turn over to a higher power things that are beyond your
control. Let Sacred Anxiety lead you to an unshakable, unconditional inner peace that does not depend on your circumstances.

Transforming questions: What would God or my
Higher Power want to say to me about this situation?
Take some time to explore the deeper questions: Who
am I? Why am I here? What is my purpose in life? How
do I conceive of God, or my ultimate source? What is
my relationship to my God?

5. *Appreciation*

Congratulate yourself for dealing with anxiety in a more creative way. Don't wait for perfection; praise any improvement. Thank anxiety for guiding you in the direction of growth. Reward yourself for accomplishment with appreciation, relaxation, and pleasure. Deepen your capacity for unconditional love for yourself and others.

The appreciation step may seem less important than the others, but it actually may be the most important. I have seen many people make real progress in mastering anxiety initially, but because they neglect to acknowledge and appreciate their own accomplishments, they never experience positive reinforcement for their efforts. Soon they become discouraged again. The Anxious Chatterbox loves to minimize achievements, point out how far you still have to go, and measure you against an impossible standard of perfection. So use Inner Talk to congratulate yourself often and enthusiastically.

Cultivate an attitude of gratitude. Anxiety is focusing on what we don't have or might lose. Gratitude is focusing on what we do have and can create. Cultivate humility and awe at the wonder of life and astonishment at the abundance of the universe. Embrace the unique adventure of your own life and let anxiety help awaken you to your true eternal self.

CARLA'S DILEMMA

When Natural Anxiety degenerates into Toxic Anxiety, the original life problem becomes hidden behind a manufactured problem and our life veers off course. The commitment to face anxiety and the willingness to experience the pain that accompanies growth can help us avoid letting the pure flow of Natural Anxiety become toxic.

A career crisis naturally triggers anxiety; the challenge is to use it productively. We are going to follow Carla, who has just been laid off from her job, through each stage of the A⁺ Formula.

Carla reacts to her unexpected unemployment, as most of us would, with a mixture of Toxic, Natural, and Sacred Anxiety. She notices that she is drinking more alcoholic beverages than usual, eating more, having trouble sleeping at night, and feeling anxious most of the day. These symptoms get her attention and she begins to apply the A+ Formula. First Carla notices her habitual resistance to change ("This is unfair. This shouldn't be happening to me.") and decides to respond with acceptance, the first step in the A+ Formula. She admits that job changes may be a fact of life for nearly everyone in today's economy and that it's natural to feel anxious as she contemplates the future.

Next she practices the second step, awareness. By sitting quietly with her anxiety she becomes aware that getting laid off has triggered old anxieties "about things never working out for me." In Carla's childhood, her relationship with her parents was filled with problems—it seemed she could never please them. Her childhood self is experiencing the layoff as a rejection by her corporate parent, and she feels discouraged and unwanted. For Carla, losing her job has immediately triggered old subconscious patterns. Her Inner Talk tapes go something like this: "This is the worst thing that could happen to me. My boss is such a monster—I knew she never liked me. It's impossible to get a job these days. I may never work again. My life is such a mess! Nothing ever works out right for me."

Carla's awareness of her emotional response enables her to analyze her options and think clearly about the situation. She realizes that it is not helping her to react to this current challenge as if she were a little kid being victimized by a bad parent.

Next she begins to think about taking positive action and starts with changing her Inner Talk. She comforts herself by telling herself that this is not a personal rejection and affirms her value and self-worth by recalling her virtues and accomplishments. She enlists her Inner Guide to develop some more productive Inner Talk: "Obviously it's very upsetting to get laid off, but it's not the end of the world. This actually could be a good opportunity for me to look for a better job in my field—or even to change careers if I want to. I'm smart and energetic and very employable. I'm a strong person and I can handle this challenge." Carla begins to think about proactive strategies she can use to cope with this unexpected development in her life.

For now Carla congratulates herself on breaking an old pattern of sabotaging herself whenever she experiences an adverse event. She is not overeating or drinking too much and she is not making herself anxious and depressed with hours of negative Inner Talk. Instead she is facing the situation in a positive way. Even though she has not yet solved the problem of finding a new job, she takes time to reinforce what she has achieved so far with appreciation. Carla tells herself, "You are doing a great job handling this. I know things will work out; just hang in there and keep believing in yourself." She also takes time to appreciate all the things that she has going for her—good health, good friends, and enough money from her savings and her severance package to live on for the next few months.

Carla has just used the A⁺ Formula to help her through a difficult passage. She has avoided falling into the swamp of Toxic Anxiety and can begin using the Natural Anxiety of being unemployed in a positive way. To meet challenges and avoid the comfort zone trap, everyone can benefit from developing and practicing skills that enable them to calm anxiety symptoms, gain insight and awareness in their inner lives, and channel the energy of anxiety into goal-achieving action.

Mastering Toxic Anxiety

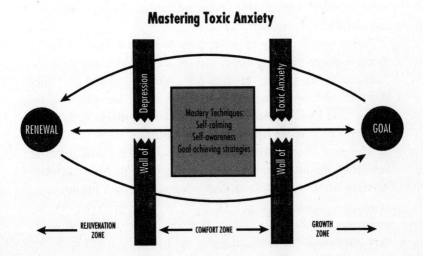

Choosing Life:
Resisting the Temptation of Toxic Anxiety

In the diagram above we see how learning basic anxiety mastery techniques can enable us to break through the wall of Toxic Anxiety, emerge into our growth zone, and meet important goals. Greater emotional and psychological self-awareness also helps us dissolve the wall of depression and relax into our rejuvenation zone, where we can experience a sense of renewal and gain greater clarity about our direction in life. In Chapter 9, we will see how this expansion of personal freedom allows us to transform the static comfort zone into a dynamic and rewarding growth cycle.

If we resist a life crisis when it occurs, the exciting, edge-of-the-seat feeling of aliveness turns into Toxic Anxiety. But if we can let the excitement flow through our nervous system, it can activate us to respond heroically, far beyond our usual capacity. The full acceptance of the Natural Anxiety of life also propels us to reach upward for spiritual strength and embrace our life unconditionally.

If Natural Anxiety works so well, why does Toxic Anxiety demonstrate such staying power in the life of individuals and societies? And, once created, why does Toxic Anxiety seem to take on a life of its own?

As human beings we crave security and wish to avoid danger. Toxic Anxiety promises us, if not security, at least less danger. "Believe in me, obsess on me, pay tribute to me with your thoughts and your energy," says the Anxiety Monster solicitously, "and I will shield you from the Dragon of Natural Anxiety, who is far more dangerous than I am."

This protection racket represents an effective form of psychic extortion. Toxic Anxiety does indeed protect us from Natural Anxiety. After we begin to mistake Natural Anxiety for our enemy, the distraction offered by Toxic Anxiety can seem like a godsend. The Monster knows that we would rather become very anxious about something that we (on some level) know is a make-believe creation of our own mind, than become even a little anxious about something real. For example, who would not prefer to obsess about being five pounds overweight than face a far more disturbing anxiety about a crumbling 20-year marriage?

Individuals who cling to their symptoms and habits, despite the presence of clear therapeutic avenues away from them, do so because at some level they know that the reward for mastering Toxic Anxiety is to advance to the real challenges of Natural Anxiety and Sacred Anxiety. Who would voluntarily choose to trade the "safety" of neurotic worries and negative fantasies for the real existential challenges revealed by honest self-awareness?

Only those with courage and a love for life.

TOXIC ANXIETY'S GIFT

We have observed that even Toxic Anxiety, the bad kind of anxiety, is potentially valuable. As Sheldon Kopp wrote, "All evil is potential vitality in need of transformation."[1] Toxic Anxiety is there for a reason; it has a message for us and it eventually gets our attention.

Those dysfunctional behaviors, those tormenting anxiety symptoms, those stress-related illnesses, and those problems, those disintegrating relationships all finally get us to stop rushing around and notice our inner life. When anxiety sends our body into panic, it forces those of us who live up in our head to realize that we have a body. When irrational thoughts and bizarre emotions erupt from out of nowhere, the dictatorship of the rational mind is confronted with the rebellion of the unconscious. In high anxiety we see our everyday reality and our personality as the fragile constructions they really are. The bizarre, phantasmagorical terrors of Toxic Anxiety are really distortions of spiritual truths—truths we have stubbornly resisted. Episodes of Toxic Anxiety are times when our denied Natural and Sacred Anxiety break through our carefully constructed defenses and provide us with a glimpse of a deeper mystery behind the daily facade.

Toxic Anxiety all too often is treated as a pathological phenomenon. It is a mental dysfunction but like all dysfunctions it bears a message—the old system is not working. Toxic Anxiety signals the need for a change in mindsets, a new model, an updated paradigm.

Asking "What is the gift behind this anxiety?" often can help us begin to change our attitude toward even the most disturbing forms of anxiety. Toxic Anxiety is an indication of an inner conflict that is seeking resolution—of disowned parts yearning to become reunited with the whole. When we resist addressing our inner conflict, the anxiety escalates and assumes more pernicious forms. As soon as we accept responsibility for our anxiety, as soon as we cease projecting it onto others or hiding it within our psyche's closet, our anxiety can begin to lead us toward healing.

Anxiety is a sign that we are trying to move to a new and higher level in our life. In both my personal and my professional life I have seen what happens when we choose to face our Toxic Anxiety and follow it to its source. We discover the Monster that has tormented us and prevented us from being who we want to be. Through facing and conquering this Monster, we discover the valuable gifts that were hidden in its cave. We find precious, long-lost parts of ourselves, which can now become integrated into a whole person. We discover goals we feel passionate about and begin to live life with greater energy, aliveness, and purpose.

THE SERENITY RESPONSE

Living with serenity in the age of anxiety does not imply living in some mono-mood of placid otherworldliness. Rather, it refers to a fully human existence that encompasses a vibrant range of emotions that is governed by a growing sense of faith and confidence. We will always be affected by the circumstances of our lives, but the nature of their impact is within our control.

This paradox of being affected by the changing world yet independent of it evokes an image of the ocean: Although the wind may whip the surface of the sea into tumultuous waves, the ocean itself remains calm below. Trying to "keep up" with everything today means that most of us tend to live ninety percent of our lives on the surface and perhaps only ten percent at a deeper level of inner awareness. What if we reversed that proportion to become more like the sea? What if we lived more deeply, more universally, more eternally within our daily lives?

In order to experience this inner peace we must cultivate "the serenity response." The serenity response is a combination of the physical relaxation response defined by Dr. Herbert Benson in the 1970s, plus the mental clarity that springs from psychoemotional intelligence and what Dr. Benson's latest research identifies as the "faith factor," a confidence borne of a deeper spiritual understanding of the nature of life. According to these clinical studies, individuals who incorporate a spiritual dimension into their relaxation practice actually have fewer medical symptoms than those who stop at simple relaxation.[2]

The serenity response, however, is not limited to periods of meditation or prayer, although such inner practices are essential for cultivating it. With experience, the serenity response becomes a way of greeting each new event in life, even those events which formerly triggered irritation, fear, anxiety, or even panic. The serenity response allows us to respond to real problems and even immediate dangers with sufficient physiological arousal and mental alertness to enable effective action, but without the sense of being threatened in any essential way.

This centered state is the hallmark of sages, saints, martial arts masters, and those ordinary men and women who remain calm and perform heroically during emergencies. The serenity response is rooted in our eternal source, and consists of a deep awareness that our essential self can never be threatened by any person, circumstance, or event. This soul self cannot be threatened by anything because it is everything.

Responding with serenity means that we answer life's episodes with acceptance and awareness—the first two steps of the A+ Formula—instead of with the ancient fight-or-flight reaction. As a result of our past conditioning, many of us experience the latter's adrenaline reaction dozens of times a day, adding to our stress levels, draining our immune systems, and fueling interpersonal conflicts. Imagine what it would be like to greet events with the serenity response instead of fight-or-flight. What if most of the stressful situations you encountered evoked serenity, instead of triggering the anxiety reaction of the past?

Anger, instead of erupting or being suppressed, could be channeled toward useful action and healthy assertiveness. Rather than degrading into depression, sadness could be consciously employed to help us accept loss and change. We could learn to reclassify our desires as preferences instead of demands. Imagine what a difference the serenity response could make in how we experience our lives: better health, greater intimacy and love, more creativity and joy. Such a shift is not only desirable, it is possible; I have witnessed it both in my own life and in the lives of hundreds of clients and workshop participants.

We begin cultivating the serenity response by transforming anxiety reactions into acceptance and awareness with the A+ Formula; eventually it becomes habitual in a greater range of situations. The serenity response is founded upon a deep sense of being loved by the universe. It results from living intimately and creatively with Sacred Anxiety on a daily basis. By facing the "Big One" each day, we deprive all the lesser anxieties of their power to threaten us. We need to train ourselves and our children to cultivate the serenity response in daily life. And, more than anything else, we need to ask ourselves how we can create the kind of just and caring society that naturally evokes the serenity response in all of its members.

Chapter Eight

MEDITATION, BREATHING,
AND BODY AWARENESS

AWARENESS THROUGH MEDITATION

Meditation is another way to deepen your awareness of Inner Talk and to gain mastery over anxiety. Meditating can help uncover subconscious programming that is stored at levels of the subconscious mind that don't come into our field of awareness simply by monitoring everyday Inner Talk. The style of meditation that I teach, "whole mind meditation," is a naturalistic approach that encourages the integration of the subconscious and the conscious mind. Instead of attempting to escape from the rational mind into a temporary state of dissociated bliss, whole mind meditation offers the opportunity to reunite powerful aspects of the mind that have become alienated from each other. Because the subconscious mind includes the whole body as well as the brain, meditation is also an opportunity to become more familiar with and more comfortable in our own bodies.

During meditation, you can listen to your Inner Talk at a deeper level and uncover and release any negative mindsets that have been hidden in your subconscious mind. Meditation is also a time to listen to your Inner Guide and gain clarity about your goals and dreams. But perhaps one of the finest gifts of meditation is taking a break from all Inner Talk, even the positive kind. You begin to notice the pauses between your Inner Talk, to focus on the silent moments and allow them to expand. Enjoying the peace of an "empty mind" can be delightfully relaxing.

The art of meditation has many levels, from enjoying basic relaxation (taking an "inner vacation") to practicing more challenging psychospiritual growth work to experiencing transcendent states of oneness. The common element of all effective meditation is awareness: becoming more aware of automatic, unconscious programs and consequently more aware of the still, small voice of inner wisdom.

Meditation also can be used to approach a problem or difficulty in your life from a new perspective. If you can stay relaxed and detached while viewing your situation, new insights may emerge. You can delve more deeply into your Inner Talk and subconscious mindsets to discover the personal laws that operate in your life. You can contemplate various themes or attributes that you want to strengthen. You might meditate on the meaning of love, truth, life, joy, compassion, forgiveness, and other timeless themes. You can further your spiritual growth by meditating on your higher self, God, or oneness. You also can meditate without any agenda, simply allowing yourself to be aware of your moment-to-moment experience, a way of focusing that is often called "mindfulness."

The following brief description will give you the basic tools you will need to begin practicing meditation, or to enhance your existing meditation practice.

HOW TO MEDITATE

Meditation is a wonderful experience that can bring diverse and rewarding benefits into your life. Among the many positive changes meditators report are better health, greater energy, clearer thinking, increased emotional self-control, deeper relaxation, enhanced self-confidence, more satisfying relationships with others, and noticeable personal and spiritual growth. Meditation takes some practice. Don't be discouraged if you can't get the results you would like at first. Keep practicing, encourage yourself with positive feedback, and learn from the obstacles you encounter. The special times when you experience deep relaxation and mental tranquillity often arrive as gifts, when you least expect them.

Detailed instruction in meditation is beyond the scope of this book, and many excellent books are available on the topic.[1] What follows is a simple breathing technique you can use to calm anxiety and to enter the meditative state.

THE ULTIMATE RELAXATION BREATH

When we are rushed, we might say, "I haven't even had time to take a breath today." External stress and pressure as well as internal emotional conflict trigger anxiety, to which we might react by tightening the chest muscles and holding our breath in an attempt to suppress the anxiety. This restricts respiration and produces shallow, rapid breathing. Shallow breathing numbs our feelings and traps the anxiety inside, which in turn triggers more physiological arousal, sending us up the anxiety escalator. Breathing naturally and fully enables us to feel our feelings and release the anxiety. One of the best ways to handle any episode of anxiety is simply to avoid resistant breathing; instead, accept the anxiety, feel the feelings, and keep breathing.

Breath is life. As the poet Elizabeth Barrett Browning wrote, "He lives most life who breathes most air." Whenever we feel we don't even have time to breathe, it is a sign that the Anxious Chatterbox has taken control of us and we are no longer acting in our own best interest. We can regain control of our lives by connecting with our calm Inner Guide and giving ourselves a simple gift—ten relaxing breaths.

The Ultimate Relaxation Breath is a method for taking time out from schedules and responsibilities and taking time in for ourselves. It is called the Ultimate Relaxation Breath for three reasons: (1) it goes beyond both the typical shallow breath and the frequently taught diaphragmatic breath to use the full capacity of the lungs; (2) it uses all the senses to create relaxation; and (3) it incorporates the spiritual dimension of breathing. This breathing technique is one of the easiest and most effective ways to reduce both biological and psychological anxiety. The whole autonomous nervous system (and through it, our internal organs and glands) takes its cue from our breathing patterns. By changing our breathing, we can influence hundreds of biochemical reactions in our body, producing more relaxing substances such as endorphins and fewer anxiety-producing ones such as adrenaline. As Inner Talk is to the mind, so breathing is to the body. Mindfulness of the breath is so effective that it is common to all meditative and prayer traditions.

Before you practice the Ultimate Relaxation Breath, take a moment to notice your habitual manner of breathing and your typical sitting posture. Breathing in your usual way, count your breaths for one minute. Make a mental note of this number.

HOW TO DO THE ULTIMATE RELAXATION BREATH

The Physical Component of the Ultimate Relaxation Breath

Most of the time, we tend to breathe shallow breaths because of habit, postural constrictions, and tense musculature. The subconscious mind associates our typical shallow, rapid breaths with danger. Deeper, longer breaths communicate safety and relaxation to the body.

Adjust your posture so that you can breathe comfortably and deeply. You can practice the Ultimate Relaxation Breath either sitting or lying down. Relax your muscles and make sure your arms and legs are not crossed and that your back is comfortably aligned.

The diaphragmatic breath improves upon the shallow breath by extending the breath from the chest down to the belly. To breathe diaphragmatically, allow your breath to descend all the way down to your abdomen so your belly expands like a balloon. Then continue breathing in so that your chest expands. Finish inhaling by breathing up into your upper chest so that your shoulders rise slightly. Now exhale by releasing your breath; finish your exhalation with a slight contraction of your abdominal muscles, thereby expelling any remaining stale air.

The diaphragmatic breath is a big improvement over the typical shallow chest breath, but it focuses only on expanding the breath vertically (upward and downward) and toward the front. To make it an Ultimate Breath, you can expand it in all directions. Try opening the entire torso and letting it expand upward and downward, toward the front and back, and out to the sides as you inhale. Breathe down into the central core of your torso and feel the breath expanding outward from this center to all directions. Avoid trying too hard. Breathing correctly is easy and natural. It is not necessary to pull the air in; just create a space for it and it will flow in effortlessly. (If chronic muscular tension in the back, shoulders, and chest restricts breathing, try some stretching and self-massage first.)

This more active form of breathing actually gives all your internal organs an inner massage and tones the muscles of the chest, back, and abdomen. The Ultimate Relaxation Breath automatically slows and harmonizes your breathing. To emphasize the relaxation effect of this breath, allow your exhalation to be longer than your inhalation. For example, count 1-2-3-4 as you inhale and 1-2-3-4-5-6 as you exhale.

As you do the Ultimate Relaxation Breath, count your breaths for one minute. Compare this number with your previous rate. Many people find they have cut their breathing rate in half and doubled their relaxation response.

The Mental Component of the Ultimate Relaxation Breath

While inhaling, say silently to yourself "Relaxation in." Imagine breathing in wonderful sensations of relaxation and feeling them going to every cell in your body.

While exhaling, say to yourself, "Anxiety (or tension) out." Imagine breathing out any feelings of anxiety, negativity, tension, or stress.

By repeating this breath 10 times, you can change an anxious or depressed mood to a positive, relaxed frame of mind—and body. If you want to activate this breath further, you can add the following sensory modes to the auditory message you are already using:

Visual: Visualize the air you are breathing in as your favorite cooling, calming, or soothing color. Imagine the tension you breathe out being a color that feels hot and stressful. Feel your mindbody changing color as you relax. You also can imagine a relaxing scene, such as a mountain lake.

Kinesthetic: Focus on really sensing the relaxing energy flowing into your body along with the oxygen molecules you are breathing in. Feel the tension and stress draining out of your body as you exhale.

Gustatory/Olfactory: Imagine breathing in a taste and aroma that feels relaxing to you. For example, as you inhale, imagine smelling the ocean air or the scent of mountain spruce. Some people associate a certain taste with well-being and relaxation—you might imagine drinking in refreshing lemonade, a minty herb tea, or raspberry-flavored sparkling water as you inhale.

Do at least 10 of these relaxing breaths, really focusing your mind on the words, images, and sensations. The more real you make it, the better it will work for you. Notice the difference in how you feel after doing 10 rhythmic, consecutive breaths.

The Spiritual Component of the Ultimate Relaxation Breath

Our word "spiritual" comes from the Latin word *spirare*, meaning "to breathe" (as in respiration). The Ultimate Relaxation Breath is a form of sacred breathing through which we celebrate this miracle and consciously receive the gift of life that surrounds us. Therefore, if you would like to enhance your experience even more, you can draw upon your spiritual resources.

To deepen your meditation, imagine a spiritual source of love and peace. This could be a religious figure such as Christ, Mohammed, or Buddha; a symbol such as a cross or star of David; a naturalistic image such as a radiant sun; or whatever it might be that symbolizes transcendent love and peace for you. Now visualize that symbol in front of you, breathe in the energy radiating out from it, and feel it entering your body. You might want to accompany the inhalation with a phrase, such as "I am breathing in divine love and peace." As you exhale, let go of your cares and concerns, and express your love and your gratitude to the source of life.

If you practice several cycles of 10 breaths at various times during each day, the Ultimate Relaxation Breath will soon become a reliable tool with which to master anxiety and find inner peace. Don't worry if this doesn't come easily to you. Focus on what works best for you in this exercise and adapt it to your needs. For most people, it is all modes working together that creates the most powerful transformation. The physiological relaxation response of relaxed breathing, the power of multiple sensory modalities, and the positive verbal suggestions can evict Toxic Anxiety from your body quickly and dramatically. The spiritual connection deepens the experience and can take you beyond relaxation to serenity.

ACTIVE AWARENESS

Along with practicing sitting meditation, you can practice meditative awareness while engaging in everyday activities, such as walking, exercising, waiting in line, having a conversation, working, and doing the dishes. We can call this "meditation in motion" or "active awareness." This type of practice is more challenging because you are combining and integrating awareness of the outside world with awareness of your inner world. In fact, the ultimate goal of meditation—if meditation can be said to have a goal—is to dissolve the illusion that there is a separation between the inner world and the outer world, between self and universe, between conscious and unconscious.

Regarding anxiety and other emotions, active awareness involves finding a way of experiencing feelings while at the same time observing them with nonattachment. Usually we either feel our feelings and allow them to dictate our behavior or control our feelings by suppressing them and ceasing to feel them. Being actively aware of emotions means experiencing the feelings without allowing them to trigger old behavior patterns; just being with physical sensations, thoughts, or feelings and allowing them to draw you deeper into your inner self. By doing so, it becomes possible for you to identify and release the mental programming behind the old patterns.

Active awareness provides a sense of freedom, a recognition of your options and choices. You can feel anxious, angry, scared, or sad and do something different with that emotional energy than you might have done previously. Awareness leads to action,

action that comes from choice, not habit. The action may be an outer one, such as talking about a conflict with your partner, or an inner one, such as nurturing a hurt part of yourself.

Active awareness, both in formal meditation practice and in daily life, is the key to becoming a more conscious, evolved human being. It helps us to wake up from our often half-asleep, habitual mental state and to use our full, conscious awareness. (If we don't use it, then Adam and Eve ate that apple for nothing!) One of the best ways to practice active awareness is, of course, paying attention to the Inner Talk we are creating and taking responsibility for it. Active awareness probably takes more courage than any other human activity because it involves facing our anxiety about life and death in the very moment we are living, directly and tangibly.

FIND YOUR ANXIETY CENTER AND CALM IT DOWN

I always try to be aware of the mindbody connection when I work with my own anxiety. One day when I was experiencing the turmoil of anxiety, I found I was not able to calm myself completely by using Inner Talk and breathing. My mind wanted to believe the positive things I was saying, but my body wasn't buying them. I noticed that my worries were accompanied by the sensation that's so often described as having butterflies in my stomach, or that sinking feeling in the pit of the stomach. It felt like something was definitely going wrong there, a churning sensation, as if the normal flow of energy had somehow shifted into reverse.

I located the center of those anxious feelings in my abdomen and applied the palm of my hand. As I rotated my hand in a clockwise direction, I found almost immediately that the anxious sensations were dissipating. With the biological component of my anxiety relieved, I resumed my Inner Talk and found that my body could now accept it. I began to teach this technique to clients and workshop participants, and I found that almost everyone could succeed in locating their main anxiety center and then calming it by using this method.

Here's how this fast, free, and effective mindbody technique can become another powerful tool in your anxiety mastery kit.

CALMING YOUR ANXIETY CENTER

Get out of your head and into your body. Notice where the sensations of anxiety are located in your body. The most common anxiety centers are located along the midline of the front of the torso and correspond to the "chakras" of yoga and the major energy centers of acupuncture. The two most common are the stomach (butterflies and nausea) and chest areas (rapid heartbeat and rapid breathing). Some people may find their anxiety center in the throat area. Worry that is unaccompanied by strong physical sensations usually indicates an anxiety center in the forehead (as indicated by the typical furrowed brow). If your main symptoms are in the arms or shoulders, use the middle of the chest as your anxiety center; if they are in the legs, use the lower abdomen.

After you locate your anxiety center, place the palm of your hand directly on the spot. Now begin gently moving your hand in a circular clockwise direction, moving downward on your left side and upward on your right side. After a minute or two, you will begin to notice a feeling of calmness replacing the sensations of anxiety.

To increase the effectiveness of this technique, combine it with positive, self-calming Inner Talk and relaxed breathing.

Remember to try the anxiety center calming technique the next time you feel any physical anxiety symptoms. You can't avoid getting butterflies in your stomach occasionally, but the next time it happens you can get them all to fly in the right direction!

Because the emotions and the body often don't listen to reason, we can use touch to calm the scared child or raging beast within. As a father, I have learned as most parents have that you can't talk a young child out of being anxious or scared, but you can often calm a child by holding it calmly or stroking its back.

When the child within you won't listen to reason, it probably has a good (emotional) reason not to. Listen to the Inner Talk and find out why. Remember that even natural methods like this one can be misused to cover up anxiety. Be sure to listen to your irrational emotional self and acknowledge any suppressed feelings lurking in your anxiety center. And use the anxiety center calming technique to communicate safety and relaxation nonverbally.

There are many ways to get in touch with subconscious feelings and memories by combining breathing and body awareness with psychotherapeutic techniques. We can learn a lot by listening to our bodies. Our bodies often know more about how we are really feeling than we do. For most of us, becoming friends with our bodies and feeling safe in our bodies is a key component of the healing process.

Part Three

HARNESSING THE POWER OF NATURAL ANXIETY

Natural Anxiety

Symbol: The Dragon

Natural Anxiety is the healthy form of anxiety that activates us to react to threats to our well-being. It also alerts and energizes us to respond to opportunities for growth. We are born with Natural Anxiety. It is rooted in the human condition and reflects our concerns regarding the possible loss of power and control. We have many needs and desires—for food, love, pleasure, approval, achievement, and self-expression. Our Natural Anxiety is realistic, for at any moment we might lack the power to fulfill the needs and desires we deem necessary to our existence as a person.

Natural Anxiety is the pivot point in life. Its purpose is to move us forward and upward—forward to personal growth and upward to spiritual evolution. Our task is to use Natural Anxiety effectively so that it does not slip backward into Toxic Anxiety, but propels us forward into life. If we learn to accept the Natural Anxieties inherent in life instead of denying them, we can experience greater peace of mind. Natural Anxiety is a powerful Dragon that we can harness to propel us toward our goals and to realize our life purpose.

Chapter Nine

FROM ANXIETY TO EXCITEMENT

A Prince Encounters Anxiety

Many years ago in a small kingdom there lived a handsome young prince who had known nothing but happiness his entire life. He had grown up within the domain of his father's castle and had always been showered with love, the best food, and the finest clothing. The air was filled with fragrant scents from the beautiful gardens within the castle's walls, and musicians played their sweet melodies daily in the courtyard. His caretakers had spared no effort in shielding the prince from anything that might disturb his happiness.

One day the young prince grew restless and began to wonder about the world outside the castle walls. The next morning, very early, he disguised himself and slipped away from the castle before anyone else was awake. As he wandered through the countryside he was astonished at what he saw. Walking through a village he was drawn by a strange sound that he had never heard before. In a room filled with the stench of sickness lay a woman with open sores all over her body. Her face was contorted in pain and she moaned in agony. The young prince realized with a jolt of horror that the physical body was subject to disease and injury.

The second sight the prince beheld was that of an outcast. The hood of the man's robe only partially concealed his misshapen face, and the prince saw that people were disturbed by his strangeness and avoided him. He knew this man had never been loved, would never marry, and would never know the joy of camaraderie and friendship. With an aching heart, the prince realized that love, acceptance, and approval did not come to all people. With another spin of fortune's wheel, it could be lost even by those who possessed it.

Next the prince saw a family living in a small, dilapidated hut. All were clothed in tattered rags and the children were emaciated. He watched the parents scour the countryside for scraps of food and any work they could find, but it was clear that it was never enough. In their dismal, downtrodden faces the prince saw how poverty had destroyed their hopes and dreams. Feeling great sadness, the prince realized that not all people possess the resources or experience the good fortune that allows them to develop their full potential in life; instead of success, some face never-ending hardship and misery.

Nearly overcome with anxiety by this exposure to the precariousness of life, the prince turned back toward the castle. Halfway there, his passage was blocked by a funeral procession. An old man's corpse passed by in an open casket. His gaze transfixed by this sight, the prince encountered the final horror: old age and death. He realized that even those abundantly blessed by health, love, and success inevitably age, wither, and die. Stunned by this revelation, the young prince shivered in the warm sunlight, sensing the transitory nature of his own mortal frame.

Trembling so much with anxiety that he was barely able to walk, the prince continued back to the castle. He saw people rushing here and there, caught up in the emotional dramas of the moment, focused on the daily realities of their existence. This sight was the most incomprehensible of all to the young prince. He thought: "With the threat of disease, poverty, abandonment, old age, and death constantly surrounding them, how can people go about their business each day and give so little thought to their ultimate fate and to the essential nature of life?"

Then in the midst of the busy marketplace, his vision became riveted upon the still figure of a monk, a holy man sitting and meditating un-

der a tree. "And how can he sit there at peace with all this suffering around him?" the prince wondered.

He returned to the castle, but he could no longer find contentment within its walls. He could not forget what he had witnessed; anxiety gnawed at him day and night. "What is the meaning or value of life if nothing lasts? Am I only this body that decays and dies? Who am I? What is the purpose of life?" The prince vowed to follow these questions wherever they might lead him. So began the great adventure of Prince Siddhartha, who ultimately penetrated the secret of life and became known as the Buddha.[1]

Buddha's quest was not inspired by a grand vision to found a new religion. His search was motivated and made necessary by his own anxiety about life. Unlike most people, he was not satisfied to make the usual compromises with the Natural Anxieties of existence. He saw that life began with the birth cry of the infant and ended with the death cry of the aged, and that in between existed all the travails of mortal life. Looking at human existence honestly and directly, Buddha declared that "Life is suffering." His anxiety about human suffering would not go away until he had followed it to its origins. Buddha's path provides an example of great courage that we too can follow as we face the challenges of Natural Anxiety and allow them to lead us where we need to go—deeper into Sacred Anxiety. Later, in Chapter 16, we will revisit Buddha's life journey and see how he transformed his anxiety into an unshakable inner peace.

HARNESSING THE ENERGY OF NATURAL ANXIETY

Disease, abandonment, failure, and death—these are the core Natural Anxieties of human life. Put another way, the holy grails for which we strive are health, love, success, and immortality. Here we will focus on the anxiety aroused by the first three of these real, universal, daily concerns of humankind.

Whether we look at psychologist Abraham Maslow's hierarchy of needs, at modern advertisements, or at records of ancient oracles and fortunetellers, we learn that human beings are continually anxious about health (physical and mental well-being); love (intimate relationships, family, friendships, social status, acceptance, and approval); and success (material prosperity, power, career development, and personal fulfillment).

Aren't these the things that you worry about on a daily basis? Almost all of us desire these and fear their loss; all the positive Inner Talk in the world cannot erase their reality.

What can we do about these Natural Anxieties? We can accept them and engage in the challenge they present. Life in this world is filled with Natural Anxiety and there is no escaping it. As we observed, the adventure into Natural Anxiety began when Adam and Eve left the Garden of Eden and were suddenly confronted with strategic survival problems. For the first time, they needed to provide their own food, clothing, and shelter. The necessity of establishing social organization, negotiating interpersonal relationships, and the quest to master the natural world commenced. And the search for meaning, the desire to understand the human predicament, and other spiritual questions leaped into awareness.

Today we, too, continually encounter new and anxiety-producing challenges on our path through life. Everyday circumstances produce a continual and copious flood of stressful events and anxious thoughts. Rather than wearing ourselves out by fighting against the tide, we can learn to ride the wave. Instead of our usual frustrating and ultimately impossible attempts to manage stress and reduce anxiety, we can use the radical approach of transforming anxiety into fuel for personal and spiritual growth. Søren Kierkegaard found anxiety to be the surest route to genuine faith. The words of this existentialist philosopher leap across a century and a half to guide us today in our search for serenity:

This is an adventure that every human being must go
through—to learn to be anxious in order that he may not

perish . . . Whoever has learned to be anxious in the right way has learned the ultimate . . . the more profoundly he is in anxiety, the greater is the man . . . Then anxiety enters into his soul and searches out everything and anxiously torments everything finite and petty out of him, and then it leads him where he wants to go . . . [Thus] the individual through anxiety is educated into faith.[2]

Kierkegaard counsels us to recognize that the greater our anxiety, the greater the opportunity for transforming anxiety into inner peace and being educated into faith. Ralph Waldo Emerson, an ocean away but writing at the same time, also recognized anxiety as "an instructor of great sagacity,"[3] a source of wisdom. In this chapter, I want to share with you some surprising and paradoxical ways by which you can learn, in Kierkegaard's phrase, "to be anxious in the right way."

INSTEAD OF TRYING SO HARD TO RELAX, WHY NOT GET BETTER AT USING ANXIETY?

While Toxic Anxiety is rampant with false alarms, overreactions, denial, blame, and inner psychological conflict, Natural Anxiety is triggered by real problems and real issues. Toxic Anxiety worries about money when there is enough money in the bank; an actual financial crisis activates Natural Anxiety. Toxic Anxiety obsesses about becoming ill; a diagnosis of cancer evokes Natural Anxiety. Toxic Anxiety magnifies a friend's thoughtless comment into an unforgivable insult; a genuine conflict of interest with another person arouses Natural Anxiety.

When we experience Toxic Anxiety, it is important for us to relax and calm down, for it does not represent a real external threat—then we can use this equanimity to look within and begin to resolve the hidden inner conflicts. Natural Anxiety, however, indicates the presence of a potential threat to which we need to respond or an opportunity of which we want to take advantage. In Natural Anxiety, it makes sense to use the energy of anxiety and turn it into action. We need its alertness and excitement to respond to the challenge at hand. When we are dealing with Natural Anxiety, it is counterproductive and even self-destructive to try to relax the anxiety away. Natural Anxiety is a gift of energy that we can use to meet the very challenge that has aroused it.

There are three keys to meeting our Natural Anxiety effectively. The first is transforming (or preventing) Toxic Anxiety. The second is using human intelligence for effective problem solving. The third is transforming Natural Anxiety to Sacred Anxiety.

THE FIRST KEY:
TRANSFORMING (AND PREVENTING) TOXIC ANXIETY

Because the purpose of Natural Anxiety is to move us onward and upward, the first key to harnessing its power for personal evolution is to prevent a descent into Toxic Anxiety. We know now that Toxic Anxiety reactions are dysfunctional responses rooted in the past. If we can stay in the present and see life without filters, we can avoid slipping backward into Toxic Anxiety's pit. If we do slip, it indicates the presence of an undigested anxiety experience that must be processed before we can be free to release it. By using the methods of Inner Talk, meditation, and the A+ Formula, we can bring awareness to the parts of our minds that are stuck in the past and heal them into the present. In this way, we transform the Toxic Anxiety back into the Natural Anxiety from which it became distorted.

When—through our lack of awareness or our temporary refusal to grow—Natural Anxiety degenerates into Toxic Anxiety, the original life problem becomes hidden behind an artificial problem and our lives veer off course. The commitment to face anxiety and the willingness to experience the pain that accom-

panies growth can help us avoid letting the pure flow of Natural Anxiety become toxic.

We noted earlier in Chapter 7 that when Carla was laid off
from her job, her Natural Anxiety triggered a barrage of Toxic
Anxiety in the form of catastrophic thoughts and self-defeating
Inner Talk. Toxic Anxiety reactions are almost always triggered
by an actual problem or challenge we are facing. By bringing
awareness to our Inner Talk, we can identify the trigger and un-
hook it from our habitual response.

Carla used the A+ Formula to become aware that losing her
job reactivated old childhood programming about things never
working out in her life. She began to remove this old tape so
that it didn't play automatically whenever she thought about her
current situation. She began to face it with what Zen Buddhists
call beginner's mind, a fresh and uncontaminated outlook that is
open to new solutions and opportunities. Carla was able to prevent a further descent into Toxic Anxiety and to transform the
portion that had been activated. Calming Toxic Anxiety reactions enables us to effectively use the Natural Anxiety aroused
by a life challenge. As Emerson so sagely noted:

> The wise man in the storm prays to God, not for safety from
> danger, but for deliverance from fear. It is the storm within
> which endangers him, not the storm without.[4]

THE SECOND KEY: USING HOLISTIC INTELLIGENCE TO USE NATURAL ANXIETY PRODUCTIVELY

The second key to using Natural Anxiety effectively involves
the full use of human intelligence for problem solving. When
we are confronted by a problem in life, we often fail to use the
full capacity of our human consciousness. Whether as individuals or as a society, we often react emotionally, based on unex-
amined assumptions and beliefs about how things "should"

work. Or we might attempt to quell our anxiety by addressing an issue in a scientific, rational manner and thus come up with a technological fix that fails to address its social and spiritual dimensions. These partial solutions simply create new, often more toxic, problems.

To catch the next wave of human progress, we need to cultivate holistic thinking—perceiving our lives in a way that encompasses the full range of our human capacities. An increasing body of empirical evidence indicates that we must learn to unite our emotional, intellectual, and spiritual intelligences to apprehend the full dimensions of a problem and to envision the most elegant and long-lasting solutions.

For each of us as individuals, and for all of us as a society, this means looking at problems and conflicts in a new, holistic way. We no longer have the luxury of indulging in feel-good solutions that simply validate our preconceptions or our emotions. Nor can we afford to rationally dissect a dilemma without addressing the emotional and social implications. We simply cannot pretend that moral and spiritual questions have no bearing on even the most mundane issues of life.

When Carla lost her job, she chose to avoid the pitfalls of Toxic Anxiety and accept the challenge with which life presented her. Using her holistic intelligence, Carla now begins to develop a strategy for channeling her anxiety productively. Her Natural Anxiety, instead of being dissipated, is ignited to provide the extra energy she needs to meet the challenge ahead of her.

Using the A+ Formula, Carla accepts that she is unemployed and that she is facing a transition period in her life filled with anxiety-producing unknowns. Bringing awareness and analysis to her dilemma, she realizes that she needs to maintain her physical and mental health during this time and to gather information and explore her options.

Based on this understanding, she takes action. Carla exercises regularly, practices meditation, reduces her expenses where possible, and continues to see her friends. In addition, she joins a networking group, works with a career counselor, reads books and magazines in her field, and regularly sends out job applications. She also uses this time to step back and take a look at her life, her career direction, and her life purpose.

In these practical ways, Carla is using holistic intelligence. She optimizes her physical health, attends to her emotional needs, and applies rational problem-solving strategies to find a new job. Each step of the way she focuses on how she can channel her Natural Anxiety toward some tangible achievement that will lead to resolving her situation. By remembering to appreciate herself and the progress she is making—as well as the other blessings in her life—Carla can keep her motivation level high and her life as enjoyable as possible during this challenging time.

Individually and collectively, we are being called to master the next challenge of human evolution—integrating the vast scientific knowledge we have now acquired with our ancient emotional heritage and our spiritual nature. This second key to mastering Natural Anxiety encourages us to use our natural, holistic intelligence to see the whole picture instead of blindly grasping short-term, quick-fix solutions that relieve the anxiety of the moment only to have it erupt later in the form of far more serious problems.

THE THIRD KEY: ASCENDING TO SACRED ANXIETY

Guided by the A+ Formula, Carla begins the process of acknowledging the sacred aspect of her life with a shift in attitude, choosing acceptance instead of denial. Carla shifts her reliance from her Anxious Chatterbox to her Inner Guide and allows herself to deepen her awareness of her inner life during this crucial time. Taking her cue from the Chinese character for "crisis" which is composed of two elements, one meaning "danger" and the other meaning "opportunity," she decides to view the loss of her old job as a potential opportunity as well as a problem.

She analyzes her situation by taking a look at the big picture and asking probing questions such as: Do I really need to work right away or can I take some time off? What is the worst that can happen? Do I still find my present career fulfilling? How do society's current needs match my skills and interests? What are my values and how am I expressing them in my work? What is my life purpose? Am I fulfilling it?

These questions are potentially much more anxiety-producing than the question of how to find a job, and it is not surprising that many people try to avoid them entirely, for they introduce issues of meaning and purpose. Climbing to the top of the ladder of success might not really be success if it is the wrong ladder. As daunting as they may seem, these questions are important ones to ask in a time of transition; they help to transform it from a grueling ordeal that must be endured into an exciting—even though uninvited—opportunity for growth. Such questions also can open the way to greater self-knowledge and deeper serenity.

Upgrading Natural Anxiety to Sacred Anxiety requires that we face the outcome we dread the most, the worst-case scenario. Even though we might use all our resources as effectively as possible, we still have no guarantee things will turn out the way we hope. For Carla, a sudden illness, a family crisis, or a deep economic recession might place her current goals temporarily, or even permanently, out of reach. Sacred Anxiety is the recognition that all our skills in mastering Toxic Anxiety and meeting Natural Anxiety still do not guarantee a conventional happy ending.

Times of personal crisis automatically trigger Sacred Anxiety. We do not need to look for it, only to acknowledge its presence. It is right there in our catastrophic thoughts that "my life will never work out right." Our task is to recognize the sacred element and untangle it from Toxic and Natural Anxiety. Crisis and loss always trigger anxiety about our ultimate fate.

To attain peace of mind during the difficult times she is experiencing, Carla needs to cultivate her spiritual life. She needs to know that she can continue to love herself and savor life even if she experiences ongoing difficulties. After she faces her worst-case scenario and can calmly accept it as a possibility—however remote—then Toxic Anxiety can no longer threaten her with its prognostications of gloom and doom.

We can never find security at the level of Natural Anxiety, for there is no guarantee that catastrophic things will not happen to us. That little voice that asks "What if . . . ?" cannot be silenced with rationalizations, insurance policies, or a large portfolio of stocks and bonds. Ultimately, the only solution to our Natural Anxiety is elevating it to Sacred Anxiety. The sacred action step of the A+ Formula is often the paradoxical one of letting go. This means letting go of our desires and even our heartfelt dreams to accept life unconditionally. In doing so, we refrain from placing requirements on life and admit our powerlessness to guarantee any specific outcome. We choose to release to a higher power those things over which we have no control. Finally, we cultivate a sacred appreciation for life that does not depend on circumstances—surely one of the most difficult yet most rewarding tasks of human life. In this way, we reach a place where our peace of mind is no longer attached to circumstances, so we can no longer be threatened by outer events. We are at peace, loving life as it is in this precious moment.

THE NATURAL GROWTH CYCLE: EVOLUTION'S ENGINE

Desire is the wellspring from which life flows, the fuel for life's fire. Spinoza called it "the essence of a man." Having a desire automatically gives rise to a goal that represents the fulfillment of that desire. Thus, our energy is always moving from a desire to a goal. (By "energy," I mean our total life energy which includes our physical, emotional, mental, and spiritual energy.)

Immediately, the problem arises of how to achieve that goal.

The problem represents the obstacles that we must overcome to reach the goal. If we cannot solve the problem, we will not be able to fulfill our desire.

Because problems are often difficult to solve, goals are not always easy to achieve. They demand an intensity of effort beyond that required for everyday routines. Whenever we try to achieve a goal, anxiety naturally arises, for we know there is never any guarantee that we will meet our goal and satisfy our desire. The more important the goal and the more it stretches our abilities, the more anxiety we will experience. But this anxiety is actually just what we need—it is the energy boost we need to achieve our goal. We will always experience Natural Anxiety whenever we move toward our growth edge because anxiety is a form of intensified energy and awareness.

People who have mastered anxiety have learned how to use Natural Anxiety as a secret power source to get to the next level in the game of life. They recognize Natural Anxiety as a sign that they are on the right track and moving toward growth. Self-actualizing people know how to transform it into the forward-moving energy of excitement and enthusiasm. If you remember some of your own positive experiences with Natural Anxiety, you will recall that it feels very different than Toxic Anxiety, which manifests itself as nervousness, negative thinking, confusion, trembling, and weakness. Natural Anxiety at its best is actually a positive, high-energy sensation that blends anxiety (a healthy appreciation for the inherent risks) with excitement (enthusiasm about the potential rewards). Natural Anxiety is what an accomplished skier feels just before pushing off to ski down a challenging slope.

The excitement in life comes from living at our growth edge. If we allow our Natural Anxiety to develop fully, it can transform into excitement and enthusiasm. Courage is not the absence of anxiety, but the ability to use it productively.

Natural Anxieties are like growing pains, the necessary discomfort that comes when we stretch ourselves to reach a goal.

The antigrowth comfort zone cycle we explored earlier in Chapter 6 is actually a dysfunctional version of a natural and healthy phenomenon: the growth cycle.

The Growth Cycle

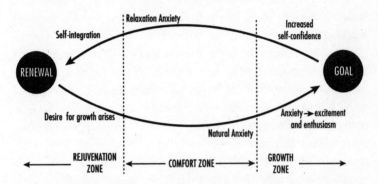

In the above diagram of the growth cycle, the lower half of the cycle represents the active phase we have been discussing, when desire leads to formulating and achieving a goal based on our inner sense of purpose. The upper half of the cycle illustrates the relaxation/integration phase of the cycle.

This growth cycle is a fundamental unit of evolutionary progress, which clearly reflects other natural cycles, such as the seasonal cycle of growth. Each phase of the growth cycle is important and enjoyable when it is in proper balance and relationship with the whole. We love the routine, comfortable, predictable familiarity of our comfort zone. And if we don't allow ourselves enough time in the comfort zone we might find that, though we accomplish a great deal, we are unable to digest, assimilate, and enjoy our experiences. If we spend too much time there, however, we become bored and stagnant.

We also crave the excitement and high-energy aliveness of the growth zone. This is the zone of peak performance, ecstatic joy, and creative breakthroughs. The people Abraham Maslow referred to as "self-actualizing" spend a large portion of their time in their growth zones. Yet if we try to do too much or fly too high, we can burn out or crash. On the other hand, if we avoid the growth zone, we stop growing and life starts to lose its meaning and purpose. When this happens, we experience an existential emptiness; life begins to look gray and taste flat.

The rejuvenation zone is a place of deep rest. Sometimes "relaxation anxiety," a resistance to letting go, may prevent us from relaxing into the rejuvenation zone. If we fight our need for renewal, we sabotage this natural cycle and become vulnerable to burnout, illness, and depression. Although not much appears to be happening on the outside during rejuvenation, a great deal of growth and change is occurring within. Internally, the body is recharging its batteries and the process of self-integration continues. We relish this "downtime," this period of rest when we relax and reconnect with ourselves at a deeper level in the rejuvenation zone. We also find that if we spend too much time here, we may become soft, sluggish, and self-centered.

However, not allowing *enough* time to relax and nurture ourselves in healthy ways is a far more frequent problem in our culture. Because "nothing happens" during rejuvenation, our achievement-oriented society generally lacks respect for the mysterious, creative resources of this vital realm and it is probably the most neglected and ignored region of our rushed and busy lives. Rejuvenation is the opposite of the active, goal-focused growth zone. Here we can simply enjoy being alive and appreciate the perfection of the present moment. Quiet contemplation, creative play, music, meditation, restful sleep, and prayer are some of the most powerful methods of tapping the treasures of the rejuvenation realm.

Heeding our desires, solving problems, and achieving goals all lead to the development of a self-actualizing character. This growth cycle is not a closed, repetitive process, as the previous diagram might suggest, but a dynamic and evolving one that is more accurately reflected in the spiral on the next page.

The Comfort Zone Expands

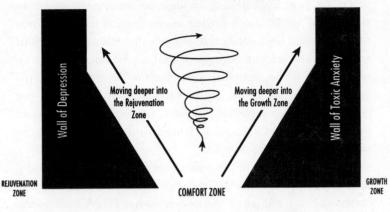

We can see that successful growth cycles build upon one an-other. Each successive revolution on the spiral represents the ful-fillment of a higher and greater desire. Our comfort zone actually expands with each cycle. We become larger and more inclusive, encompassing a wider variety of experiences and viewpoints, and with each cycle we train ourselves to be able to withstand higher currents of energy and greater creativity. We also learn to trust and let go to our inner wisdom. This growth cycle suggests that our ultimate destiny is to become infinite.

Honoring our highest desires and the anxiety they evoke propels us into the active, purposeful participation in the world that gives our life meaning. As D. H. Lawrence observed, ". . . from the unknown, profound desires enter in upon us, and the fulfilling of these desires is the fulfilling of creation."

MEANWHILE, BACK IN THE COMFORT ZONE . . .

We *can* escape from the comfort zone—no matter how long we have been trapped in it—and transform it back into the healthy growth cycle it is meant to be. The pull of the past and the self-sabotage habit may be strong, but the desire for growth and for life is potentially far stronger.

Eventually in the comfort zone cycle, we reach the point where we have felt bad long enough. Something shifts. We realize that if we go much further in our current negative direction, we might lose our health, our job, our relationship, or our remaining self-esteem. Somehow we have beaten ourselves up enough and we begin to feel hopeful again. We get ourselves together and try again; we begin that journey back toward our goal. We lose excess pounds, we sober up, we pay off the credit cards, we ask life for another chance. And then, tragically, the same cycle often begins again.

My greatest regret in life is that I spent as much time as I did shuttling back and forth within my comfort zone while actually believing that I was going somewhere. When I look back on the events of my life, I can see my comfort zone operating behind the scenes, keeping me from achieving my deepest desires. It made me work very diligently to get things I would later realize that I didn't really want in the first place, while setting me up to sabotage myself whenever I aimed for my true goals.

Every day in my counseling practice, I witness the suffering caused by the anxiety Monster keeping people trapped in their comfort zones. I feel tremendous compassion for the suffering I see because I have been there myself. This toxic cycle produces heartrending consequences in the lives of all the people who spend too many valuable years trapped in alcoholism, workaholism, perfectionism, unhealthy relationships, and the countless other melodramas that distract us from the true adventure of our lives.

It is tragic when good, sincere people try valiantly time after time to move forward and each time are thrown back into their comfort zones without knowing how it happened. We continue to make decisions based on our preference for dealing with predictable anxiety patterns (the devil we know) rather than facing the anxiety that accompanies moving into the unknown territory of our growth zone (the devil we don't know). In addition, a kind of comfort-zone amnesia seems to develop between cycles, and this keeps us from learning from our mistakes or seeing the self-destructive pattern. We begin each cycle hopeful but not much wiser, gradually becoming more hopeless and depressed with each round.

DESPERATION OR INSPIRATION?

Practically speaking, how can we become motivated to move beyond our comfort zone? How do we get out of a rut—whether the rut we have chosen is the fast track or the breakdown lane? We have two choices: desperation or inspiration.

We have noted that after enough repetitions, this comfort zone cycle spirals downward and reaches a critical point. We might become frustrated and angry with it or we might encounter a real life-threatening crisis, but in any case, we hit bottom. We realize that living in this comfort zone system is truly hopeless. All too often this important realization gets filtered through the Anxious Chatterbox, and we misinterpret it to mean that life is hopeless or that we are hopeless. This mistake easily can trap us at the depression end of the comfort zone. Depression, like anxiety, often has its toxic and healthy strands tangled up. We need to separate them so we can understand the healthy message hidden within depression: The old system is truly hopeless, but life is far from hopeless. This message enables us to finally face the harsh reality that if we stay within our comfort zone, we will never have the life we want, never reach our most important goals in life, and never be the person we were meant to be.

Depression can be a great motivator if we use it correctly. Like anxiety, despair can paralyze us or energize us. It's a choice. Desperation can provoke us to be willing to do whatever it takes to get beyond the boundary of our comfort zone. If we use despair positively, we might start to feel that facing our anxiety begins to look pretty good compared with staying in the living hell of our old comfort zone.

In fact, despair can be much more productive than the feel-good illusion we usually call hope. This positive use of desperation was celebrated by the poet Andrew Marvell when he wrote that the highest love is "begotten by despair/ Upon impossibility."

> *Magnanimous despair alone*
> *Could show me so divine a thing,*
> *Where feeble hope could ne'er have flown*
> *But vainly flapped its tinsel wing.*[5]

After we give up the self-sabotaging hopeful attitude that somehow things will get better in the comfort zone, a temporary depression might follow. But it is only from this bracing reconnection with reality that the power of magnanimous despair can emerge to show us the way out.

Inspiration is another route out of the comfort zone. We might find an inspiring goal that makes facing our anxiety appear worth it for the first time. Long-buried dreams may resurface. We become enthusiastic. We might find a goal, a project, or a cause worth living for. We might decide to face our anxiety and the Dragon that guards the growth zone because we love our kids and our spouse and we don't want to let them down. We might do it because we decide to love ourselves enough to live the life we were born to live.

Being trapped in the comfort zone is like being stuck in a dark tunnel. But if we can see a light at the end of the tunnel (inspiration), it can become worth the risk. Hearing a train coming though the tunnel behind us (desperation) will probably get us moving, too! It often takes a combination of inspiration and desperation before we are willing to go where we have never gone before. Our fears push us from behind while our dreams pull us forward.

TURNING ANXIETY INTO ACTION AND EXCITEMENT

Would you like to change your relationship with your comfort zone so that it becomes a healthy home base instead of an inner prison? The first step is to acquire reliable ways of calming your anxiety reactions; you can use Inner Talk, the Ultimate Relaxation Breath, and the other effective methods detailed earlier. Through diligent practice, you will find that you are able to experience Natural Anxiety without turning it into Toxic Anxiety. You can reinterpret the little shocks of anxiety you'll experience as a positive sign that you are breaking free from the comfort zone and moving toward growth.

The next phase is turning anxiety into energy and excitement. Because it's difficult to think clearly when anxiety arises, clarity regarding how to achieve your goals provides you with an essential light at the end of the tunnel. Develop a step-by-step strategy to guide you, so that when anxiety arises, you can channel its energy toward accomplishing a practical next step.

Intelligent action is the key to upgrading Toxic Anxiety into Natural Anxiety. "Do the thing you fear to do, and the death of fear is absolutely certain," wrote Emerson. Take action. Do it. Turn anxiety into action and excitement.

For many of us, it is easy to remember the times that we failed to live up to our expectations. But we can benefit greatly from recalling the many times when we have triumphed over anxiety and pushed beyond our comfort zone. Each of us has within ourselves deep, and mostly untapped, resources of great courage and perseverance. In the following exercise, you will have an opportunity to remember—and build upon—your successes.

YOUR COMFORT ZONE BREAKTHROUGHS

Draw the growth cycle diagram on a sheet of paper. Close your eyes and review a time in your life when you did show courage, when you got to the edge of the comfort zone and kept on going.

Open your eyes and plot that experience onto your diagram, making notes at each point in the process. Was it inspiration or desperation (or both) that got you moving? Identify what motivated you. What was anxiety doing to scare or threaten you? What new skills did you develop or find you had inside? What was the goal you aimed at? Do you remember how it felt to turn anxiety into excitement—or to feel anxious but move forward anyway?

You might enjoy recalling several of these courageous times and diagramming them. Your Anxious Chatterbox might try to minimize these incidents ("Yeah, sure, but these were exceptions"). Don't let it get away with that. The courageous part of you is your real self.

After drawing, and learning from, past breakthroughs, bring your focus to the present. Imagine being able to tap into the fearless warrior inside you and get some help with a current challenge. Focus on a comfort zone that is limiting you today and then diagram how you could turn it into a dynamic growth cycle.

THE RIGHT GOALS CAN PULL US OUT OF EVEN THE STICKIEST COMFORT ZONES

Even highly successful people have had to struggle to break free of their comfort zones. Oprah Winfrey's highly visible battle with her weight could not be won until she recognized that the problem was not weight or food, but an underlying anxiety. She began looking deeper than diets—into herself:

For years, I'd been saying on my show that you are . . .
responsible for your life . . . So I asked myself, "If you want [to
be thin] so much, then why are you still fat?"[6]

The answer Oprah received from her inner self: "I was still
afraid, even after all those years of talking about overcoming
fears. I was afraid people wouldn't like me if I were thin, that
the audience would turn on me. I was just so afraid to change.
But I was also just tired of being stuck."

Oprah had reached that crucial point where desperation and
inspiration intersected. She decided to face the anxiety that had
kept her trapped in self-sabotaging patterns. She realized that
overeating and dieting were just two sides of the same problem.
She stopped focusing on food and weight and reexamined her
purpose and her goal. She redefined her purpose from losing
weight to personal growth, and she focused her energy on a
challenging goal that she could get excited about. Oprah decided to run a marathon, something that required a high level of
fitness and self-discipline:

I have always been undisciplined . . . just sort of going with
the flow. But running the marathon required goals, and daily
discipline, and follow-through. And I did it.[7]

In training for the marathon, Oprah found that her excess
weight began to melt away. But even more important, her excess Toxic Anxiety melted away, too. She was able to develop
healthy lifestyle habits and tap inner resources that finally allowed her to live naturally and comfortably at her optimal
weight.

Oprah Winfrey continues to demonstrate her willingness to
transform anxiety into personal growth. When other talk shows
gained viewers with increasingly sensationalized topics, Oprah
turned worries about ratings into spiritual concerns about
meaning and purpose. She listened to her higher self and reaf-
firmed her commitment to produce programs that were honest,

uplifting, and life-affirming. As a result, millions of viewers followed Oprah into her growth zone. By sharing her discoveries and allowing others to witness both her trials and her triumphs, Oprah communicates the excitement of living life on our growth edge.

Each of us has the perfect challenge waiting for us, the one we need right now in order to grow personally and spiritually: It may be the annoying, anxiety-producing problem we've been wishing would just go away—or it could be that secret dream we hardly dare to dream. It is probably sitting on our doorstep at this very moment, waiting for us to invite it in.

Chapter Ten

CHANGING YOUR
INNER WORRIER INTO
AN INNER WARRIOR

WORRY—THE ROBBER WE KEEP INVITING BACK

Would you like to change the anxious worrier in your head into an inner warrior who can face life with confidence and equanimity? This chapter explores several methods for avoiding unproductive worry and using Natural Anxiety effectively. In the process you will learn more about how your mind works—and how to get it working for you, instead of against you.

Every day of our lives is an opportunity to enjoy the gift of life—to breathe freely and deeply, to smile, to love, to work creatively, and to experience the wonder of creation. So why don't we experience life in this way more often? Worry is one of the chief culprits. It robs us of our happiness and security, and it often does so with impunity. Worry is like paying exorbitant interest on a loan we have not yet received.

We not only allow worry to rob us, we invite it in. Mark Twain brought his fine sense of irony and humor to this topic when he wrote:

> My life has been filled with terrible misfortunes—most of
> which never happened. Life does not consist mainly—or even
> largely—of facts and happenings. It consists mainly of the
> storm of thoughts that is forever blowing through one's head.

We dignify this storm of thoughts that blows through our heads
with the name of worry. Although worry is a form of Toxic
Anxiety, I have included it in this section because most of our
worries are about real possibilities, about Natural Anxieties.
Worry is so fiendishly difficult to deal with because it takes legitimate, reasonable concerns and then hands them over to the
Anxious Chatterbox, who intensifies and exaggerates them, instead of referring them to the Inner Guide who could help us
deal with them effectively.

As Mark Twain suggests, we often live more in our self-
created world of dire images than in the real world. Isn't it
strange that we prefer living in the much more treacherous
world of self-generated worry than the relatively benign everyday world where personal catastrophes are far more rare? Perhaps it is one more indication of the ego's overriding need to
feel in control; our mental world may be filled with dangers but
at least they are our dangers. Like Dr. Frankenstein, we prefer to
create our own monsters and then battle them rather than face
our powerlessness to determine exactly which difficulties fate
will present us with.

Worry deprives us of our right to enjoy our life without giving us anything in return. Let's take a look at a typical day in
Kelly's life:

Kelly happens to be in good health, gainfully employed, married to a
man who loves her, and free from any great problems. Does she spend
the day filled with pleasure and gratitude about how much is going right
with her life? Unfortunately not. Instead, old habit patterns induce
Kelly to spend the minutes and hours of her day worrying. On her way
to work she becomes anxious about arriving a few minutes late. During
the morning she frets about whether the report she is writing is really

good enough. At lunch she worries that she is going to eat a little too much (she is always trying to lose five pounds).

After work, at her health club, Kelly recalls a fitness article she read in the newspaper and worries that she may not be exercising vigorously enough to get the maximum health benefits from her 45-minute work-out. At home, she spends the evening engaging in "freestyle worrying" as her thoughts poke and prod at the potential trouble spots of her life, like a suspicious shopper squeezing a tomato until it becomes thoroughly bruised. Is her marriage really and truly fulfilling? Are she and Brad saving enough for retirement? Will things go OK when her mother comes to visit in two weeks? Should she talk to Brad again about having a child or wait until he's under less pressure at work? This storm of thoughts continues even in Kelly's sleep, giving rise to anxious, unresolved dreams.

Throughout this entire day, as on most other days, worry has robbed Kelly of the inherent joy of living. She has lived entirely in her head and in her own mental world, never once stopping to smell the fresh morning air when she opened the front door, never enjoying the feeling of aliveness in her body while she exercised, and never savoring the connections she has with her co-workers or even with Brad.

It may well be that Kelly needs to address some of the issues she worries so much about. Yet worrying about problems is not an effective approach, even though it is by far the most popular one. Worry, by definition, fails to address issues productively. To worry about something means to anxiously turn it over in one's mind. And then to turn it over again. And again—without ever coming to a decision or course of action.

We use the word "worry" to describe this common type of unproductive mental activity. An older meaning of this word gives us a clue to its underlying nature. In the past, "worry" was commonly used to describe the process of playing or toying with an object without ever fully grasping it. Worry fiddles around with problems but never stops to examine them in an organized, intelligent fashion. Worry becomes a substitute for thoughtful examination and self-reflection.

Subconsciously we may even believe in the superstition that worrying about something keeps it from happening. Let me illustrate this point with a quick story.

There was a man who always walked down the street waving his arms around. Someone finally came up to him and asked him why he was waving his arms. The man replied, "To keep the tigers away, of course!"

The other person said in astonishment, "But there aren't any tigers around here."

"See, it works!" the man responded proudly.

Why not call the Anxious Chatterbox's bluff and take a break from unproductive worrying? You just might discover that it is your Anxious Chatterbox who has been creating the tigers it is supposedly protecting you from.

Worrying gives us the illusion that we are doing something, yet it is an illusion and one that actually keeps us from taking effective action. We worry about a pain rather than make an appointment with the doctor. We worry about our son's distractibility and nag him, instead of having a calm and compassionate conversation with him about it.

We often joke about how stupid it is to worry, yet we accept it as inevitable. As Ogden Nash wryly observed, "He who is ridden by a conscience/Worries about a lot of nonscience." In the ultimate irony, we may even worry about the fact that we worry too much. But worry is not just a minor bad habit; it has a sinister aspect that must be faced. Worry is the most common method we use to create Toxic Anxiety, and it is the mechanism by which we manufacture the chronic stress that leads to illness.

Worry's Middle English ancestor, *worien,* originally meant to viciously strangle or bite and was used to describe the way a wolf attacks and kills a sheep. This powerful image more accurately conveys the actual role worry plays in our mental life and the way it injures our body. Interestingly, both the English word "worry" and the Latin root of the word "anxiety" originally meant to torment by strangulation.

How can we keep worry from hijacking our legitimate concerns and turning them into Toxic Anxiety instead of allowing Natural Anxiety to move them forward into action? All worry is unproductive Inner Talk. Using the basic principles outlined earlier for changing self-defeating Inner Talk into growth-promoting Inner Talk will help defeat the worry habit. But we can do much more as well, especially regarding our worries about the future. We can't just stop thinking about the future; that would be foolish. However, we can get better at using our minds when we do think about the future—and almost all worry consists of anticipating the future.

ANTICIPATION: HALF THE PLEASURE, HALF THE PAIN

Anticipating a pleasurable experience is half the fun: We enjoy dreaming about an upcoming vacation for weeks ahead of time. Smelling the aromas of food cooking not only captures our attention but physiologically prepares our body for digestion. Watching our lover seductively disrobing can rival the excitement of actual lovemaking.

If the joys of anticipation are often half the fun, the distress of anticipating an unpleasant experience can be half the pain— or even all of the pain, if the dreaded event never occurs. Anticipatory anxiety, the feeling that we will be unable to handle some future event, is one of the most dreaded forms of anxiety. How can we fight a threat that hides in the future? As Marlow asks in Joseph Conrad's *Lord Jim:*

> How does one kill fear, I wonder? How do you shoot a spectre
> through the heart, slash off its spectral head, take it by its
> spectral throat?

202 Finding Serenity in the Age of Anxiety

Suspense writers know that while a threat lurks ominously in the shadows, its power to frighten is far greater than when it actually appears. As the master of suspense Alfred Hitchcock noted, "There is no terror in a bang, only in the anticipation of it."

Even anticipating positive events can become a problem if we overdo it. It's healthy and natural to look forward to enjoyable events. But some people go too far; they anticipate desirable occasions so often and so grandly that the actual experience inevitably becomes a letdown. Anticipating too much also imposes preconceived ideas about how things should go, which can leave us unable to enjoy the unexpected. If we go too far in the opposite direction and allow anxiety to block the positive anticipation of an upcoming event, we rob ourselves of the gradually building excitement and invest too little of ourselves in the experience. If we want to maximize our enjoyment of living, we need to be consciously in charge of our anticipatory faculties and find a balance.

POSITIVE ALTERNATIVES TO WORRY— PLANNING AND VISUALIZATION

Because we are so frequently anticipating the future, we might as well learn to do it wisely. Instead of engaging in the worry habit we can use two powerful tools—planning and visualization.

To **worry** is to anxiously imagine a negative future, resulting in inaction or unproductive activity.

To **plan** is to confidently anticipate the future by taking practical steps to meet personal goals and turn potential problems into opportunities.

To **visualize** is to create a positive vision of the future—a best-case scenario.

Common sense dictates that we will benefit from anticipating future problems in a realistic manner and trying to prevent them or minimize their impact. This calls not for worrying, but planning. We can preview various possibilities and then develop strategies to deal with them. I have noticed that many chronic worriers actually avoid planning for the future because they are afraid it will trigger anxiety. If we don't address our Natural Anxiety during the day, it will attack us as Toxic Anxiety at night. Worrying in bed at night when fatigue interferes with clear thinking is the least effective recourse. But by taking responsibility and addressing our Natural Anxieties proactively, we rob worry of the chance to hijack them.

One major difference between intelligent planning and toxic worrying is that worry often concerns itself with possibilities that are beyond our sphere of control, while planning involves itself with areas that we can do something about.

Recognizing that worry robs people of joy, many spiritual teachers have spoken about it. When Jesus asked his listeners if they could add an inch to their height by worrying, he was pointing out that some things are beyond individual control. Anything within our control calls for responsible planning. Anything outside our control can be released to a higher power. The "Serenity Prayer" says it well: "Grant me the courage to change the things I can change, the serenity to accept the things I cannot change, and the wisdom to know the difference." As we shall see later, those anxiety-producing possibilities that we can do nothing to prevent are especially appropriate to address at the level of Sacred Anxiety.

After we have done whatever reasonable planning seems appropriate we can enjoy using the power of visualization to create a positive vision of the future. Worry is really nothing more than negative fantasies. Doesn't it make a lot more sense to use the power of our imagination to visualize what we desire rather than what we fear? Our thoughts about our future influence our actual future more than any other single factor within our control. We seed the future with our thoughts.

If we are going to spend time fantasizing about the future, why not visualize things going right—achieving our goals and expressing our true essence? This can make a world of difference in how we experience our life. Engaging in positive visualization includes being aware of potential problems, but perceives how they can lead to creative solutions. Olympic athletes, artists, and successful entrepreneurs all use visualization to imagine their best-case scenario. By visualizing a perfect performance or an ideal outcome we seed our minds with the potential for maximum success. Our minds begin looking for ways to make our dreams come true, instead of worrying about all the ways they might not.

For those times when the worry habit has dug its teeth in and won't let go, we can at least minimize its damage. One useful technique is setting aside 15 minutes a day and doing all your worrying at that time—a kind of one-stop-shopping approach to worry. You also can get your Anxious Chatterbox to stop harassing you with unproductive worry by making a personal commitment to confront an issue you've been avoiding: You can do some active, responsible planning by exploring various strategies on paper or talk about the problem in a solution-oriented manner with a good friend or a counselor. Here's another method, paradoxical in nature, that I call The Three Minute Catastrophe: Focus steadily on your worries for three minutes, intensifying and exaggerating them until you reach your ultimate, worst-case apocalyptic catastrophe. Then accept the worst that can happen, laugh at it, and let it go. You have just condensed a whole week of gnawing, gradually escalating worries into a few concentrated minutes—and stolen all of the Anxious Chatterbox's thunder.

Although most worries are about the future, some are about the past. Worries about the past often are concerned with feeling guilty about something we have done. They also may have to do with feeling angry or hurt about something another person has done to us. If we continue worrying, obsessing, and resenting, we allow the past to poison the present. We can choose to forgive ourselves and others for past hurts, make amends where needed, and return to focus on the present.

We spend far too much time anticipating the future or regretting the past—and not nearly enough time living in the present moment. One of the best antidotes to dread, regret, and resentment is simply to bring our awareness back to the present moment and all the blessings it contains. On an existential level, we can never prepare for "It"—all we can do is live the moment that we are in, in the way we want to live any future moment.

MINDSETS: THE GLASSES THROUGH WHICH WE VIEW OUR WORLD

How does anxiety interfere with solving problems and then manage to create unnecessary ones as well? It does so by affecting the cognitive process itself, by distorting reality, and by inhibiting learning and problem solving. Another clear path to mastering the worry habit is to become aware of how important mindsets—our attitudes, assumptions, beliefs, and worldviews—are to our thinking.

The following mental exercise will help you grasp the role that a mindset plays in how we perceive our environment. In the figure below there are four arrows. What color are they?

A simple question, right? It's very obvious: Anyone can see that the arrows are black. Or are those black arrows simply the product of a particular mindset?

Where you see four black arrows on a white background, someone else, with a different mindset, looking at the same diagram, could see a black square with four white arrows pointing toward the center. Can you switch mindsets and see the white arrows?

So are the arrows really white or black? It all depends on your mindset, doesn't it? Notice how you can now switch back and forth much more easily between those two mindsets when you gaze at the diagram. Being able to acknowledge other mindsets and see things from different points of view greatly expands our options in life, for being able to match the most appropriate mindset to a problem multiplies our chances of solving it. In fact, this approach constitutes the essence of the scientific method.

Periods of disequilibrium occur when one recognizes that an old mindset doesn't work and a new one has not yet been constructed; they are periods of confusion, doubt, and insecurity. Not having a working model is like traveling in unfamiliar territory without a map. In other words, disequilibrium is anxiety producing.

This is the by-now-familiar Natural Anxiety that accompanies personal growth. Ideally, this anxiety should energize the cognitive process and aid the revision of an old mindset or the formation of a new one. But what happens to someone who has not learned how to use this anxiety productively and experiences even small amounts of anxiety as threatening or overwhelming? Instead of adapting the old mindset to reality, the temptation arises to reduce the anxiety by using the quick fix method of distorting reality to fit the old model. This is a variation on the Cain complex: abusing the power of consciousness to construct false realities to preserve the personality's worldview.

Forcing present experiences to fit old mindsets is also the

root of prejudice. Prejudice is prejudging a person or situation on the basis of a rigid mindset derived from past programming, rather than forming an opinion based on our actual experience in the present. Toxic Anxiety keeps people trapped in old mindsets because they cannot or will not deal with the anxiety produced by changing them.

Our dilemma as human beings is that mindsets can be both growth promoting and growth inhibiting. The capacity to build models of reality is vital to all learning. Yet the very models that enable progress eventually become themselves limits to further evolution. This is why scientific theories need to be modified periodically when new experimental data becomes available. The healthiest response to this dilemma is to use our mindsets responsibly and flexibly. We must be able to change or discard a mindset when it no longer serves our personal evolution. Above all, we need to avoid mistaking even the most revered mindset for reality (the map is not the territory).

Consequently, the following skills can aid us tremendously in mastering the art of living: (1) the ability to construct and utilize mindsets effectively (and to change and discard outdated mindsets); (2) the awareness that mindsets are merely models of reality, not reality itself; and (3) the ability to suspend all mindsets and experience the creative state of beginner's mind.

People who operate with flexible mindsets use anxiety as a growth-promoting friend. In his poem, "The Age of Anxiety," W. H. Auden describes the choice we all have to "climb the cross of the moment/And let our illusions die," or to "refuse the tasks of time" and cling to our familiar yet outworn mindsets. All too often, Auden observes, "We would rather be ruined than changed."

FINDING SERENITY IN REALITY

"What, me worry?"

Was Alfred E. Neuman right? Is the only way to avoid worry to be slightly mad? Some observers certainly draw that conclusion. Ernest Becker believed that the "full apprehension of man's condition would drive him insane." Many philosophers have noted that it is necessary to be somewhat crazy—out of touch with the reality of our natural vulnerabilities and ultimate mortality—to function in the world, for living in the kind of world we do, we would be crazy not to be anxious. Pascal expressed this existential double bind quite succinctly: "Men are so necessarily mad that not to be mad would amount to another form of madness."

While recognizing the worldly wisdom in the view that too much reality can drive us crazy, this book offers an alternative possibility—the full awareness of our human condition can drive us to enlightenment! Although it may seem logical that the less we think about negative possibilities, the happier we will be, the sacred path to peace leads in quite a different direction. Serenity does not exclude unpalatable realities; it includes them. On the surface, someone who relies on denial ("Bad things can't happen to me") may seem as free of anxiety as the person who is truly at peace ("When bad things happen, I can use them for spiritual growth"). Yet denial offers only a fragile and superficial peace. Acceptance of life's realities, including the tragic aspect of human existence, is the only path to genuine inner peace. We can find serenity in reality.

Avoiding our existential reality on a daily basis often leads to the formation of certain dysfunctional mindsets that reflect a fundamental unwillingness to accept life on its own terms. Emerson observed that "Life invests itself with inevitable conditions, which the unwise seek to dodge."[1] We often prefer to ignore these anxiety-producing conditions or pretend that we are somehow exempt from them (the illusion of specialness). Upon reflection, most of us will accept the more unpleasant facts of life intellectually or in general; what appears to be difficult for us is accepting them emotionally and personally. I have summarized some of the more disturbing ones as The Least Favorite Laws of Life.[2] This is not intended as a complete or balanced list of life's laws, only a few of our least favorite ones. If you can accept all of these, you are well on your way to unshakable inner peace.

You may have some of your own laws to add to the list. Are there any listed here that you believe are not true? If you are in-

---

THE LEAST FAVORITE LAWS OF LIFE

Life is suffering.

God loves us, but that does not entitle us to special treatment because God loves everyone else just as much.

Life does not come with any guarantees.

Our bodies can malfunction and are subject to injury and illness.

Bad things happen to good people.

There are no magic potions, no panaceas.

Not everyone we meet will like us.

The more we genuinely love and care about another human being, the more anxiety we experience concerning their well-being.

Every advantage is accompanied by a disadvantage.

The disasters that actually befall us in life are often ones we never even considered.

Money, even lots of money, can only buy things that can be bought.

Sometimes our worst fears do come true.

Everything changes.

Just because we love someone, it does not mean that they will love us in return.

Some of our most cherished dreams may not come true, no matter how much we want them to.

The chances are very high that we never got all our important needs met in childhood. Nevertheless, we are completely responsible for who we are today.

Sometimes there are no second chances.

Despite the human relationships we have, we remain separate individuals and face life (and death) alone.

Life is not always fair, at least in the short run of one lifetime.

Evil exists.

We will never be free of problems because every solution inevitably creates a new problem.

Our defenses keep us from experiencing love and peace.

Without our defenses we would feel absolutely terrified.

Because we inevitably hurt and are hurt by one another, we need to forgive ourselves and each other endlessly.

We really are going to die.

Our time of death is unknown; it may occur today.

Our manner of death is also unknown; it may be painful.

Because life involves anxiety, pain, and suffering, we desperately need each other's love and acceptance.

The Least Favorite Laws of Life apply to all of us.

terested in a direct route to greater peace of mind, reread the list, noticing which laws are most disturbing to you, and then meditate on them until you can embrace them with joy and acceptance. Buddhists take a similarly paradoxical approach to serenity when they meditate upon the disintegration of their own corpse until the image no longer has the power to disturb their mind.

TRANSFORMING PROBLEMS FROM OBSTACLES TO STEPPING-STONES

Some people view the uncertainties of life and the natural difficulties that accompany human growth with resentment, anger, hopelessness, or fear. When these negative reactions occur, the Natural Anxiety that normally helps energize and propel us forward begins to turn against us. One of the reasons many of us fail to deal with Natural Anxiety effectively is because we have trouble welcoming problems as part of life. When we resent problems or think of them as unfair, we already have taken our first step away from healthy Natural Anxiety and back toward Toxic Anxiety.

The word "problem" generally has a negative connotation; we seldom say, "I've got a big problem on my hands!" in a joyful manner. I, too, had always looked at problems as obstacles that kept me from achieving my goals. For years I hoped that next year the problems that were hassling me would be resolved and I could finally relax and be happy, that soon this difficult phase of my life would be over and the good times would start to roll in—if I could just get through this hassle-filled day, just get through this difficult year.

After getting through many years this way, the horrible thought began to gnaw at me that maybe the good times I hoped for might never come. Maybe this was it. Maybe life was one of those what-you-see-is-what-you-get propositions. I was reminded of the wry observation, "Life is what happens to you while you're making other plans." My first reaction was disillusionment and depression. What's the point of keeping on if life is just one damn problem after another?

Gradually, it dawned on me that maybe my problems weren't the problem. After all, the dictionary defines a problem as "a question to be answered," and I recalled that it was by solving math problems that I had learned to do math. Perhaps it was my attitude to problems that was the real problem. I began to understand that problems are learning experiences that help us move forward in life. This realization transformed the problems that I had seen as boulders blocking my path into the very stepping-stones that enabled me to move forward. By solving life problems, we learn to live. Life becomes one blessed problem after another.

Through changing our attitude to life's problems, we no longer need to experience them as surprise attacks, but can approach them as mysterious opportunities. We naturally would prefer certain kinds of problems (What's the best way to handle all the exciting opportunities success has brought me?) over others (How can I survive this failure?). But a deeper wisdom than our conscious mind seems to guide our lives. Whether we like it or not, life seems uncannily adept at presenting us with the very problems we require for our spiritual growth. Resenting problems is like resenting life itself.

When a problem appears, we can learn to respond, "Thank you very much." Welcoming problems as opportunities enables us to relax with them and uncover the priceless gift hidden at the center of even the most undesirable situation. We possess the power to transform problems into opportunities, and opportunities into problems. The choice is ours.

ARISTOTLE'S METHOD FOR MASTERING ANXIETY

To face problems and the unpalatable truths listed in the Least Favorite Laws of Life, we need a method we can use to deal with both Toxic and Natural Anxiety. The following cognitive method for mastering anxiety comes to us from insights thousands of years old. In the *Nichomachean Ethics,* Aristotle wrote extensively on the role of the emotions in human happiness. He discovered that certain conditions were required for anxiety to occur. I have adapted his insights and developed them into a technique for mastering anxiety that I call Aristotle's Method in honor of this ancient Greek philosopher who first identified the essential ingredients of anxiety:

1. **Threat:** We perceive an object or situation as a threat to our self.
2. **Imminence:** We perceive (consciously or subconsciously) the threat as about to occur in the immediate future.
3. **Powerlessness:** We feel impotent to prevent the threat.
4. **Helplessness:** We feel unable to handle the threat if it does occur.

Aristotle's insights are borne out by my clinical and personal experience. The greater and more imminent the threat appears, and the more powerless and helpless the individual feels, the greater will be the ensuing anxiety. I have discovered that Aristotle's insights lead to a therapeutic protocol for mastering anxiety that is as simple as it is profound: A positive change in one or more of the four components of anxiety will reduce Toxic Anxiety symptoms and allow the energy of Natural Anxiety to be used creatively. We will take a look at how each ingredient contributes to anxiety and how to use each one to further our personal growth.

1. Threat into opportunity The threat is the stimulus that triggers anxiety. It may be an external threat (being laid off from work) or an internal threat (a negative thought or an unpleasant physical sensation). In some types of anxiety the threat may be unknown ("I don't know why I'm feeling so anxious").

The greater the threat, the greater the anxiety. But it is mainly our perception of the threat that determines its degree—or even if it is a threat at all. In Toxic Anxiety (such as a fear of flying), a nonexistent or relatively minimal threat is manufactured and magnified. An anxiety about flying in an airplane can be reduced through the process of identifying the anxiety-producing Inner Talk and changing it to self-calming Inner Talk.

On the level of Natural Anxiety, the threat can be more precisely identified and then separated from any excessive or exaggerated worry. For example, receiving only an average review at work when we have been expecting an outstanding one is cause for concern and does pose a threat to our self-image. The situation calls for self-examination and discussion, but not for self-flagellation and panic.

Being willing to be honest about which aspect of the self feels threatened gives us the option of letting go of that aspect of our self-image, thereby letting go of the threat. For example, if we experience Toxic Anxiety in the form of worry and frustration because our child's grades are not up to our expectations, perhaps it is because our self-image as a good parent is dependent upon having our child excel in school. Being willing to let go of that particular definition of being a good parent eliminates the threat and the Toxic Anxiety. Then our actions can be directed calmly and intelligently to being helpful and supportive to our child.

To gain mastery over a threat, we can change our perception of it: We can shrink a greatly magnified threat down to its actual size. We can focus on more clearly identifying a vague threat. Then we can transform what we perceive as a threat into an opportunity for growth, thereby changing anxiety into excitement and positive energy.

2. *Imminent danger into present safety* A fascinating aspect of all anxiety—including, for example, anxiety about not having enough money to retire on thirty years from now—is that

subconsciously that threat is experienced as imminent. Whenever we vividly picture a threatening situation, our subconscious mind experiences it in the present, prompting our emotions and our body to react as if we were already in the midst of the situation we are dreading.

Unless we are actually in a situation that presents a clear and immediate danger (in which case anxiety would become focused into a specific fear), the object of our anxiety is never immediately present. Even feeling anxious 10 minutes before giving a talk is about something in the future.

Intellectually, we know that worries are about situations we may experience in the future, and we may be puzzled about why they give us a headache or queasy stomach in the present. The reason is that when we obsess upon a future threat, our subconscious mind begins to perceive it as imminent and our body gets fooled into thinking it is dealing with an immediate danger. Then, because our body is not given any recourse to action in the present, the tension builds and the anxiety feeds on itself.

"Imminence" comes from a Latin word that means "hanging over." Like the sword of Damocles, our anxious thoughts hang over us and appear to pose an immediate threat to our well-being. Understanding the imminence factor provides another vital key to mastering anxiety. Because anxieties are usually about the future but are subconsciously perceived to be in the present, we can push them back into the future where they belong and thereby feel safe in the present. Even in a situation of extreme danger, such as hearing an intruder outside our bedroom door, it helps to remember that we are safe right now; staying calm and thinking clearly will enable us to mount the most effective response.

We have learned how Inner Talk provides a practical tool for influencing our subconscious mind and that we can replace catastrophic messages with accurate and truthful ones, such as, "I am safe now," and "Any threat I perceive is in the future and I am safe in the present." We also can visualize the anxiety situation literally receding from its position in the foreground of our mind out into the distance.

We also can use the imminence factor positively. Allowing our anxiety to motivate us to take an action in the present may help us meet a future challenge. For example, if we are worried about a trend to layoffs in our profession, instead of putting it out of our mind, we can vividly visualize what it would be like to be unemployed and get anxious productively right now, letting the energy of anxiety motivate us to learn new skills.

Remember, anxiety only affects us if we perceive it as imminent. By placing anxiety about the future in the future, we can experience safety and calm in the present. And by letting imminence motivate us to take appropriate action in the present, we can create the best possible future for ourselves.

3. Powerlessness into empowerment The more powerless we feel in relationship to a threat, the greater our anxiety. And as soon as we become anxious we tend to magnify any threat and minimize our own skills and resources. Reducing the magnitude of the threat to realistic proportions and seeing the opportunities it contains automatically makes us feel more powerful simply by comparison. Changing our mindset—our definition of the threat or problem—will greatly increase our sense of power relative to the challenge facing us.

Naturally, the more empowered we feel, the less anxiety we will experience. We can use Inner Talk to change powerless "I can't" statements into powerful "I can" affirmations. We can empower ourselves by concentrating our energies on what we do have control over, instead of focusing on factors beyond our control. Trying to change things we have little or no control over (like other people) is a set-up for anxiety. For example, the wife of an alcoholic can feel anxious and powerless by obsessing on how she can't get him to stop drinking. Or she can feel empowered by focusing her attention on things she can do—get counseling, join a support group, develop plans to live separately if he continues to drink, etc.

An honest and accurate appraisal of our power enables us to use it effectively and to obtain any additional help, information, or training that we need to deal with the situation. In all situations, and especially those that constitute a grave threat to our well-being, we can call upon our deeper spiritual resources to find the inner power we require to meet the challenge at hand.

4. *Helplessness into confidence* Much of the time we underestimate our ability to meet life's challenges. But the reality is that we may not be able to prevent certain threats from occurring. Perhaps our spouse will never stop drinking; perhaps we or someone we love may develop a fatal form of cancer; perhaps no matter how hard we work, we will lose our job.

In all such cases, we need to develop a basic sense of self-confidence, the inner knowledge that we can handle whatever life presents us. Great difficulties, such as illness or loss, can temper our souls. Even experiences that wound us can ultimately strengthen us through the healing of those wounds. We need to know that even if we cannot achieve the outcome we prefer, we still will feel good about the way we responded to the situation, that our integrity and self-esteem will remain intact.

It is immensely important to realize that we are seldom as anxious about the dreaded event itself as we are about how we will make ourselves feel when the event occurs. The greatest threat to any human being, perhaps even greater than death itself, is the ultimate loss of love and self-esteem. This dread lies at the root of our negative fantasies that some particular outcome will be the "death of me" or the "end of the world." What we really fear is our own catastrophic, self-critical, and self-shaming Inner Talk. Making a pledge to ourselves that nothing will ever stop us from loving and accepting ourselves can restore a feeling of serenity in even the most trying circumstances.

Aristotle's primary contribution to the philosophy of living the good life was the concept of the Golden Mean. Applied to the emotions, the Golden Mean represents a balanced midpoint between extremes. Aristotle's ideal consisted in using emotions "to the right degree, at the right time, for the right purpose, and in the right way." And, he sagely observed, "this is not easy."

The spectrum of anxiety runs from the extreme of cowardice (too much Toxic Anxiety) to the opposite extreme of arrogance (too little Sacred Anxiety). The Golden Mean of Anxiety can be called courage or self-confidence—the ability to make effective use of the Natural and Sacred Anxieties that arise as we move forward toward our goals in life.

The word "confidence" comes from the same root as the word "faith." Ultimately, mastering anxiety depends upon developing a deep and abiding sense of faith that one participates in the life of the universe in a way that never ends.

Chapter Eleven

BRINGING PASSION TO
THE ADVENTURE OF LIFE

OUR SACRED PURPOSE

Having a great and passionate mission in life is the animating force that carries us through anxiety. We are willing to risk anxiety for what we love, and we will risk great anxiety for what we love greatly: The flames of a burning house have no power to stop a mother from rescuing her child who is trapped inside; the rushing waters of an icy river cannot deter the ordinary hero who dives in to rescue a stranger who has slipped and fallen into the current. Love is stronger than anxiety.

What do we love enough to live for and die for?

Helen Keller, born deaf and blind, was able to see certain things much more clearly than many people blessed with perfect eyesight. In her book, *The Open Door,* she wrote:

> Security is mostly a superstition. It does not exist in nature, nor do the children of man as a whole experience it. Avoiding danger is no safer in the long run than outright exposure. Life is either a daring adventure or it is nothing.[1]

Then what is the purpose of this adventure?

We need goals—clear goals with a magnetic pull that draws us out of our comfort zone. But what kind of goals have the magnetism that arouses the passion and courage we need to face the fire-breathing dragons that lie in wait for us?

There is nothing the matter with ordinary goals such as buying a new car, finding a more fulfilling job, or having a healthy baby. The question is what end do these goals serve? If we envision our goals in conventionally limited ways, we remain constantly threatened by the Natural Anxiety of not achieving them. Goals are not the same as a life purpose. Our life purpose is the organizing principle of our existence, and if our goals are ends in themselves they become dead ends; achieving them fails to satisfy our hunger for meaning in life, and we fall prey to Toxic Anxiety. To find a deeper meaning, our goals must be connected to—and organized to serve—a greater life purpose.

Our life purpose begins to take shape when we ask ourselves the most basic questions: Who am I? Why am I here? If material success were our purpose, then much of humanity would be condemned to fail at fulfilling the purpose of life. Yet life is not designed to fail. We are all here to succeed. The only life purpose that can take us beyond Natural Anxiety is a higher purpose, a sacred purpose: spiritual growth and evolution. This planet is a school for souls—a place to learn and grow, to expand our capacity for unconditional love. It is this perspective that enables us to feel genuine acceptance, even gratitude, for the Natural Anxieties of life.

Every goal short of spiritual growth leaves us at the mercy of Natural Anxiety, but when our life purpose is spiritual growth we can always be accomplishing it, for there is never a situation in which we cannot grow. We may not always be able to grow in the way we want to, and we may not even be able to see the growth opportunity at first, but we can discover it if we search for it. Even within the hell of a concentration camp, Viktor Frankl found an opportunity for spiritual growth. There he "grasped the meaning of the greatest secret . . . The salvation of man is through love and in love."[2] Such revelations often come when we face death, the ultimate Natural Anxiety, and cross over into Sacred Anxiety.

"I believe that every person is a spiritual being having a human experience . . . And that the point of our brief time on earth is to come to grips with what is eternal inside us."[3] This was not written by a philosopher or a theologian but by Scott O'Grady, the U.S. Air Force pilot who was shot out of the sky in June 1995. Landing behind enemy lines in war-torn Bosnia, he amazed an anxiously watching world with his ability to survive in a hostile countryside for six days until he was rescued. An experience that might have traumatized someone else became transformative for him. He attributed his courageous spirit to the belief that his life had a higher purpose, one he could work on anywhere.

HEALTH, LOVE, AND SUCCESS ANXIETIES REVISITED

If we look at life from a spiritual perspective—that our primary purpose is the evolution of our soul—the most basic Natural Anxieties take on new meanings and paradoxical dimensions.

HEALTH ANXIETY

Mastering our anxieties about our health and survival moves us in two directions—greater health and greater acceptance of the lack of it. We need to become more open to vibrant health and pleasure in our life, to define health as a sense of positive well-being, not merely the absence of disease. In this way we can open ourselves to more energy, more vitality, and more aliveness. We can learn to handle the excitement and ecstasy that lie beyond the comfort zone. When good health emanates not merely from genetic good fortune, but radiates from a passionate encounter with the source of life, it becomes a spiritual experience.

We also need to become more accepting of pain and illness. Health and illness, pleasure and pain, are interrelated; they are all part of normal life. Acceptance of discomfort enables us to exercise vigorously, to go out into the cold or the heat, and to stay a little hungry—challenging our body and making us hardier and healthier. The ability to experience physical pleasure helps us to manage pain. In working with people who suffer from chronic pain, I have found that many of them had been concentrating their attention on the 10 percent of their body that was in pain and ignoring the 90 percent of their body that still felt good. Shifting the focus of attention allows relaxation and maximum enjoyment of life and often aids the healing process.

It is natural to prefer health over disease. Yet if disease strikes us, it too can become a way to grow. Often illness comes when we have ignored our body or our emotions for too long. Like anxiety, illness often functions as a safety mechanism, calling us back to our body and our inner life. Even illness or accidental injury that appears random and undeserved must be accepted before one can heal.

Catastrophic illness or accident presents us with perhaps the ultimate challenge. We suddenly face a life radically different from the one we'd planned on. The agenda we had set for our career, our family life, and our personal development may be rendered impossible by disease. Yet our spiritual life, which is the truest and deepest level of our being, can never be thwarted, even by death. Bernie Siegel, the Yale surgeon and author of many books on spiritual healing, has observed:

> The healing mechanisms are the same for all diseases and for
> all patients . . . We must all confront the reality that no one
> lives forever. Illness and death are not signs of failure; what is a
> failure is not living. Our goal is learning to live—joyously and
> lovingly. Disease can often teach us to do that.

LOVE ANXIETY

Love anxiety is both the fear of abandonment and the fear of being suffocated or controlled by others. Emotional isolation and psychological alienation is a lonely hell, but some people would argue that being trapped in a bad relationship is a far worse fate. To relax more deeply with the natural social anxieties that are part of human existence, we need to cultivate both an inner independence and an ability to connect intimately and deeply with others. Possessing these two complementary skills enables us to navigate the sea of human relationships with as much pleasure and equanimity as possible.

If we know that we can embrace any social interaction as a learning experience, then our social anxieties diminish greatly. If we can accept times of solitude and isolation as opportunities to deepen our connection to our inner self and to our God, then we need not fear being alone. Although fate can deprive us of those we love, it cannot deprive us of our ability to feel love and express love. Being more concerned with the giving of love and less with the getting of it assures us of a constant flow of love through our being. Then we can grow equally from receiving love from others and being deprived of it. In the following chapter on relationships, we will explore this apparent paradox in greater depth.

SUCCESS ANXIETY

We often imagine that we will experience peace of mind only with the achievement of a long-sought success. Yet when we realize that success has wrecked as many people's lives as has failure, we can begin to understand that it is we, not fate, who control our destiny. Both success and failure can derail our life and both can promote growth.

When we define success in the conventional way to mean "accomplishing what we set out to do," then the possibility of failure always looms in the thicket of circumstances beyond our control. We can help ourselves transcend the usual anxieties about success and failure by evolving a spiritual definition of success: to wholeheartedly endeavor to accomplish a life goal and to learn from the experience. Then nothing can ever wrest true success from our grasp except our own unwillingness to embrace the experience. Thomas Edison failed to find the right elements to create a reliable light bulb thousands of times. But because he had learned something from each attempt, he considered each experiment a success, not a failure. Only if armed with such an invincible attitude could he persevere through the many trials required to find the right combination.

If our planet is a school for spiritual growth, then both failure and success are esteemed members of the faculty. Success is certainly the more popular teacher, yet it provokes just as much anxiety as failure. The arrival of a long-sought opportunity brings elation and excitement but also anxiety about greater expectations and responsibilities. What if we blow it or, even worse, what if we do our very best and are found wanting? Successfully accomplishing a goal does not relieve anxiety and may even increase it—each success simply raises the bar a notch.

What is important is that our successes and our failures are our own. On the spiritual level, to succeed in meeting our parents' expectations or those of society may represent an abject failure, for to succeed at things we have no passion for accomplishing teaches us little. Only by following our deepest anxiety and deepest desire can we find genuine success. All truly successful people have defined success for themselves.

When we become too attached to a limited definition of success, like getting a certain job, marrying a particular person, winning a prize, or excelling in the eyes of our peers, we are signing up for Toxic Anxiety. Success is not a distant goal, but a process, a state of mind, and a way of living life. To know that we can handle anything—to know that we can turn everything into an opportunity for spiritual growth—that is living successfully.

THE HERO'S JOURNEY

We all have a need to be the hero or heroine of our own life story. Ernest Becker believed that the most important question for every human being is "how conscious is he of what he is doing to earn his feeling of heroism?"[4]

The true hero is the man or woman who heeds the call to adventure, who is willing to confront the guardians of the threshold that attempt to use the terrors of anxiety to frighten seekers away from the path. Anxiety can subvert the hero's quest in two ways: It can prevent us from embarking on the journey in the first place and it can tempt us into seeking a false heroism that is cheaply bought by distorting reality. Life requires us to pay a price for true heroism—facing our anxiety. Joseph Campbell wrote:

> The hero, therefore, is the man or woman who has been able
> to battle past his personal and local historical limitations to the
> [true] human forms.[5]

If we are to travel this road, we must find our way past what our mother and father expect us to be, past what our peers want us to be, and even beyond the forms imprinted upon us by our culture. This is the hero's journey, to return to the wellspring of human consciousness and find out what it means to be a man and what it means to be a woman. Instead of merely copying stories we have heard, we need to write our own story. Each of us deserves to be the author of our own life.

The great heroes of history are those who have faced anxiety, not just for themselves but for an entire culture. We call soldiers who fight for their country's freedom heroes because they face death on behalf of a greater cause. Galileo and Darwin faced anxiety for their own epochs, eventually transforming major cultural beliefs about the nature of life. In a deeper sense, Moses, Jesus, Buddha, Mohammed, and the world's other great spiritual teachers became perennial heroes by facing Sacred Anxiety for all of humanity.

According to Campbell, the hero's task is to die to his cultural form and be reborn as an "eternal man." The hero must "return then to us, transfigured, and teach the lesson he has learned of life renewed."[6] Each of us, wherever we find ourselves in society, are heroes and heroines, and it is upon us that the future of the universe depends. The fate of this planet depends upon our willingness to listen to the call of adventure and seek our most interesting, most exciting (and most anxiety-arousing) challenges. And then to return and share our story with our companions, to listen to their stories, and to weave new stories and new myths that bring new life.

Have You Drawn Your Life Map Yet?

How can we find these marvelous, inspiring life goals that help us face anxiety? Does everyone have them or are they reserved for a chosen few?

Most of us do not have the type of mission or talent that will put us on the cover of *Time* magazine. We are trying to pay the bills, meet our personal goals, treat others decently, and—if all goes well—enjoy our lives as much as possible. Sometimes it is hard to find the heroic element in our lives. All too often we seek our heroes in books and on movie screens. Yet the heroic is there in our own lives, we only need to take the time to look for it and to reaffirm it.

One way we can search for spiritual direction is to draw a Life Map. Few of us can take the time to reflect on our life by writing an entire autobiography, but drawing a Life Map can render many of the same benefits. I still remember the feeling of astonishment I had when I drew my first Life Map and saw my whole life represented on one large piece of paper. I was amazed at how patterns emerged, how I could begin to see some design and direction in what had often seemed to be a confused, winding path filled with detours, mistakes, and failures. After drawing a Life Map of my past, I drew a Life Map of my future, which helped me become more conscious of my dreams and aspirations.

The technology for drawing your own Life Map is simple and inexpensive. All you need is a large sheet of paper or poster board and an assortment of colored markers, plus your memory and your imagination. The defining structure of the Life Map is the lifeline, which represents the path your life has taken or will take. It can be expressed as a straight line, a series of steps, a spiral, or any freeform design you choose. The lifeline of your past Life Map begins at birth and ends at the present. You can show the ups and downs of your life, the forks in the road, and the roads not taken. You can use symbols, pictures, and words to mark important events. Color can be used to differentiate phases of your life.

Before drawing your map, take some time to reflect about your life. Close your eyes and begin to let your lifeline take form in your imagination before you draw it on paper. Remember as you visualize your past that there is no right or wrong way to look at your life. You have been telling yourself a certain story about your life up to this point, and by drawing your map you have the chance to become more aware of your story and to rewrite it if you wish. The stories we tell about our life become our truth. They give our life the meaning, or lack of meaning that it has; they create our identity.

Unless we take the time to become consciously aware of our stories, we continue to repeat the stories we have heard others tell about us, including our family members, our peers, and our culture—stories that may induce anxiety, shame, low self-esteem, and a severely limited identity. A major task of effective psychotherapy is to help people change the stories they tell about themselves. When anxious or depressed clients come into my office, I help them see how they have been telling themselves anxiety-filled stories about their lives and how they are busy writing depressing scenarios about their futures. I remind them that they can take back, from their parents and other cultural authority figures, the power to write their own stories and become the authors of their own lives. Often after just one session they walk out of my office feeling much better about themselves. Nothing has changed yet in their outer lives, but they have begun to write a more positive story. Instead of playing the role of helpless victims, they begin to see themselves as heroes and heroines who have overcome many obstacles and survived. They begin to write stories of their futures that inspire them to live.

When you visualize your Life Map, remember that your story is also the story of all humanity. Your life partakes of all the great myths and legends. You can envision your life as a great adventure. What is it that has motivated you throughout your life? What is the secret quest you are on? When you were a young boy or girl you had not yet lost the sense of life as a glorious adventure. When you perceive the spiritual quest contained in even the humblest of lives, you can transform the mundane into the transcendent. Whether you are trying to earn a degree, pay your bills, raise a family, start a business, or adjust to a major life change brought about by illness, divorce, or job loss, remember that you are on a spiritual quest. Your life matters to the cosmos.

FINDING YOUR HIDDEN TREASURE

When you have drawn your past Life Map, you can meditate on it. You can draw other versions of it; sometimes it helps to draw your most negative story about your life so you can see how toxic it is—and then ceremonially burn it. You can begin to sense what has been guiding your life and the stories you have been telling yourself. Somewhere in your Life Map, where you may least expect it, you will find a hidden treasure.

Our greatest gift often comes from the place where we have been wounded the most deeply. Many creative and successful people are "wounded healers"—people who overcame a problem and transformed it into their life's work. Bill Wilson founded one of the most successful organizations in history through facing his own wounds. Today millions of people benefit from Alcoholics Anonymous and similar programs. My client, Paolo, deeply anguished by his daughter's disability, put his computer savvy to work and founded a company that designs and produces computer-assisted communication devices for the disabled. Another client, Vanessa, a talented secretary who found her path to executive positions blocked by gender bias, opened her own consulting practice, providing career development training for office workers seeking to reach their full potential. Such people bring passionate enthusiasm and a sense of purpose to their work because they listened when their "inner voice" called them to take on a challenge.

When Joseph Campbell advised students looking for direction in life to "follow your bliss," he chose his words carefully. He didn't tell them to follow their obvious talents, their social expectations, their ego gratification, or even their happiness. He used the word "bliss," a word we associate with a state of passionate spiritual ecstasy. Like many before you, you may discover your greatest treasure where you least expect to find it. To find your greatest gift, search in the dark regions where you have hidden your wounds and your passions.

Find a way to love your life. If you are living a life that does not feel like your "real life," because your work is unfulfilling or your relationships are unsatisfying, don't stop loving your life. When life feels off-track, it is easy to give in to self-pity, bitterness, shame, or vague hopes. Anxiety can trick us into misinterpreting our dissatisfaction as a sign of our unworthiness when it is actually evidence of our greater potential. Nonjudgmental acceptance of where you are is the first step to moving forward. Avoid the comfort-zone trap and use your desperation creatively. Develop what Steven Covey calls a "principle-centered" way of living, based on your highest values. The best formula for change: Love the life you have and create the life you love.

Follow Your Passion in
Drawing Your Future Life Map

The goal of the quest, the hidden treasure in the world's most resonant myths, is always greater aliveness and abundant life. The treasure is the gift of life: the Holy Grail in the King Arthur legend, the living waters that bring healing. Yet it is not the acquisition of the treasure that transforms the protagonist into a hero or heroine—it is the quest itself.

The right quest generates passion. It is in searching that we come alive with the inner passion that gives life its color and vibrancy. Passion is the fire of human life, the fire in the belly that propels us forward through challenges. And anxiety is passion's fuel; embracing anxiety in the right way transforms it into passionate energy. The more willing we are to experience the sacred shivers of passion, the less susceptible we become to the toxic trembles of worry, panic, and depression. When we suppress and smother our passion, boredom and ennui sap our will, and fatigue overcomes our body. Instead of fire, we get the gray smoke of Toxic Anxiety. But if we consciously breathe into our anxiety, it reignites into a divine and passionate flame.

Passion can burn as well as warm. Enthusiasm can be harnessed to unworthy ends. When we allow passion to rage uncontrolled, it can lead to burnout, madness, and violence. The fires of passion and enthusiasm fuel our spiritual growth when they serve our life purpose instead of our momentary desires.

True enthusiasm for life is a nourishing of the spirit. Enthusiasm comes from the Greek word *entheos,* meaning "the god within." Deep, enduring enthusiasm, unlike momentary excitement, comes only when we have aligned our life with a higher purpose. This means opening up to the deeper flow of wisdom in our psyche. Thoreau advised, "Dwell as near as possible to the channel in which your life flows."

After reflecting on your Life Map, you can take the awesome responsibility of creating your own future by drawing a future Life Map. This map begins with the present moment and ends with your death. Yes, death. It's going to happen some day. Sooner or later, we will reach the end of our lifeline. As Samuel Johnson wryly observed, the prospect of death "concentrates the mind most wonderfully."

What do you want to experience between now and then? Be bold, dream big dreams. Let your first map be the hero's map, unfettered by the limiting lie we call reality. Your future Life Map can be one of many, as you explore alternate futures that emphasize different aspects of yourself. After you express your deepest, wildest, most creative dreams you can focus them into more down-to-earth maps that help you plan the next year or the next month.

Drawing a Life Map becomes a small way station on our journey, a brief time to stop amidst the noisy rush of everyday life, to gaze back at where we have come from and to envision our future. And, perhaps most important, to ask why we are on the path. Our stories represent the archetypal human journey, an age-old quest for meaning and fulfillment, our own unique variation on the universal theme of being human. Where we were before our individual lifeline began and where we go after it ends is ultimately a mystery—our life on earth is enveloped by this vast mystery.

SACRED SUFFERING OR TOXIC SUFFERING

In the past, passion was often looked upon as a base emotion, associated with evil, and was contrasted with the nobility of reason. Today passion has acquired almost too positive a connotation: we pursue passionate sex; we admire a passionate advocate for justice; we dream of happily pursuing goals we feel passionate about.

Passion does have this connotation of a positive and intense emotional state, a kind of ecstasy. Yet this is only half of passion's nature. The "Passion of Christ" refers not to his dynamic ministry but to his crucifixion. The word "passion" (from the Latin *passus*) actually means to undergo suffering, and older uses of the word include martyrdom and surrender.

It is important that we integrate both meanings of the passionate life, the agony and the ecstasy. Passion is a high-energy state of great joy, but this state is entered through surrendering to the greater life force, a process that may cause us great pain as we let go of our defenses, as we surrender the desire for comfort to the higher passion for growth. As we feel rigid ego boundaries dissolving in the flood of passion, we may experience great anxiety.

We may, like Jesus, Nelson Mandela, or Martin Luther King, Jr., have to endure suffering and persecution when we surrender to our passion. Yet the passionate life is the only life worthy of a hero or heroine. Living heroically might mean hanging in there and working things out in a difficult marriage. Or standing up to a tyrannical boss. Or staying connected with our children even after a bitter divorce. Being a hero does not mean overcoming others. It is not swaggering around with a gun or a big bank account. Being a hero means being willing to do what is most difficult for us—to face our own fears and anxieties honestly and to follow our true calling in life, no matter what.

Suffering is not highly respected today. Much of our culture considers suffering the province of losers, something to be avoided, a punishment for making mistakes in life. As with anxiety, suffering has both a healthy and an unhealthy dimension. The key question is: Are we suffering because we are facing our anxiety or because we are fleeing our anxiety?

When we suffer because we are trying to avoid Natural or Sacred Anxiety, then our suffering becomes repetitive and meaningless. We sense that we have been here before and we feel irritated, angry, or guilty. This kind of suffering is actually an attempt to manipulate suffering, for we prefer old familiar suffering to suffering that is new and therefore more anxiety producing. This artificial suffering is a kind of antisuffering that only leads us further into our own delusions.

But when we suffer because we are facing our anxiety, we enter the realm of sacred suffering. Sacred suffering is a blessing, a sign that anxiety is working on us, whittling away at everything nonessential. The blessing of suffering brings us deeper into our spiritual life. The word "suffer" comes from the Latin *sufferre,* meaning "to carry below"; suffering brings us deeper. If we did not have suffering to carry us deeper, we would always stay on the surface of life, for the good life is so enchanting, so entertaining. There are beautiful new clothes to buy, clever technological machines and gadgets to entertain us, bright new appliances to give us a sense of progress, new cars that bestow freedom and power, new people to meet, and new places to go. Yet there is no escaping suffering. The "good life" eventually leads to boredom, illness, guilt, and meaninglessness. Mother Teresa once commented that the spiritual suffering she observed in the prosperous West rivaled the physical suffering of the poor in the slums of Calcutta.

The day I realized that my first marriage was breaking up, my whole world fell apart. I remember the feeling of suddenly plunging deeper below the surface of life. On another occasion, when my daughter was being rushed to the hospital by ambulance, I experienced the same feeling. The familiar everyday scenery, the streets, stores, and houses of my everyday world were all still there, but they had become mere props on a stage; their ordinariness no longer reassured me that I knew the world. I was forced to go deeper. Those who have experienced divorce, serious illness, or financial reversals, or who have lost a loved one, or who have struggled with psychological problems may consider themselves blessed. These can be received as gifts, not curses.

At times I still forget the truth about suffering and allow it to make me feel punished, angry, ashamed, and unloved. But in moments of clarity, I feel truly grateful for my suffering. I have been blessed by many problems and difficulties over the years. I know myself well enough to know that without this suffering I would never have gone deeper. Suffering is the universe's way of drawing us back when we wander astray.

Gradually I've been learning to accept the unguaranteed life. Difficulties will continue to visit me throughout my life, and I understand now that my power lies not in resisting them but in embracing them. I have learned to approach potential crises with a win/win mentality. Either things turn out the way I want and I win what I want or they don't, and I win a chance to master anxiety and experience serenity at a deeper level. Either way, I can grow. To know we can grow spiritually through both success and failure frees us from toxic suffering and ushers us into the realm of sacred suffering.

The story of Job is a classic illustration of sacred suffering. God had blessed Job with prosperity. He was rich beyond measure. He enjoyed a happy family and good health. Job loved God and worshipped faithfully. Yet as great as his faith was, God knew it was the faith of the fortunate. True faith demands a deeper test, and God wished to temper Job's faith in the fire of suffering. Job was anguished by the suffering God visited upon him and also was profoundly confused by it. Not knowing why he was suffering was even more disturbing to him than the terrible calamities themselves. Nietzsche wrote, "He who has a why to live for can bear with almost any how." Job searched for the meaning of his suffering.

What I admire about Job is that, unlike his friends, he could discern that his suffering was not toxic suffering, not punishment for misdeeds; he sensed that somehow his suffering was God's way of teaching him about life. Job reminds us that it is all right to be angry about our suffering; it is OK to be angry with God. The important thing is to have a conversation with our God about our suffering. Through our dialogue with God, our suffering acquires meaning, and only when our suffering is redeemed with meaning does it become transformative. God was blessing Job with suffering, suffering that brought him to a deeper understanding and greater faith.

Now that we have ventured into the territory that marks the boundary between the Natural and the Sacred, we can examine the effects of anxiety upon personal relationships and upon society as a whole. Later we will complete our journey by entering the transcendent realm of the soul as we explore Sacred Anxiety.

Part Four

ANXIETY
AND
SOCIETY

Chapter Twelve

RELATIONSHIPS:
THE ANXIETY AND
THE ECSTASY

NAVIGATING BETWEEN THE POLES OF
SEPARATION AND FUSION

Anxiety and relationships are intimate companions. It is anxiety about being alone that prods us to seek connection with another person, yet our anxiety about becoming too dependent may keep us from the deeper intimacy for which we yearn.

Our anxiety regarding love begins with our relationship with our parents and the basic question: "Do you love me for who I really am?" Later this anxiety extends to our siblings, our friends, and to society at large and is usually referred to as social anxiety. Social anxiety manifests itself as separation anxiety (the fear of being abandoned by others) and fusion anxiety (the fear of being suffocated or dominated by them). It encompasses the desire to win social acceptance and approval, to feel important and respected. Social anxiety provides the fuel for embarrassment, lying, shame, guilt, shyness, scapegoating, rebelliousness, and conformity.

This is what Robert Frost called "the fear of Man—the fear

that men won't understand us and we shall be cut off from them." We need social recognition to feel that we are somebody. Without it we feel like a nobody. Yet we also dread becoming enmeshed in suffocating or abusive relationships. We fear being controlled, defined, overpowered, or hurt by other people. This anxiety is often expressed as, "Do I have to give up my self to be loved by you?"

The dual anxieties of separation and fusion present us with an existential polarity that can all too easily degenerate into a toxic double bind if we do not accept it and navigate it consciously. Because love and intimacy are the deepest desires of the human heart, they create some of our most profound dilemmas. For example, the deeper the connection with another, and the more we allow ourselves to be truly known, the more vulnerable we become to being hurt. And the more important we become to other people, the more painful it is when we cannot meet their expectations. We dread never finding love, and fear giving ourselves completely to love. Ultimately we are just as anxious about being loved as not being loved.

Our first and most formative relationship is the powerful emotional connection we have with our parents. By its very nature, it is one that is often fraught with anxiety as well as love and it influences all our subsequent relationships.

As adults, we first enter into an intimate relationship hoping it will relieve much of the anxiety we feel in our life. We hope to find love, lasting security, and unconditional acceptance. Yet the most miserable people I have met have not been those without partners, but people who are entangled in destructive relationships. For although we are quite capable of inflicting unhappiness upon ourselves, it is mild indeed compared with the misery we can experience through the expert assistance of another human being who knows us intimately!

Although I have learned a great deal from counseling couples, my deepest learning has naturally come from my own search for love. Intimate relationships are like pressure cookers. The container of marriage can cook or mature us far more quickly than is generally possible on our own. For the daily pressure of intimacy evokes our deepest anxieties and opens us to the healing power of love. Yet the pressure generated also can implode upon one's individuality or explode into mutual destruction. If a couple unconsciously begins to project their anxiety onto each other, they will soon find themselves thrashing about in a steaming cauldron of rage, confusion, and pain.

Our intimate relationships can provide the most intense and valuable paths to personal growth. It is here that we can work through our deepest inner conflicts. Yet our urge to merge continually fights with our fusion anxiety; our need for independence vies against our separation anxiety. Not surprisingly, we often get trapped in a relationship comfort zone. In this chapter, we will explore how we can use relationships to cultivate awareness and master anxiety, so that they can become sanctuaries of safety and love in our lives.[1]

GETTING OUT OF THE TOXIC RELATIONSHIP CYCLE

Although some of us may make a conscious life choice not to travel the path of an intimate sexual relationship, many more desire love and intimacy but find their way blocked by the fear of getting hurt, the worry of commitment, and the dread of abandonment—in short, by anxiety. Behavior patterns that are neither too close to trigger fusion anxiety nor too distant to trigger separation anxiety form the boundaries of our relationship comfort zone. Because they were determined in our childhood, these boundaries seldom expand without conscious awareness and they tend to create patterns that can lead to a toxic relationship cycle.

In a toxic relationship cycle, power struggles are endlessly reenacted without any resolution: Intimacy inevitably begets conflicts and leads to anxiety. In turn, conflict and anxiety lead to arguments, hurt feelings, and withdrawal (the "silent treatment" and "being in the doghouse"). While withdrawal might bring momentary relief, eventually it turns into loneliness and isolation, triggering anxiety about abandonment. This separation anxiety leads to new overtures and renewed intimacy. The intimacy relieves the separation anxiety and is followed by a honeymoon period as the couple traverses their comfort zone. Before long, however, the increasing closeness triggers fusion anxiety for one or both parties. Conflict ensues, and the cycle repeats once again.

Unless couples can become conscious of such patterns and change them, chronic conflict will eventually undermine the positive elements of their relationship. Some couples spend a lifetime bickering, nagging, and criticizing each other without ever resolving anything. Some couples withdraw permanently, ending the painful conflict by divorcing. Many other couples choose to avoid conflict by retreating from the challenge of marriage into an arrangement, living separate lives under the same roof.

Many of the conflicts in our relationships are the product of different comfort zone settings. When one person is reaching the boundary of their comfort zone and is already experiencing fusion anxiety, the other person may just be reaching a desirable depth of intimacy. As the first person reverses direction and heads back into his or her comfort zone, the partner experiences abandonment; their mutual anxiety explodes and accusations fly.

For far too many of us, lack of awareness about the role of anxiety in our intimate relationships dooms us to these kinds of hurtful, repetitive encounters. But if we are willing to face our own anxiety, we can transform a comfort zone relationship into a healthy, growing relationship, one characterized by a mutually reinforcing process of growth. One phase of this positive cycle strengthens the growth of our selfhood; the other phase deepens our sense of couplehood.

The key to changing a static comfort zone relationship into a dynamic, growing relationship lies primarily in how we handle conflict. We can train ourselves to stop in the midst of conflict—or at the least, immediately afterward—and engage in a process of self-awareness. We can do this by asking ourselves, "What triggered this conflict? What am I anxious about? How am I feeling threatened?"

Asking these questions enables us to use our relationship as a path to self-knowledge and deeper serenity. Intimate relationships arouse our deepest anxieties and, therefore, when used intelligently, can help us grow personally and spiritually in a most remarkable way.

USING THE ANXIETY IN RELATIONSHIPS FOR PERSONAL GROWTH

As we learned earlier, a diffuse and undifferentiated anxiety is often our initial unconscious reaction to anything that we perceive as a threat to our self-image. As I studied my own responses in daily life, I began to realize that I had often experienced this diffuse anxiety but, because of its primal and fleeting nature, I had been largely unaware of it. Only the more developed emotions were strong enough or loud enough to get my attention. It was not until this primal anxiety had metamorphosed into fear or anger, sadness or joy that I realized I was feeling something. But by then my emotional state had already developed to the point where I had little control over it. It had me; it was me—by then "I" was angry; "I" was sad. This emotional energy quickly followed timeworn channels into habitual behaviors, which all too often were far from being the most effective responses to the situation.

Gradually I learned to relax and detach sufficiently to practice self-awareness. I soon found that I was able to catch the emotion before it developed completely and to then trace it back to the primal anxiety. This enabled me to ask myself the crucial question, "How am I feeling threatened?" The answer to this question enabled me to choose a response more consciously. For instance, if I found myself starting to feel angry in response to something my wife Christine said or did, I would attempt to relax with the anger and trace it back. Invariably I found that primal anxiety—a vague sense of my self-image being threatened—was my initial reaction. I also noticed that this anxiety almost always had to do with core emotional patterns from my childhood. Some part of me would feel hurt and in danger of further injury. This sense of being threatened would either lead to my withdrawing into a passive, introverted response, in which I would feel hurt, victimized, and hopeless, or mobilizing an active, extroverted counterattack using weapons such as criticism and blame.

What I found, to my occasional delight, was that during some episodes I could maintain enough awareness to consciously attend to my primal anxiety. This enabled me to take responsibility for my own inner state, instead of being convinced that the other person was causing me to feel angry or hurt. In other words, I learned that I had choices. I could choose to identify the threatened part of me and, drawing upon psychological and spiritual resources, restore a feeling of existential safety to my threatened inner world. I could identify inner conflicts and take responsibility for resolving them instead of projecting them onto my relationship with my wife or my children. I also could discuss troubling issues more calmly and productively. I discovered that I could be in charge of the energy of primal anxiety and decide how to use it, instead of unconsciously allowing it to travel along certain well-worn channels that always led to the same painfully familiar scenarios.

As Norman Lear observed, intimate relationships involve "real people in real conflict, with all their fear rubbing against their love for one another." The important thing is whether a couple learns to use that rubbing constructively. By getting our anxiety and our love to work together, Christine and I allowed our conflict to serve as a kind of psychic sandpaper that smoothed our rough edges. Gradually our defenses became worn away and we learned to surrender more gracefully.

Without love, fighting can become destructive. Our fighting was transformed by the coexistence of love. We both began to use conflict to bring our own anxiety into sharper relief and to take responsibility for it instead of projecting it. In the past, I had tried to solve relationship problems by focusing my magnifying glass on the other person; now I was discovering that a mirror was a much more effective tool.

I realized that all conflict between people arises from anxiety. Conflict occurs when we try to reduce our anxiety by changing the other person's behavior. The other person naturally resists and counterattacks, resulting in an escalation, not a reduction, of the anxiety. I learned that, although my wife might trigger my anxiety, its roots lay much deeper, within myself and my past. After I accepted this, I was able to retrain myself to avoid letting my anxiety follow old patterns of blame, such as making Christine wrong, criticizing her, or feeling that I was an innocent victim. By my not allowing my anxiety easy release through unconscious behaviors, my anxiety took me deeper inside my own psyche. There I discovered my basic anxieties, the ones that lay underneath every conflict, every judgment.

What I found there was a dread of abandonment and a fear of fusion; that if I were truly myself then my lover would leave me (or that I would leave her) and, if I surrendered to love, that my essential selfhood would somehow be obliterated. Every relationship problem is nothing but a variation on these two themes. Our intimate relationships present us with an opportunity to deepen these existential wounds or to heal them.

THE ANXIETY AND THE ECSTASY

Intimate emotional sharing, sexual passion, lovemaking itself, is the purest and most transcendent expression of love for many couples. In the naked simplicity of sexuality we encounter each other's essence most directly and profoundly. But the powerful forcefield of love also brings everything to the surface: Old hurts, deeply buried wounds, and primitive anxieties also arise in the midst of love's cleansing power.

This happens to every couple, yet the process is often misunderstood. The doubts, the guilt, the shame, and the fear disturb the romanticism and seem to threaten the relationship. Yet it is only through this sometimes painful purification process that a couple's love can reach a higher level of authentic commitment and greater passion. If a couple begins to hide from each other at this point, the journey to intimacy becomes detoured, passion fades, and sexual problems may develop.

The sexual dimension of intimacy can be one of the most sublime and pleasurable ways to practice mastering anxiety and experiencing serenity. Sexual problems can be more easily resolved if we accept that anxiety and ecstasy are intertwined. Both anxiety and ecstasy are forms of the "shivers." The greater our ability to master anxiety, the greater the ecstasy we can attain. All too often a sense of shame and an unspoken cultural taboo prevent couples from talking openly with each other during lovemaking. Individuals and couples can benefit by shedding their culturally programmed notions of what lovemaking should be like and approach lovemaking with a beginner's mind. Each person, each couple, has their own unique style of loving. Pretending that we have no idea about how it "should" be can open up new possibilities. Discovering and co-creating original, spontaneous, playful sexual self-expression can become an ongoing adventure.

Sexual encounter is an I/Thou encounter of the deepest sort. In the intense heat of the sexual crucible, the most profound anxieties will bubble up to the surface. Couples need to be willing at all times to shift gears—to move from pleasure to pain, from play to healing, and back again. Childhood wounds, past traumas, personal insecurities, and spiritual anxiety may all be loosened up by our nakedness and our love.

Sexuality is the most entrancing gateway to Sacred Anxiety. Gazing at the face of our beloved, we glimpse the invisible face of God. Through the embrace of our beloved, we are enveloped by God's loving presence. Sexual ecstasy takes us to the edge of life and death. The more alive we feel, the closer to death we feel. In the moment of climax we disappear for a moment, experiencing the temporary death of the self. We surrender to each other, and surrender together to a unity that is greater than both of us.

Our sexual relationship can become a high sacrament—a tangible manifestation of divine love. In this sacred ritual of transcendence, we die to our self-image, we die to the world, and partake of the eternal and the infinite. It is an unbounded time of mystery, wonder, and gratitude. In that moment we glimpse, not the possibility of a heavenly paradise, but the living presence of an earthly one.

Merging the Couple's Path with the Spiritual Journey

Although they are the least frequently recognized, issues of Sacred Anxiety lie at the heart of all intimate relationships. The need for love and acceptance is a spiritual need as much as it is an emotional one. Many couples unconsciously project their existential anxiety onto their mate. They expect the other person to provide a level of unconditional love and security far beyond that which is humanly possible and, as a result, continually feel betrayed. Couples who practice self-awareness in their relationships take responsibility for their own Natural and Sacred Anxiety and look to their mate as a cherished companion on the path, not as a savior.

In our fragmented society, many of us now expect the marriage relationship to deliver the sense of security and connection that was previously provided by religion and community. We want our partner to be a secure haven from a competitive, uncaring society and a cold, godless universe. When we place these expectations on someone, they will eventually feel inadequate, anxious, and resentful.

By facing our own anxieties openly and honestly on all levels, we can transform intimate relationships from bloody battlefields or sterile stalemates into vibrant arenas for spiritual growth. We can own our Toxic Anxiety and trace it back to our childhood emotional programming. We can face our Natural Anxieties instead of dumping our own job stresses, health worries, and personal frustrations onto our partner. We can accept our Sacred Anxiety about life, death, and existence and not expect our mate to somehow magically make us happy. We all need unconditional love. But unconsciously demanding it ready-made from our mate is just another way of avoiding our own intimate encounter with God.

Anxiety owned is easy to listen to with empathy. Anxiety projected is experienced as attack and provokes counterattack. Taking responsibility for our anxieties as they arise in our relationship draws us closer to our partner and reinforces a deep sense of safety, love, and acceptance. Paradoxically, when we take responsibility for our own anxiety, it vastly increases the possibilities of both giving and receiving unconditional love, or as close to it as humanly possible.

LOVE AND ANXIETY

Until we bring awareness to our relationships, most of us live in love's comfort zone—close enough to take the edge off loneliness, and distant enough to preserve our sense of being able to live without the other person. The tragedy is that many people who love each other are unable to express that love fully because they are unaware of how anxiety throttles and distorts their love. They feel, but not too deeply; they hold back, unable to make the final commitment. Yet those who protect themselves from the loss of love by blocking out love already are suffering from what they most dread. Forgoing love in the present out of anxiety about losing it in the future is a fool's bargain.

At the extreme, unconscious anxiety can turn even love to hate. When one wants another and feels unworthy or unable to win their love, or fears being manipulated and hurt, anxiety can distort love into either hate or indifference. Hate is injured love, and it may be inflamed through anger into violence. Indifference is injured love retreating into numb withdrawal.

How can we respond to the anxiety that love provokes—to this deep dread of abandonment? The answer is not to love less, but to love more. Although the object of our love can be taken away, our ability to love can never be lost or taken from us. And if our ultimate love object includes the source of life itself, no one can ever take away the object of our love. The path to serenity is to love so much, so deeply, and so unconditionally that we can never be without love. We can let our love for a spouse or a child or a parent expand far beyond our past self-imposed limits. We can let love become a reflex, a habit, an impulse that cannot be denied. Just as the answer to anxiety in general is not less anxiety, but greater and more meaningful anxiety, the answer to our anxiety about love is not less love but more love and greater love.

Anxiety is love's limit, but not its enemy. Our anxiety guides us to the edge of our love. Our task is to keep changing anxiety into love—to have the courage to love passionately, universally, and eternally.

Chapter Thirteen

LIVING IN THE AGE
OF ANXIETY

AMERICA'S ANXIETY ATTACK

We are living in an unprecedented Age of Anxiety. Our individual lives, our families, and our neighborhoods all float upon a vast, roiling sea of deep cultural anxiety. During the last few years, the word "anxiety" has escaped the bounds of psychology and leaped into the larger social, economic, and political arena.

Pollsters barrage us with statistics showing that people are losing their faith in government and in venerable social institutions such as corporations, schools, and churches. Two-thirds of the population believe that the American Dream has become harder to achieve during the past decade.[1] Eighty percent believe it will be even harder for the next generation.[2] Establishment apologists tell us that "It's really not that bad," pointing to millions of new jobs that have been created. A harried working mother replies, "Yes, and I have three of them."

Too often, politicians prefer to smooth over public anxiety with platitudes and hollow reassurance or pander to it with extremist rhetoric. Pundits rush to identify the causes of our discontent and propose cures that range up and down the political spectrum. The cacophony of strident and contradictory voices only heightens the general anxiety. Disillusioned voters either stay home or vote unenthusiastically, as the voting public increasingly answers "none of the above." Today winning an election is no longer a sign of being the most popular candidate, but merely the least unpopular.

Meanwhile, the powerful engine of capitalism churns out a bountiful supply of food, consumer products, and electronic entertainment—modern bread and circuses—that distract us from our anxiety. And underneath all the hubbub and commotion lies a deep depression, a profound sense of disillusionment about modern life, that is accompanied by a gnawing hopelessness about the future.

I began this book with the statement that true serenity may be both more necessary and more possible in today's Age of Anxiety than at any other time in history. This chapter, and those that follow, explore the unique opportunities for spiritual growth with which this Age of Anxiety presents us.

WHY IS THIS THE AGE OF ANXIETY?

What's really going on? Why are we so anxious in the midst of peace and prosperity? We can find lamentations bemoaning the breakdown of society going back to Greek and Roman times. Yet something differentiates this time in history from previous eras of anxiety: This is the first time that we are facing not a local epidemic of anxiety, but a global one. The truth is that, to borrow from Charles Dickens, this is the best of times and the worst of times. The contradictions and confusions of our time create a sense of uncertainty and anxiety that pervade every level of society.

The causes of the anxiety epidemic can be found across a wide spectrum—biological, social, economic, political, and spiritual. Biological factors include the destructive effects of generations of alcoholism, smoking, and drug addiction, of accumulated environmental toxins, and the increasing consumption of highly processed artificial foods. Our fast-paced urban and suburban lifestyles, attuned to digital clocks instead of the rhythms of nature and our own bodies, also upset the delicate physiological balances upon which our mental tranquillity depends.

The industrialization and centralization of economic life has forced most people to labor for vast corporate and governmental entities instead of being self-employed as craftspeople, farmers, bakers, carpenters, shopkeepers, or doctors. The juggernaut of urbanization has fostered the growth of the city and spawned the mega-metropolis—vast areas such as New York, Los Angeles, and Tokyo. The resulting overcrowding, noise, crime, pollution, impersonal social interactions, and loss of contact with nature has undoubtedly added to our daily anxiety.

Michael Sandel, Harvard professor of government, identifies two concerns that lie "at the heart of our discontent."

> One is the fear that, individually and collectively, we are losing
> control of the forces that govern our lives. The other is the
> sense that, from family to neighborhood to nation, the moral
> fabric of community is unraveling around us. These two fears
> define the anxiety of the age. It is an anxiety that the pre-
> vailing political agenda has failed to answer or even address.[3]

Few people seem immune to this pervasive sense of loss of control. Parents feel they have lost their children to the media, the schools, and the street. Young people feel that the world is spinning out of control and their dreams for the future are receding out of reach. Business owners feel that big government is tying them up in red tape. Employees feel they are at the mercy of gigantic corporations, technological change, and a ruthless global marketplace.

The breakdown of family and community structures and the resulting confusion regarding customs and roles create uncertainty, anxiety, and conflict. The human capacity to adapt to change is being stretched to its limit by the rapid rate of technological change. Economic anxiety, caused by decreasing real incomes combined with longer work days, corporate downsizing, global competition, and unemployment leaves many people in a state of constant anxiety about an unpredictable financial future.

Government and the political process appear unable to provide solutions for these real concerns. Instead, the acrimonious, divisive, and indecisive conduct of politics increases the public's anxiety that no political party really has the answer. Every proposed solution, whether in the direction of more government or less government, seems to create a new set of problems.

Spiritually and morally, society appears to have lost its compass. Signs of moral and ethical decay are all too obvious, from impoverished, crime-infested ghettos to our most revered institutions. This unease about our moral foundations may be the most disturbing anxiety for many today. The commercialization of every aspect of life and the disconnection of individual freedom from social responsibility have created a secular jungle where "anything goes." History is replete with examples of mighty empires that have decayed from within once they lost their spiritual and moral underpinnings.

This pervasive sense of meaninglessness and hopelessness offers fertile ground for the mass-media conglomerates that have become the storytellers and meaning-makers of our culture. The daily news is delivered by the media's Anxious Chatterboxes, who, in a frenzy of anxiety-driven competition, barrage the public with anxiety-producing topics ("The Ten Most Toxic Products Found in Every Home"), promising to relieve the anxiety they have just created with yet more information. Advertisements inundate us with messages carefully crafted to activate our anxieties about not looking good enough or not owning the latest, newest, and best. The high-tech world of commerce requires workers to digest mountains of new information each week just to keep apace with never-ending changes. Overstimulated and overloaded with hundreds of often-contradictory messages each day, we suffer from the modern malady of "info-anxiety."

The pace is unrelenting. Much of our anxiety stems from the sense that it is all just *too much*. Many of my clients tell me that there is just too much going on in their lives, more than they can handle comfortably. And this *is* an age of too much—too much information to process, too many possibilities to choose from, too much change happening too fast, too much stuff in the mail and the malls (and in our closets), and much too much to do.

Yet we love the choices and the possibilities. Even though it is too much, we don't want to give any of it up! However, in order to handle this age of too much, we need to relearn the ancient concept of *enough*. More and more people are opting for voluntary simplicity, making a conscious choice to buy only what they truly need. Many people are deciding to redefine their economic lives after discovering how quickly a consumer's heaven of infinite products can become a consumer's hell of eternal debt; still others have sensed the emptiness of acquiring more and more in a world where most people do not have enough.

HOW TO HAVE ALL THE TIME IN THE WORLD

It is all too easy to become so overcommitted that every day becomes an experience of too much. We instinctively resist recognizing our limits because to do so triggers our suppressed Sacred Anxiety. We like to pretend we have unlimited potential and that we will live forever. Yet in reality we have limited energy and a finite lifespan. Admitting we can't do it all today is admitting we won't be able to have it all and do it all during this lifetime either.

Perhaps the most common complaint I hear from my clients is that they don't have enough time. Several commentators, including the physicians Larry Dossey and Stephan Rechtschaffen, have written extensively about the effect of time sickness on our physical and mental health.[4] Modern rushaholics are always racing, always out of breath, always feeling behind schedule, always striving, but seldom managing to get ahead. The stressful impact of this way of life on the neurohormonal, digestive, and cardiovascular systems is immediate.

When we are playing beat the clock, time is our enemy and every second becomes fraught with anxiety. In the daily ticking of the clock, we hear our anxiety about both life and death. Even closer to home, our heartbeat signals our aliveness, while the silence between beats reminds us of our mortality. Time is running after us, ready to devour us if we fall behind. Time is out in front, promising us relief if we can just catch up with it. Our anxious, time-hounded existence gives rise to both a feverish beat-the-clock mentality and the rebellious reaction we call procrastination. We dread running out of time. We experience time as a scarce commodity; even people who are financially wealthy often suffer from time poverty. Existentially we know that one day we will truly run out of time. Death is the ultimate deadline, the dreaded Day of Judgment. In our heart of hearts, we dread that we may be found wanting, not quite good enough at the end of the day, at the end of our life, at the end of time.

Such an existence is antithetical to spiritual growth. To use anxiety for spiritual growth, we need to be willing to look within, to liberate ourselves from the pressured sense that there is not enough time. We may choose to return to the joyful attitude that is expressed so exuberantly by the psalmist:

> This is the day the Lord hath made; we will rejoice and be
> glad in it.[5]

Today is this unique, miraculous, once-in-a-lifetime day we are living, and it is also the eternal day in which we live forever. We can change our time sense to a far more serene concept of time that includes an awareness of timelessness, of having all the time in the world, because we (in the larger sense of our nonself soul) do have all the time in the world. Having the security of eternity enables us to relax enough to appreciate the preciousness of each fleeting moment. This day we are living is precious and unique in the history of the universe and will never come again. It invites us to live with full awareness and full gratitude, giving it everything we have.

Taking time to honor the inner life of the soul has always been important, but never has it been more important than in today's nonstop society. The ancient advice to "honor the Sabbath and keep it holy" reminds us to respect our need for a day of rest. Paradoxically, the same too-much syndrome that forces us to recognize our limitations may also inspire us to search for the boundless and the infinite.

OUTDATED MYTHS AND DYING GODS

The modern myth of human progress through worshipping the gods of science, technology, democracy, and capitalism has fallen on hard times. Despite the extraordinary expansion of knowledge and a cornucopia of inventions, it is becoming disturbingly apparent that things have not turned out the way we had anticipated.

On a psychological level, our global anxiety is closely related to the fact that human beings today no longer grow up with one universally accepted cultural myth. A culture's myth, traditionally in the form of religion, provided a common lens of fundamental beliefs, values, icons, and images through which its members viewed reality. In today's global village, the ordinary person now has hundreds of such myths and paradigms competing for his or her loyalty.

Whether a peasant farmer in a remote African village or an office worker in an American metropolis, each inhabitant of this planet is exposed to an unprecedented variety of belief systems. Our minds are oversaturated with contradictory worldviews.

Anxiety thrives on this uncertainty and confusion. Joseph Campbell speculated that:

> The failure of mythology and ritual to function effectively in our civilization may account for the high incidence among us of the malaise that has led to the characterization of our time as "The Age of Anxiety."[6]

Now, in the waning moments of the twentieth century, end-of-the-millennium anxiety is accelerating exponentially. There is a disquieting feeling in the air that we are at the end of an era. We read that we are living in a postmodern culture, in a postindustrial economy, with posttraditional lifestyles. We are basically "post" everything that is familiar to us. We are skewered somewhere in between the modern era that is passing away and a future era that has yet to take form.

The ability to utilize anxiety effectively may prove to be the most essential survival skill as we enter the twenty-first century. Our collective response to this raging cultural anxiety will determine whether we descend into a paranoid and destructive divisiveness or evolve to a new level of human society.

SOCIAL ACTION AND SOCIAL CHANGE

Societies are subject to the effects of Toxic Anxiety just as individuals are. Anxiety can divide a country, and it usually does. The rampant anxiety in 1930s Germany led to the genocide of Jews and other minorities. People in an anxious nation become more defensive, numb, and shortsighted. They have an urge to cling even tighter to old belief systems, to seek simple answers. Throughout history, anxious populations have been all too willing to seek relief from uncertainty and change by putting their faith in demagogues.

Kurt Goldstein, a psychiatrist who witnessed Hitler's manipulation of German anxiety wrote: "There is no better means . . .

of enslaving people and destroying democracy . . . than to create in people a state of anxiety. One of the basic pillars of fascism . . . is anxiety."[7] As a society, we must untangle the knot of anxiety that binds and paralyzes us in the face of the crises we face. We need cultural healing for the Toxic Anxiety that divides us, clear collective thinking to meet the Natural Anxiety issues that challenge us, and spiritual awareness of the Sacred Anxiety that can unite us.

No amount of psychotherapy and no amount of medication will reduce the societal component of our anxiety. Instead of searching endlessly for personal neuroses, we need to place this portion of our anxiety out there where it belongs—and channel it into social action. We need to get anxious about larger issues such as social injustice, economic inequality, and ecological threats. Society developed to help its members manage anxiety more effectively. When society exacerbates and provokes individual anxiety, as it does today, it no longer performs its primary function successfully.

Will our anxiety unite or divide us? Anxiety can unite us if, instead of projecting it onto another person (or group), we examine the outdated myths, paradigms, and systems that are oppressing both ourselves and our neighbors. Sometimes catastrophe and hardship bring out the best in people and engender the feeling that we are all in it together, dealing with a common danger or hardship. The greatest moments in history have been those when people set aside the personal anxieties that divided them and saw the big picture, the greater anxiety that could unite them.

The main characteristic of authentic leaders is their willingness to tell the truth. Can our leaders respond creatively to our anxiety? Can we allow new visionary leaders to come forward, or will we run from difficult truths to follow demagogues who proffer simplistic solutions and convenient scapegoats? As individuals and as nations, our most challenging task is to become anxious about the right things in the right way.

Nelson Mandela provides an inspiring example of a man

who, subjected to hardship and persecution, succeeded in mastering anxiety to such a degree that later he was able to calm an entire nation in the grip of fear and panic. He guided his deeply divided country, on the verge of erupting into all-out racial war, into a peaceful transition to democracy.

Gandhi and Martin Luther King, Jr. provide other recent examples of ordinary people who mastered their anxiety to such an extent that they were able to inspire millions. Instead of allowing anxiety to paralyze them or to provoke them to violence, they channeled their anxiety into powerful, peaceful action. These modern miracles are testaments to the power for good that is liberated by just one person who insists upon rising above the mortal anxiety reaction and approaches even injustice and potential catastrophe with the spiritual strength of serenity.

THE OPPORTUNITY OF THE APOCALYPSE

Is the millennium just a calendrical coincidence, or are we truly at the end of an era? Is this the Age of Anxiety because we are in the midst of a major transition in human history—one we have barely begun to acknowledge? Below the surface of our lives swirls a disquieting sense that things are spinning out of control.

We associate the word "apocalypse" with its secular meaning of great cataclysmic destruction. And there is indeed a very real and frightening disintegration taking place in the world. Yet, apocalypse also has a spiritual meaning: It signifies a revelation of what has been hidden (the Greek root means "to uncover"). Apocalypse can be a time of spiritual renewal and revolution, of great and fundamental change in our understanding of the purpose of life.

The frightening disintegration we see going on around us is also a kind of letting go, a loosening, an opening. We are in the midst of a creative confusion that could culminate in a global tragedy, or lead us to a new Golden Age if we are willing to attend to the anxiety that permeates our civilization and our souls. Which perennial truths handed down from our ancestors need to be preserved and re-expressed in relevant forms? What new visions are struggling to be born and need to be nurtured?

The gift that this Age of Anxiety offers us is its very anxiety and profusion of possibilities. The spiritual advantage of our anxious postmodern age is that our cultural defenses are breaking down. There is no universal myth left to believe in. This vacuum of belief systems creates great anxiety but it is also an opportunity that seldom comes in history, the opportunity to become anxious at a deeper level, a level beyond cultural myth, that can lead to a deeper peace. As individuals we can recognize and accept that we are living in an Age of Anxiety. Instead of numbing to our anxiety, feeling ashamed of it, or seeking easy answers, we can let our anxiety work on us.

This *is* the best of times and the worst of times. The problems are real, but so are the opportunities. We are in the midst of a wrenching and traumatic disintegration of the regional cultures that have sustained humanity for millennia. It is far more difficult than ever before to find security in our personal circumstances, our institutions, and our cultural belief systems. But there is also a rebirth and reintegration taking place. New cultures of knowledge are being created from an unprecedented cross-fertilization. For the first time, our whole planet is connected through a global nervous system made of fiber optic cables and communications satellites.

Amidst the bewildering confusion of belief systems lie the riches of an entire planet's knowledge. Today for the first time in history the grand scope of human learning and experience is available to us. We can read the words of the wisest spiritual teachers from every era and every land. We can learn to unite the remarkable discoveries of science and the productive capacity of industry with perennial ethical truths. We can broaden our vision with the literature, myths, and cosmologies of ancient civilizations.

Our present challenge is to become more alive to the wonders and possibilities of our times. This invitation can feel overwhelming, yet it is also tremendously exciting. We are, each of us, part of this adventure, part of this Age of Opportunity. Crumbling belief systems and traditions force us to search for their essence, to return to the source from which they sprang. The serenity we find within ourselves as a result of this quest will be far more nourishing than any sense of security that depends upon outer circumstances or external belief systems.

Our challenge today is essentially the same as it has been in any age, only more so—to find our own core values and to live by them. Living our lives in harmony with our highest values—values which unite us with one another rather than divide us from one another—brings serenity. Perhaps the revelation of this apocalypse is that the eternal quest which unites us is far greater than the individual differences which divide us. This Age of Anxiety invites us, even forces us, to enter the spiritual dimension of Sacred Anxiety to find the serenity and faith we need in order to live.

Part Five

EMBRACING
SACRED
ANXIETY

SACRED ANXIETY

Symbol: The Angel

Sacred Anxiety is the mysterious existential and spiritual experience that religions have called the fear of God. According to a traditional religious proverb, "If you fear God you will fear nothing else, but if you do not fear God you will fear everything else." In other words, if we ignore the sacred dimension of life, we will be tormented continually by life's changing circumstances. But if we embrace Sacred Anxiety, it can free us from Toxic Anxiety and instill a deeper faith that helps us to meet Natural Anxiety with serenity.

Sacred Anxiety came into being when Adam and Eve bit into the apple and became self-conscious, thinking beings. It arose with our awareness that we will inevitably lose our personal existence to death and that our death can occur at any moment. It concerns our existential powerlessness against fate.

Sacred Anxiety cuts through our everyday personality like a double-edged sword. One edge of the blade is life anxiety, the anxiety of Being, in which we experience the terror of conscious selfhood. The other edge, death anxiety, is the dread of Non-Being, of losing our individual selfhood and being reabsorbed into the universe.

The Hebrew psalmist tells us that, "The fear of God is the beginning of wisdom."[1] The purpose of Sacred Anxiety is to call us to awareness of the deeper spiritual issues in our life and our relationship with God. Issues of morality, meaning, values, life purpose, and the ultimate questions of death and the afterlife exist within the realm of Sacred Anxiety. Embracing Sacred Anxiety leads us to wisdom, serenity, and joy in living.

Chapter Fourteen

CULTIVATING THE
SACRED IN LIFE

Let one who seeks not stop seeking until one finds.
When one finds, one will become anxious.
When one is anxious, one will be awestruck
and will enter the kingdom.[2]

FOLLOWING ANXIETY ALL THE WAY TO SERENITY

This intriguing quotation is the first saying of Jesus in the *Gospel of Thomas,* one of the Nag Hammadi scrolls. In these three brief sentences, he beautifully articulates the spiritual quest in which ordinary anxiety is elevated into Sacred Anxiety and higher consciousness. The quest commences with a search for the truth. Through persistent seeking, and the suffering that inevitably accompanies it, we gradually find the truth about life. Confronted with the truth, our limited worldview and our former self-image begin to fall apart; we experience a stage of great confusion and anxiety—a dark night of the soul.

If we allow this anxiety to deepen, we are led into the realm of Sacred Anxiety and the source of our being. Our first impulse is to flee from the holy terror that we initially experience. Too often we become frightened and fail to follow anxiety all the way to serenity. Yet when we finally embrace Sacred Anxiety, it transforms into astonishment, awe, and ecstasy—what the Jewish theologian Abraham Heschel called "radical amazement." Through this sacred shivering, our old skin is cast off and we are reborn as co-creators of life. At that moment we know all, are one with all, love all, and are at peace with all.

Emerging into Sacred Anxiety

We have seen how greatly we can benefit from becoming aware of the way in which our daily anxieties reflect our deeper concerns about life and death. All our anxieties revolve around either a dread of letting go or a fear of becoming more alive. Rachel's story helps illustrate the process of opening ourselves to Sacred Anxiety.

Despite her pain, Rachel's eyes were clear and bright and looked directly into mine. "I don't know if you can help me, but I'm willing to give it a try."

At 66, Rachel had never been to a psychotherapist before and this was clearly something she thought she would never do. But none of the many medications she had tried were able to relieve her debilitating migraines; even the maximum dosage barely took the edge off the pain. Biofeedback, herbs, acupuncture, and chiropractic had not helped either. Rachel suffered from insomnia and was trapped in a cycle of worry and depression. She knew that I used meditation and hypnosis in my practice and hoped I might be able to help her get to the root of her problem.

Rachel began telling me more about her life. Her husband had died three years earlier, leaving a gaping hole in her life. A year after his death, she had been diagnosed with cancer. It was in remission now, but it was a type of cancer that was incurable and would likely prove fatal when it returned.

Rachel had lived a full life; she had enjoyed a long and happy marriage, raised two sons during her twenties and thirties, and had developed a successful career as a clothing designer during her forties and fifties. Life had not always been easy, but it had been good. Now, instead of the rewarding golden years she had expected to enjoy with her husband, she faced each day alone, tormented by migraines, and with a future clouded by cancer. Over the past two years, Rachel had become more and more entangled in anxiety's knot—so much so, she told me, that "Sometimes I feel like I'm losing my mind."

I began by helping Rachel sort out the three levels of anxiety so that she could work with them more productively. She began to see that because of the overwhelming nature of the changes in her life, she had become caught in a Toxic Anxiety pattern of worry, confusion, hopelessness, pain, and paralysis.

Through practicing meditation, she learned how to relax in the midst of all the fears and uncertainties, finding the still center within. She worked on accepting her migraines, a lifelong affliction that had become much worse after her husband's death. Instead of becoming angry or frightened when the first signs appeared, she trained herself to relax with them. To her surprise, the headaches became milder and less frequent. She began sleeping more soundly and feeling more energetic.

As her Toxic Anxiety symptoms lessened, Rachel was able to deal with her Natural Anxiety. She began to process the many emotions she had suppressed in the midst of the catastrophic events of the past few years and was able to cry and grieve. She then turned her renewed energy to the many practical tasks that needed to be accomplished—selling her home and moving into a condominium and organizing her financial and legal affairs. She also was able to accept the fact that she was alone now. Although they cared deeply about her, her sons lived far away and frequent visits were impractical. Rachel became more active in her synagogue, joining discussion groups and mentoring teenage girls. She also began to attend a support group for cancer patients at a local hospital. She was surprised at the depth of the connections she was making through these activities.

As her life began to stabilize somewhat, Rachel regained the sense of empowerment and confidence that she had lost. One day she sat down and announced, "I've been pretending that I don't have cancer because I've been feeling so good. But I know that I do and that I'm probably going to die in the next few years. I want to get ready for it." We began to delve more deeply into her anxiety about death and to explore her Sacred Anxiety.

We were using hypnosis to understand the roots of her migraine headaches when a memory surfaced. Rachel recalled her first migraine at the age of 14 and realized that it coincided with the time that her mother had died. Her mother had died of cancer, in the most painfully agonizing way. She had wanted so much to help her mother and had chastised herself for having been unable to prevent her painful death. Rachel realized that her migraines were associated with death, pain, powerlessness, and guilt. Over the course of several sessions, Rachel was able to heal this traumatic memory. As she saw the truth of the situation, she was able to release these negative emotions, and her migraines became rare occurrences rather than daily torments.

Her mother's death had left a toxic imprint on Rachel's relationship with God. Angry at God for making her mother suffer and for taking her away, Rachel had stopped believing in a higher power. "I specifically remember thinking that I didn't want to believe in a God who could let something like that happen," she told me. From that time on, her religion had taken the form of a social custom rather than serving as a spiritual path.

Rachel now faced her Sacred Anxiety regarding death and the meaning of her life. She returned to the scriptures and the teachings of Judaism and, through prayer and meditation, began a dialogue with God about her mother's death and her own death. She joined a writing group and composed her spiritual autobiography, through which she shared her life journey with others.

"I realize that our last task in life is to prepare for our death," she told me. Rachel's cancer returned, and with a vengeance this time. But she found an excellent hospice program and was able to use both meditation and medication to deal with the pain.

Several weeks before she died, Rachel told me, "I know I'm going to die soon. I don't believe I'm going to sprout wings and fly to heaven. But I'm not afraid like I used to be of falling into a horrid black hole either. Death's a mystery, and somehow I feel like it's a good mystery—one I'm ready for."

FACING THE BIG ONE

Sacred Anxiety strikes at the very root of the human predicament. It addresses our deepest dread, our terror in the face of the "Big One." In colloquial usage, this phrase often refers to death, the ultimate catastrophe for a living organism. On a spiritual level, the Big One is our encounter with God, our relationship to the universe as a whole. Death has traditionally been regarded as the moment in which we return to our source and meet our Maker.

Kierkegaard astutely pointed out that Sacred Anxiety is anxiety, and feels like anxiety but,

> not in the sense usually understood, in which anxiety is about something external, about something outside a person, but in the sense that he himself produces the anxiety.[3]

Sacred Anxiety originates in the awareness of our existential human predicament and ultimate fate. Here we enter a realm that science and psychology generally avoid—the realm of ultimate meanings. This is the realm of myth, mysticism, religion, and philosophy, our collective attempts to deal with the Sacred Anxiety that has troubled and fascinated human beings since the dawn of consciousness.

It is Sacred Anxiety that confronts us when we dare to ask ultimate questions: *Who am I?* and its companion question, *Who is God?* Is there someone or something greater than me to whom I am accountable? Sacred Anxiety is potentially far more challenging than either Toxic or Natural Anxiety because it questions the very foundation of our lives. For example, while Natural Anxiety worries about being able to achieve personal goals, Sacred Anxiety questions our very concept of success and asks, "Who is this person who is trying to achieve those goals?"

The image of the Angel serves as a symbol of Sacred Anxiety: not the cute, cherubic angel of popular culture, but the powerful, awe-inspiring messenger of God. (Our word "angel" comes from the Greek word *angelos,* meaning "messenger.") Angels are traditionally considered sources of spiritual wisdom and guidance. Yet they may initially appear as fierce and terrifying adversaries, as in the Biblical story of Jacob wrestling with the angel.

We naturally feel profound anxiety when we are visited by these divine emissaries. Sometimes it happens outside our awareness; we brush up against Sacred Anxiety's Angel on numerous occasions without realizing it, without paying attention to it. When we fail to recognize it, this powerful Angel can ignite a firestorm of Toxic Anxiety or supercharge our Natural Anxiety to an explosive level. Sacred Anxiety may attempt to get our attention through the underlying hum of anxiety that forms the background static in our daily awareness. It may hover just outside our consciousness as an amorphous feeling that we are somehow not quite good enough or that we have lost our way. More positively, it may visit us on occasion as a sense of awe or wonder.

Sacred Anxiety troubles us when major decisions loom— whether to marry a certain person or whether to take a new job in a distant city—and we feel unreconciled values tugging us in different directions. We experience Sacred Anxiety during those disconcerting episodes when we seem to lose our sense of who we are and what we are here for; we feel hollow and unreal. It may then descend upon us as panic, nervous breakdown, hysteria, or bottomless despair.

Sacred Anxiety rushes up from the unconscious whenever we are confronted with death, especially the death of someone close to us, and, most of all, when we encounter our own death.

It is the sudden, sinking dread we feel in our stomach when the biopsy results come back and the answer is not the one we had wanted to hear. Even a car accident that leaves us with only a minor injury can rip aside our customary veil of imagined security, exposing the transitory and uncertain nature of life.

There are times in all our lives when things appear to be spinning out of control and we fear we are losing our grip. Often our instinctive response is to clutch even more tightly in desperation. Yet these episodes actually may be moments when the universe is asking us to let go so that something better can come into our life. During a crisis, the Angel of Sacred Anxiety invites us to release our tight, controlling grip—the holding on for dear life that prevents the Angel from carrying us where we may truly need to go. Sacred Anxiety, when we begin to recognize it as an Angel that wishes to guide us, can become our most reliable companion, a source of wisdom, joy, love, and peace.

AWE IS THE DOORWAY TO GOD

It will be helpful to pause here a moment to consider the profound and emotionally charged word, "God." Although I use this traditional term, I do so in the broadest sense, as a symbol of the transcendent mystery, wholeness, and intelligence of the universe. But as God is ultimately undefinable, our definition of God is not nearly as important as our relationship with God. "Who do you say that I am?" is God's invitation to begin a conversation.

Therefore, the most challenging response to this question, and a perspective that is embraced by a growing number of spiritually conscious people from backgrounds both religious and nonreligious, is to engage in an ongoing conversation with God as an unfolding mystery, a dialogue in which we deepen our understanding of who God is and who we are. This conversation is as important to God as it is to us. The universe needs each of us in order to be whole.

In our exploration of the Eden myth, we found that Adam and Eve first experienced Sacred Anxiety after eating the apple of consciousness and meeting God in the garden. The encounter between the naked, finite human self and the ultimate of existence always evokes the emotion of Sacred Anxiety. Emily Dickinson, no stranger to this feeling, wrote:

I do not know the man so bold
He dare in lonely Place
That awful stranger Consciousness
Deliberately face—[4]

In religious terms, this experience is traditionally called the fear of God. When I was a child, this phrase troubled me. Why should I be scared of a loving God? The only kind of God I could imagine being afraid of was a wrathful, punishing deity, and I could never understand why having a fear of God was considered a good thing. Only much later did I understand that this disturbing phrase, which suffered from the use of the word "fear," was misleading. A much more accurate rendering of this vital concept would be "the awe of God," which refers to the unsettling yet uplifting blend of reverence, dread, and wonder evoked by the *mysterium tremendum:* the sublime apprehension of the vast universal intelligence that is beyond our understanding. This is the numinous dread-ecstasy that sends shivers up our spine when we stand in the presence of the ultimate reality.

Awe induces the bodily sensation of spiritual shivering that we witnessed in Adam and Eve's first encounter with God. This is the quaking of the Quakers and the shaking of the Shakers. Rudolf Otto, the German theologian, observed that this emotion "is something more than 'natural,' ordinary fear. It implies that the mysterious is already beginning to loom before the mind, to touch the feelings."[5] Plato described it in this way: "First a shudder runs through you, and then the old awe creeps over you."[6]

The difference between the worldly emotion of Natural

Anxiety and the spiritual experience of Sacred Anxiety is not simply one of degree or intensity. As Otto observed, "The awe or 'dread' may indeed be so overwhelmingly great that it seems to penetrate to the very marrow," such as during a time of great crisis or ecstatic experience. "But it may also steal upon [us] almost unobserved as the gentlest of agitations, a mere fleeting shadow passing across [our] mood."[7] This is the gentler and more subtle shivering that may come over us as we quietly watch an especially magnificent sunset. Or it may overtake us during a tender moment perhaps, as we hold a sleeping infant.

Few people, even the most scientifically inclined, are unfamiliar with this mysterious emotion. Microsoft's Bill Gates admitted, "Even though I am not religious, the amazement and wonder I have about the human mind is closer to religious awe than dispassionate analysis."[8]

An overwhelming feeling of gratitude often accompanies these experiences; the natural and ordinary human emotions become elevated into transcendent sensations of spiritual awe, the majestic, the inexorable, the overwhelming, and the inexpressible. Though it frightens us, it also fascinates us. We want to turn away, and we do; yet a moment later we turn to it again.

To be able to live with Sacred Anxiety is a sign of spiritual wisdom. The Taoist sage Lao Tzu must have shocked his contemporaries, as he does us today, with his paradoxical description of the enlightened master: "trembling like one who wades through an icy stream, insecure like one who is afraid of everything, humble like a guest in awe of his host."[9]

Goethe wrote that "Awe is the best of man"; yet, "the world's misprizing of the feeling" prevents us from surrendering to it. When we fight the feelings of Sacred Anxiety, they can transmogrify into mindless horror and terror beyond imagining. Our reaction is illustrated by how we have altered the meaning of the word itself: The word "aweful," meaning full of awe, has, with the passage of centuries, become the word "awful," meaning "terribly bad." When we resist awe, it turns awful.

The Shakers characterized the rigid ego whose prideful resistance prevents the infusion of divine grace as "Old Stiff." Rigidity and hardening of the self were equated with death and alienation from God. Surrender to the sacred shivering brought union with God and eternal life. Yet this surrender scares us to death, for it requires giving up the self. This death of the self must occur before we can be born again to our true nature. If we resist this temporary disappearance of the personal self, we find ourselves struggling against the most terrifying feelings of falling apart and going crazy. We feel attacked by a nameless dread that something horrible is about to happen.

Sacred Anxiety does not affect us only on rare occasions. It is something we live with, a subtle awareness that hums in the background of every moment of our existence. Awe invites us into God's presence, yet we often turn down the opportunity because we have not learned to trust the Angel to lead us home.

RESTORING A SENSE OF SACRED ANXIETY TO SOCIETY

Sacred Anxiety arose when we became conscious; it lives within us today as our conscience. Sacred Anxiety is the source of the classic human virtues, of a moral and ethical sensibility. It gives rise to the sacred guilt and sacred shame that guide us in doing the right thing even when no one is watching, because we feel the gaze of our higher self. (Natural Anxiety makes us do the right thing because we fear the worldly consequences if others find out. Sacred Anxiety makes us do the right thing because we are aware of the spiritual consequences of our actions.)

We live in an Age of Toxic Anxiety partly because we do not allow it to be an Age of Sacred Anxiety. Having a sense of the sacred restrains our human tendency to hubris. It guides us as stewards of the planet to keep the world in balance and our works in just proportion. This delicate balance between humanity and God has been a universal theme throughout the ages and across cultures. We find it in the saga of the Israelites and

Jehovah and in the histories of the ancient Chinese dynasties. When our human tendency to self-inflation leads to the construction of a Tower of Babel, the gods soon restore balance by sowing anxiety and confusion. When a civilization loses its way, a flood comes to cleanse the earth.

Today the reigning triumvirate of science, technology, and capitalism recognizes no limits to human activity: If we can do it, we will do it. This "anything goes" mentality has now saturated our entire culture. Modesty, the profound sense of self-chosen limits that lies at the heart of all spiritual and ethical systems, is no longer valued. Its companion virtue of humility, the noblest essence of humanity, reminds us that simply because we can do something does not mean that we should do it.

One of the reasons we are so anxious today is that the perennial moral qualities have been so devalued and their polar opposites have become highly rewarded by society and the media. Brashness, extremism, shamelessness, pandering, ambition, self-promotion, and greed swirl throughout our society. From the drug addict who kills with no remorse to the corporate executive who decimates an entire town with a factory closing and says it was just a business decision, we sense a chilling lack of conscience throughout society, an absence of healthy Sacred Anxiety.

The Cain complex has reached its apotheosis in certain aspects of modern civilization. Cain not only misused his power and destroyed his brother, but he brazenly lied to God about it. "Am I my brother's keeper?" is still one of the most relevant questions for humanity today. More than anything else, we need to restore a profound sense of Sacred Anxiety to our personal and public life today. Without it we will surely lose our way.

JUDGMENT DAY: NOT BEING GOOD ENOUGH

The very thought of our encountering God is anxiety producing. We much prefer to search for God than to actually meet

God. As C. S. Lewis dryly observed, the very moment we feel that we are about to meet our Creator, we "suddenly draw back. Supposing we really found Him? We never meant it to come to *that!*"[10]

Why do we draw back? The reason is as profound as it is simple. We do not feel we are good enough. We fear being judged by our Creator, a phenomenon the major Western religions have institutionalized as the Day of Judgment. Robert Frost described this existential dread: "There is the fear that we shan't prove worthy in the eyes of someone who knows us at least as well as we know ourselves. That is the fear of God."

Why is the feeling of not being good enough so nearly universal? Ironically, the one thing the homeless alcoholic and the high-achieving professional may have in common is their inner sense of not being quite good enough. Many successful people feel that whatever they do, it's never quite good enough to get the Anxious Chatterbox off their backs for long. The "impostor syndrome," the anxiety that others will find out we are not really who we present ourselves to be, is another manifestation of not feeling good enough.

Unless we understand the sacred roots of this feeling, we will never escape it and we will never feel good enough. From a spiritual perspective, we do not feel good enough because we are trying to play God and we know we are inadequate to the role. The Cain complex, as we saw earlier, is a dysfunctional reaction to Sacred Anxiety. It is an attempt to make our own self-image into God, to make the part into the whole. We try to assume the traditional attributes of God: We feel we must always know all the answers (omniscience); we must be able to do everything and fix everything (omnipotence); and we should be able to be everywhere at once and be everything to all people (omnipresence). No wonder we feel so much pressure in our lives!

And no wonder we end up feeling not good enough. When we attempt to be infinite and omnipotent, we are doomed to fail. Ultimately, the only remedy for this feeling of not being good enough is to admit that we are not good enough—that the part can never claim to be the whole. Our existential guilt is that we try to usurp God's role and pretend our small self is eternal and infinite. Our existential shame is that we continually fail. And our existential anxiety is that we will be found out.

If we are willing to face our Sacred Anxiety about our mortality and our limitations and surrender to the whole, then the universe can take us back. We can let go of the need to be God and simply be human. Paradoxically, as soon as we stop trying to be the whole, we can again feel one with the whole.

Our urge to avoid our Sacred Anxiety by inflating our self-image is so strong that we need to surrender the Cain complex daily. Here meditation and prayer become essential ways to surrender to Sacred Anxiety. This is why all religions foster prayer, warn against pride, and encourage humility. Islam (which means "surrender to God") urges its adherents to kneel and pray to Allah five times each day, continually interrupting the habit of self-inflation with surrender to the whole. Much of the effectiveness of the twelve-step programs such as Alcoholics Anonymous is based in the participants' willingness to admit this existential powerlessness and to acknowledge their shortcomings.

By listening to our guilt and shame in a different way, we can elevate them to the sacred level and use them as entry points to reconnecting with a loving and forgiving higher reality that is always ready to welcome us.

CULTIVATING SACRED ANXIETY

Unless we consciously create a place and a time for the sacred in our busy lives, we will not be able to receive the gifts the Angel wants to bestow upon us: gifts of faith, serenity, and joy. But before we can receive its gifts, we may need to wrestle with the Angel and experience the deep yet enlivening anxiety that the sacred evokes in us. The time spent working and keeping up with everything required for full membership in modern society makes it difficult to create sacred time for most of us.

Even Benedictine monks, who traditionally supported themselves with simple monastic labor, must now work outside the monastery to make ends meet. "Monastics have become workaholics, always rushing around. I don't think our life is any different from anyone else's," observes Father Timothy Joyce of Glastonbury Abbey in Hingham, Massachusetts.[11] If those who have chosen a monastic life must struggle today to find room for their spiritual lives, we can have compassion for ourselves as we attempt to create sacred space and time for our souls. The following practices can serve to deepen our relationship with the sacred realm.

SOLITUDE Solitude is different than being alone, and it is worlds apart from loneliness. Solitude is the paradoxical experience of feeling one's separate individuality most acutely while at the same time being imbued with a sense of oneness with the universe. We need to experience a space and time that is just our own. Lacking solitude, we build emotional walls to keep others at a distance.

Solitude enables us to develop a direct relationship with the infinite. Daily interactions focus us on the horizontal plane of life; in solitude we can cultivate the vertical axis through which the sacred enters our life. In the absence of outside attractions, the gravitational pull to our center can take us straight to our inner self. We usually avoid solitude because we are uncomfortable with our existential separateness—it evokes our Sacred Anxiety. Yet only when we find the courage to stand alone can we find our true self.

In solitude you meet your self. In the silence, you can listen to the "still, small voice" of your soul and hear the roar of infinity. Regain the joy of being a young girl or boy absorbed in solitary play. Reminisce and become absorbed in the story of your life. Dream and envision the future. Free yourself from the social shame and stigma that often prevents people in our society from feeling good about being alone or doing things alone. Solitude and friendship enhance each other rather than detract.

Solitude is the celebration of our aliveness as a conscious, independent self embraced by a loving universe.

NATURE Nature is our mother; being in nature is going home. The divine design is most apparent in the natural landscape. Nature's power to nurture us and to destroy us provokes our Sacred Anxiety. Whether we are feeling gratitude for the food on our plate or being awed by the force of a winter storm, we sense our vulnerability, our smallness, and our dependence on something greater.

We can cultivate the natural in our lives by going on a hike in the country, taking our dog for a walk around the neighborhood, or meditating on the flowers in a vase. We can even commune with nature by getting in touch with our own body and emotions, for we, too, are a force of nature. Nature has always been a haven for those seeking the sacred dimension of life, and she is ever ready to receive us.

SERVICE The sacred is made evident to us by service. It is through being of service to our fellow human beings that we affirm our oneness with them. The spirit of service is often sadly lacking in our economic interactions today. We may work hard and do a lot for others (and receive much from them), but if the spirit of service is absent, then work fails in its essential purpose: to bring us closer to the sacred.

Service is a tangible expression of the understanding that you and I are one. By serving each other, we open channels that affirm our essential oneness despite our separate forms. When we work primarily to earn money, we lose the sacred dimension of work. But we can restore the sacred to our activities by refusing to allow the material aspect to obscure the spiritual dimension.

As you work, ask yourself how sacred service manifests in what you do. Focus on your desire to benefit other people's lives in a way that expresses your unique gifts. It is in being creative that you align yourself with the creative force of the universe. Whatever you do can be done as service, your contribution to creation. Likewise, when you receive a service or a product, take time to recognize the life energy that someone else is contributing to you. You also can volunteer your time and energy to help others and to further causes you believe in. Service is the web that connects us with each other and with the sacred.

UNCONDITIONAL ACCEPTANCE To heal the not-good-enough sickness that afflicts us, we need to understand that it stems from our habit of judging. When we fear that something bad is going to happen or when we get upset because "everything went wrong today," we are suffering from our own judgments. Refraining from judging and blaming enables us to enter the sacred realm of unconditional acceptance where we are always good enough and nothing "bad" will ever happen to us.

We are addicted to judging because it is the prime function of the personal self; it validates our self-created reality. Adam and Eve began judging the moment they ate from the Tree of Knowledge of Good and Evil. The practice of nonjudging ushers us into the realm of Sacred Anxiety, a place in which we admit that we do not know enough to judge anyone or anything. Nonjudging reopens the gates of Eden. The great gift that nonjudging bestows upon us is the peace that passes understanding, the unconditional peace that comes when we stop trying to figure it out.

When we judge ourselves or others we are playing God again. Yet, ironically, even God is not judgmental. "He maketh his sun to rise on the evil and the good, and sendeth rain on the just and on the unjust."[12] The universe condemns nothing and accepts everything. If we truly want to emulate the divine, we will cultivate unconditional acceptance.

We feel powerful when we sit in judgment and make things "wrong" and "bad"; the ironic consequence is that we then begin to live in a bad world that is filled with things going wrong.

Perceiving the world in this way makes us feel unsafe and anxious. Jesus understood that judgment is a double-edged sword that injures us as well as others. He advised, "Judge not, that ye be not judged, For with what judgment ye judge, ye shall be judged."[13] And as we accept, so shall we be accepted.

Most of us have an idea of how we *want* things to turn out that quickly becomes the way we believe things *should* turn out. And of course if they don't, we think something has gone wrong or something bad has happened. When you boil down most of our fears and anxieties, what's left at the bottom is our fundamental dread about not having it our way. Every worry, every anxiety is a variation on this basic concern.

Buddha called this desire the root of all human suffering. As soon as we want things to be a certain way, we become anxious that they might not turn out that way. All spiritual traditions counsel us that the way to peace of mind involves letting go of having it "my way." We don't really know how our life will unfold. Misfortune often leads to deep inner growth and eventual success; good fortune can destroy a person. We need to cultivate the ability to experience the normal emotions that accompany the ups and downs of life, along with an awareness of a deeper security, beyond the fluctuations of circumstance. Serenity only comes when we accept the unguaranteed life and say, "not my way, but thy way." Cultivating the sacred attitude of acceptance assures that nothing bad will ever happen to us because we use every circumstance to increase our ability to love unconditionally.

BEING AND NONDOING If there is one thing we are good at, it's getting things done. Modern humanity has gotten more done in the last hundred years than in all the previous centuries combined. We are the can-do civilization: We have discovered more, built more, invented more, and produced more.

Doing binds us closer to the material world. When Adam and Eve were expelled from Eden they had to begin doing in order to survive. But today we have overdone doing—we lament the fact that there is too much to do every day and too little time to enjoy it. We have allowed ourselves to become "human doings" instead of human beings. We have lost sight of the old wisdom that there is a time for doing and a time for being.

To cultivate the sacred, we need to restore balance in our lives by practicing nondoing. Nondoing does not refer to either action or inaction, but to the motivating source behind either one. We've observed that both workaholism and procrastination are examples of the anxious, controlling ego; nondoing springs from serenity and enables the universe to act through us. It means that instead of automatically doing something, we ask if it needs to be done, if it should be done. Nondoing is doing the right things in the right way at the right time. It also means doing less and feeling more—letting go of anxiously trying to fix everything and simply being. Sometimes doing nothing is the wisest and most courageous response.

"Just do it" has been the motto of the twentieth century. If we are to survive and thrive in the coming century we need to add another guiding credo: Just let it be. We need to change our daily agenda from "How much can I get done today?" to "How can I find the right balance between doing and being in my life today?"

The difference between doing and nondoing is the difference between "my way" and "thy way." In various spiritual traditions, thy way is often simply called the Way. Buddhism and Taoism speak of the Way in terms that are both mystical and practical.[14] Before Christianity became known as Christianity it was also called the Way.[15] The Way refers to the mysterious process by which the universe is evolving. On a practical level, discerning the Way in any situation means that instead of limiting ourselves to the view from the self's little window, we step outside and look at the big picture. Letting go of having it my way means that the universe can begin to act through us and our life can begin to flow more effortlessly.

It is important to understand that nondoing should never be misinterpreted to mean being a doormat, being passive or wishy-washy, or being indifferent to injustice. Laziness is not nondoing, and apathy is not acceptance. Moral integrity, clear goals, and passionate commitment are needed to synchronize our doing with our being. The art of living requires us to develop the paradoxical capacity to go for it 100 percent while letting go 100 percent. This is the great challenge of life: to work toward our highest goals while being willing to let our goals (and even our life) go in an instant. It's a tough balancing act to learn, which is why we get a whole lifetime (and maybe more) to practice it.

When we become willing to let go of having it our way, our true self can emerge more fully into the world. We can align our goals with our higher purpose. True acceptance frees us to be even more energetic, courageous, effective, loving, and creative because we are no longer handicapped by our fears. The best antidote to the anxiety of not having it our way is to love "The Way It Is" and to work energetically toward our highest vision of "The Way It Can Be."

BLESSING This final way of cultivating the sacred in our lives involves recognizing our true purpose as human beings. We are here to bless the world and to bless each other.

Strangely, though we seldom hesitate to "damn" things, we often hesitate to bless them. We have been conditioned to imitate a harsh judgmental God instead of emulating a loving God. To bless means literally "to make sacred," to recognize the sacred dimension in all things. Damning takes away the sacred, blessing restores it. To love someone is to bless them.

For the sacred to become manifest it must at some point become a communal experience. Through the ages, worship and celebration have helped communities transcend individual differences and reconnect with their sacred source. Community rituals for blessing have largely disappeared from the modern world. Most of our communal experiences now consist of events such as the Super Bowl and TV sitcoms. Sacred celebration has become a lost art. Find a way to revive it. Join a meditation group, attend religious services, enjoy a concert, take a walk in nature with a friend, or create your own ritual of sacred celebration.

If you want to live in a loving world, bless it. Bless your neighbor as you bless yourself. The greatest gift you can give your children is your blessing. Bless your problems. Bless your anxiety and let it lead you home.

Chapter Fifteen

LIVING BETWEEN
LIFE AND DEATH

THE TWIN POLES OF EXISTENCE:
LIFE ANXIETY AND DEATH ANXIETY

We discovered earlier that anxiety could not be mastered until we viewed it through a trifocal lens that revealed its three strands. Now we can focus on Sacred Anxiety at its deepest root: Because human beings are individual organisms conscious of their separateness from one another and the universe, we are simultaneously confronted with both life anxiety and death anxiety. Our life anxiety is our fear of fully experiencing our aliveness, our creative power, and our existential isolation. Our death anxiety is about the dreaded annihilation of the self: losing power, being absorbed back into the universe, and ceasing to exist as an independent individual.

KERRY SLIPS ON AN EXISTENTIAL BANANA PEEL

Kerry, 28, had worked for seven years as a repairman for the phone company. His employer had recently merged with a larger corporation, and Kerry was suddenly without a job. This unexpected event reactivated certain anxiety symptoms that he had experienced in the past. He had been quite comfortable with the routine of his previous job and was unprepared for the soul-searching this job loss had forced upon him. He wasn't sure whether to set his sights on a solid career in the communications industry or to gratify his passion for sports by opening a sporting goods store with his friend Lorenzo, who also had been laid off. Meanwhile, he was living with the anxiety of being unemployed.

"I really don't know what I want to do," Kerry told me with evident frustration. "I thought I knew who I was, but now I realize that I don't, really." He said he wanted to explore issues of self-identity, yet looking within made him exceedingly uncomfortable. He had been vacillating within his comfort zone, unable to decide on a direction, but his unemployment compensation would be running out soon.

At his next evening appointment Kerry told me, "Today I did a job with this buddy of mine who's still working for the phone company. He had a complicated repair job to do at a supermarket. Because they let so many people go, now they're sending out one guy to do a two-man job, and I thought by going along I'd help him out and keep myself busy."

Several hours into their work, the store manager came up to Kerry and asked him a question about the repair. Kerry had become surprisingly flustered. He was able to refer the manager to his friend, but the manager's question had triggered a panic attack. For a few minutes Kerry had felt "dizzy, weird, panicky."

"I was sweating like crazy and my heart was racing a mile a minute," he recalled. "The supermarket scene looked unreal, like I was watching a movie. I felt like I was going to die." He had survived the episode using some of the anxiety mastery techniques he had learned, but he was still very troubled that such an ordinary question had shaken him so deeply.

On the surface level, Kerry had become anxious because he was pretending to be the phone company employee that he no longer was; he was concerned that the store manager might see through his façade. That could account for feeling some mild anxiety, but the sheer panic could only come from a deeper stratum of Kerry's being. As we delved into the mystery, it became clear that the manager's simple question had activated feelings of Sacred Anxiety in Kerry as he suddenly faced the overwhelming question that his conscious mind was trying so hard to avoid: "Who am I?" While he was at this suburban supermarket, Kerry had slipped on an existential banana peel and plunged free-falling into the twilight dimension of Non-Being.

TURNING THE CURSE OF PANIC INTO THE GIFT OF PEACE

Seeing through these temporary rips in the veil of consensual reality can actually be a gift that helps us find the true realm of inner peace. Although Toxic Anxiety is the least healthy form of anxiety and Sacred Anxiety is the most evolved form, the two have an eerie similarity, for both diverge from the province of culturally sanctioned reality. People who are undergoing an anxiety attack no longer see the world or experience themselves in the normal way. They experience unreality, the feeling Kerry had that the world around him was not real—a stage set, a movie. He felt that he was no longer participating in the world but observing it from a detached perspective.

In extreme anxiety, people also experience depersonalization, the sense that they don't feel like themselves. They may feel like robots, as if an alien force is controlling their body. Or they may feel disconnected from themselves, as if they are standing outside themselves, observing themselves. Depersonalization is the temporary loss of connection with one's sense of personal selfhood.

Anxiety often appears to threaten the fragile house we call our personality, the image that we build to validate our selfhood. When the flames of anxiety begin to lick at the walls of our house, we usually panic and try to put them out. And of course each time we manage to stifle them, it seems to work; at least for the moment the fire subsides and we repair the damage. The problem is that we thereby doom ourselves to be rushing around for our entire lives, putting out little fires here and there. The house we built as protection against anxiety becomes a prison of perpetual anxiety. And we live with the knowledge that, in the end, death will destroy our precious house forever.

People who experience panic are privy to an existential secret that most people are not: that one's self-identity can disintegrate at any moment because it is an illusion in the first place. During panic attacks people often feel that they are losing it, going crazy, or going to die. This feeling of being on the very brink of the gaping chasm of Non-Being is an utterly terrifying sensation that can best be understood as a near-death experience. When, in the grip of panic, they are feeling that they are going to die, it doesn't help very much to know that no one has ever died during a panic attack. It doesn't even help to remember from their own experience that they may have survived many such anxiety attacks.

Why is it that these intelligent people, when subject to anxiety attacks, cannot seem to learn from their own experience and that of others? This puzzling phenomenon occurs because it is difficult to overcome a nonrational experience with logic alone. People who panic will say they know it up here, pointing to their head but not down here, pointing to their body. No one would shake uncontrollably and have their heart rate zoom to twice their normal rate and experience more terror than ever before unless they truly feared they were dying. The reason they feel that they're dying is because they are dying. Instead of trying to get them to fit the consensual reality that they are not dying, we should ask instead: In what way are they dying?

Although they are not dying a physical death, these individuals are dying a psychological death. Their death throes signal the death of their everyday self and their customary reality, for their self-image as a rational, competent, in-control person has fallen to pieces. Their body feels like an alien entity, completely out of their control. Their normal world has been replaced by a terrifying vacuum that is about to suck them away into noth-ingness.

The more a person's sense of security is identified with stay-ing in control, the more frightening the experience will be. An extreme need to be in control is usually the result of an emo-tionally insecure childhood and represents the child's attempt to salvage some sense of personal power within an anxiety-producing environment. People who have panic attacks need to be reassured that they are not physically dying, but their death anxiety also needs to be taken seriously. Panic must be recog-nized as a very real type of psychological near-death experi-ence. Only then can concerns about identity, the beyond, and spirituality be addressed. This is not a substitute for coping skills and behavioral treatments, but it adds a layer that is essential for deeper healing.

Kerry's parents had both been alcoholics, and his childhood home had been an unsafe environment in which verbal and physical abuse was a daily possibility. His religious training had reinforced his feeling of living in an unsafe universe in which a strict God was waiting to punish him for doing anything wrong. While Kerry was growing up, it was not safe for him to feel or express his emotions nor to acknowledge the physical sensations that arose in his body; they had to be controlled at all costs. As a teenager, Kerry had also experienced the death of his adored grandparents and had been in a serious car acci-dent himself. One year prior to his first visit to me, his father had died. Like many people, Kerry did not have a healthy way to grieve these losses. Subconsciously, he viewed death as a black hole that could suck people—including himself—away at any moment.

The legacy of all these experiences for Kerry was that he lived in a hostile universe. Letting go meant letting go to chaos and terror, and that was exactly what his panic attacks felt like. Echoing the possessed-by-demons language of centuries ago,

Kerry told me, "I feel like if I let go, the anxiety will just rush in from out of nowhere and take over my whole body."

For Kerry, anxiety was a hostile, alien, and supremely destructive force that could invade his body and mind at any time. We have only to look at the popularity of many science fiction stories and horror movies that involve an alien life form invading and taking over the bodies of human beings to understand that this archetypal dread is not limited to people who experience panic; it reveals an unconscious anxiety that is widespread and perhaps universal.

In working with Kerry, I saw that he was caught between—and paralyzed by—his life and death anxiety. His deep fear of death made him anxious about letting go and relaxing, and his fear of life kept him from feeling his feelings, expressing his emotions, and making decisions. He needed to move forward in his life and make career choices, but he was avoiding doing so because he was afraid of making a mistake. Kerry needed to move inward and make peace with his own emotional history but instead he engaged in creating distractions. The more he tried to avoid anxiety, the more it oppressed him. His panic, while an extreme response to not having examined these issues, was a highly intense manifestation of the anxiety all of us experience in addressing these polar anxieties of life and death. We will return to Kerry later in this chapter to see how he began taking steps to resolve these issues.

DEATH ANXIETY: THE BOTTOMLESS ABYSS OF NON-BEING

In his landmark book, *The Denial of Death,* Ernest Becker presented the radical view that the main force driving human beings and human culture is our awareness of our own mortality. Early humans were so conscious of their own vulnerability to death that they named themselves mortals—literally "those who die." Immortality was reserved for the gods alone. Death is the ultimate failure for an organism committed to its own self-preservation. In its most biological aspect, Sacred Anxiety is simply the terror experienced by a living organism aware of its own inevitable death. Becker further argued that modern society, to a far greater degree than preceding ones, has tried to deny the power death has over our lives. The demise of traditional cultures, mythologies, and religions has left us with even more to fear from death. "What characterizes modern life is the failure of all traditional immortality ideologies," Becker wrote.

The knowledge that we will die implants death anxiety ineradicably in our mind. The awareness that we do not know the time or manner of our death intensifies it even more. Our terror escalates further when we realize that we do not know what will happen to us after we die. This anxiety is unique to human beings. Animals do not worry about dying; one day they simply die. We think about dying, or suppress our thoughts about it, many times throughout our life. It has been said that an animal dies a single death, but human beings die ten thousand deaths. No wonder death is our ultimate repression, so bone-rattlingly terrifying that few of us allow its here-and-now possibility to enter our minds.

Rollo May astutely identified our paramount concern to be our "existence as a personality." Therefore, the ultimate threat to the self must be its own nonexistence. Behind every threat of personal failure lies the deeper threat to the personality—the final failure of death. Every loss, every anxiety about any potential loss, reverberates within our unconscious mind down to the level of Non-Being. These upwellings of Sacred Anxiety do not require a definable trigger. They often occur out of the blue, for no discernible reason—which makes them even more terrifying to the cause-fixated rational mind. Yet our unconscious mind often knows more than our rational mind can notice.

The simple but profound truth that the self fears is that the ultimate growth of the self is to become non-self. When an apple seed succeeds in fulfilling its destiny of growing into an apple tree, it also succeeds in destroying itself as a seed; in the same way, the destiny of the self is to grow beyond itself. And at the moment it does so, the personal self is transformed or, from the self's perspective, destroyed. To truly succeed in achieving our ultimate purpose as human beings is to disappear as an individual. Naturally, most of us have mixed feelings about that.

From the self's limited perspective, both Being and Non-Being mean one thing: destruction and death. Although a seed has no free will and cannot resist its transformation into a tree, a human being can and usually does resist transformation. Part of our resistance is because we associate the loss of self-identity with both insanity and death. Yet letting go of a limiting self-identity is also the only way to salvation and oneness.

The most challenging way for us to regard death is to courageously explore its here-and-now reality, to converse with the mystery of our human existence. If what we dread most about death is the possibility of losing our self, then death—the dissolution of the personality—can occur at any moment. As mystics and spiritual teachers have told us for centuries, this experience of non-self also can be one of the most direct routes to enlightenment and serenity. We must lose our life to find it.

LIFE ANXIETY: THE BLAZING LIGHT OF BEING

Life anxiety is often harder to understand than death anxiety because we are all supposedly in favor of living. We want to live; we want prosperity, success, abundance, and eternal life. We appear to want it all. But do we really? Or do we want just a little more than we have now? This reluctance to move too far out of our comfort zone is illustrated by a poll that found that most people, when asked how much money they would like to make, name a figure only $10,000 to $20,000 higher than their current income.

Do we really want eternal life, infinite wealth, and power? Do we really want to be as gods? Or are we overwhelmed by our infinite, eternal potential?

As a psychotherapist, I have seen the power of self-sabotage at work in scores of talented men and women. In the public arena of politics, sports, and entertainment, we have observed that the rich and famous suffer from self-sabotage along with everyone else. It seems that even at the moment of our greatest success, when life energy begins to course through us at a higher voltage and we sense we are about to jump to a higher level, all too often our nervous system short-circuits at the very instant of transformation.

The existential basis of our life anxiety, the fear of success, is the trepidation we feel when we approach the godlike state of becoming true co-creators of reality. The more that things go our way, the more afraid we become of our own power: We become afraid of becoming "too big for our britches" and "getting a swelled head." With greater power comes greater responsibility and greater expectations; we begin to feel that it is all too much, that more energy is rushing into us than we can handle. We feel in danger of bursting, falling apart. While death anxiety is the dread of collapsing into nothingness, life anxiety is the terror of exploding into everythingness.

This terror of flying too high is well-illustrated in such myths as Phaethon and Icarus. The gods punish hubris, chastising those who try to make the self into something bigger than it is. Even the familiar children's rhyme about Humpty Dumpty addresses this fear of heights and suggests that it begins very early in life. The anxiety described here is that of falling apart and never being put back together again. Our self-image has fallen to pieces and even the royal forces of the conscious mind cannot restore wholeness:

Humpty Dumpty sat on a wall.
Humpty Dumpty had a great fall.
All the king's horses and all the king's men
Couldn't put Humpty together again.

Yet as with death anxiety, our true life anxiety is not about some future overexpansion or explosion; it is about the fact that our self-image, our personality, could fall apart at any moment.

If we look carefully, we will discover that life and death anxiety are two sides of the same coin—a coin that can flip back and forth with tremendous speed. Life anxiety evokes death anxiety, and vice versa. The more alive we feel, the more aware we become of the possibility of death; the closer we come to death, the more vividly we experience our aliveness. Although the extremes of life and death provoke us to terror, perhaps the most excruciating place to be is precisely where we find ourselves: always in between the two.

DEATH IN THE MIDST OF LIFE

Life and death anxiety can attack us in a terrifyingly immediate way as the threat of existential Being and Non-Being, for both threaten the existence of the self. They haunt every moment of our existence, just as the disturbing nothingness of quantum physics lurks within the reassuringly solid world around us. Throughout our life, we unconsciously sense that at any moment the illusion of selfhood can dissolve or be torn away, revealing our nothingness. We constructed our personality to cover our psychological nakedness, our feeling of being nothing in the face of God, or the universe, and we live with the constant anxiety that we will dissolve back into the nothingness from which we emerged. It is not only the destruction of the personality that we dread, but the realization that it is a self-constructed illusion and never actually existed in the first place! This is the essential self-knowledge that Buddha reminds us we are so busy ignoring.

So the terrifying fact is that even short of death we can lose our selfhood. When we declare, "I almost died of embarrassment," it is not physical death, but self-image death that we feel we have so narrowly escaped. If even the slight threats to our self-image that we term embarrassments can feel so life-threatening, what of true madness, insanity? For even more than death, we fear losing our mind or going crazy. If I become physically ill, my sense of "I" can remain healthy. But if I become mentally ill, it is my very sense of "I" that is affected.

Our anxiety about our own Non-Being is a major reason we become trapped in the comfort zone. We recoil from relaxing too deeply into the rejuvenation zone because it lies next to the abyss of Non-Being. It is not merely anxiety about revealing our faults and inadequacies that keeps us from growing. What we dread most is revealing the nonexistence of our very self—exposing the fiction of our carefully constructed personality. As the American philosopher Eric Hoffer observed:

> Our greatest pretenses are built up not to hide the evil and the ugly in us, but our emptiness. The hardest thing to hide is something that is not there.[1]

In fact, that is an excellent definition of the personality: the "something that is not there."

The well-adjusted normal personality generally can manage quite successfully to keep the terror of Non-Being out of awareness and maintain the social fiction of being an individual self. The healthy defenses of normality protect us from becoming conscious of the strange realms beyond our ego boundaries. But the more fragile and fragmented personality that has never quite formed completely because of childhood deprivation or trauma is not nearly so well-defended against the existential vastness of outer space. Those who are subjected to the altered states of anxiety and depression are much more in touch with the anxiety of Non-Being than most people. This is why they may live with the daily dread of falling apart, and experience the heart-stopping panic of near-death experiences as they teeter on the brink of the abyss of nothingness.

THE WISDOM OF PANIC

Anxiety attacks are an invitation to personal and spiritual growth. When the healthy, self-renewing process of psychological death and rebirth is blocked by Toxic Anxiety, the pressure for growth builds up and can erupt into panic and then collapse into depression. Psychological panic, the kind that erupts during an anxiety attack, is the revenge of the repressed. It strikes when we have become dangerously estranged from our body and our true feelings. It is the mindbody's attempt to restore balance in a situation of extreme alienation, usually associated with prior trauma or deprivation.

When Pan, god of the primitive emotions, has been suppressed for too long, he gets our attention with an earth-shaking tantrum we refer to as "panic." The ancient Greeks visualized Pan as a half human and half animal figure. He symbolizes the uneasy balance we strive to maintain between the emotional animal self that dwells in the brain's limbic system and the more evolved rational, socialized self that resides in the cerebrum.

People who experience panic can learn to acknowledge their feelings of dying and know that these feelings signal a kind of psychological death, not an imminent physical death. We can begin to ask: What parts of me need to die? Which old, limiting self-images do I want to let go of? What are the obsolete models of life and death that I am operating under?

Panic is not only an experience of dying but also an awareness of acute aliveness! It is a simultaneous encounter with both life and death anxiety. We can also ask: Which parts of me want to become more alive? Could I see this not just as a death experience, but as an experience of rebirth, the arrival of a new self struggling to be born? Panic, this dysfunctional state of Toxic Anxiety, often can be transformed into an invaluable opportunity to explore the realm of Sacred Anxiety. In traditional cultures, people who were touched by such altered states often were selected for special spiritual training and became the shamans of the tribe.

Experiences of high anxiety and panic bring us the awareness that we can die at any moment and that death can lead to rebirth. They remind us that our personality is just a convenient construction we use to get around in the world, a wonderful fiction that enables us to write our life story—and one we need to let go of often so that we can remember our greater self. Certainly, experiencing trauma, especially in childhood, can become a handicap in dealing with anxiety. Yet many people have learned to use trauma as an accelerated course in life's school of anxiety. When Toxic and Sacred Anxiety are mixed together, as they were in Kerry's case, the most important course of action is to unravel these from one another. The toxic residue from the past can be healed and transformed, while the sacred can be embraced.

KERRY'S HEALING

Kerry and I began to peel back the layers of defenses that he had built up within himself. He began to recognize how and when he slammed the lid down on his emotional self. Gradually, he was able to restrain the impulse to suppress his inner self. He learned, through meditation and relaxation exercises, that it was finally safe to be in his body and safe to feel his feelings.

Kerry was able to become much more confident about letting go of his tight grip on his emotions and the desperate need to control his body after one particular counseling session. During a guided meditation, Kerry—with surprising ease for one so afraid of letting go—was able to imagine himself dying. He felt his spirit floating out of his body, drifting up above the clouds and into the warmth of the sunny blue sky. The blissful smile on his face confirmed that he was enjoying his expanded awareness. He practiced coming back into his physical body and then drifting upward again.

Through this experience Kerry was able to connect with the part of himself that knew the universe could be a friendly place and that letting go of his body could usher in feelings of happiness and well-being. Having ventured into this higher aspect of his consciousness, he began the process of decontaminating his spiritual life from the toxic conditioning he had received earlier in life. His panic attacks diminished and then disappeared. He was able to face his death anxiety without going numb; he accepted it and enjoyed the positive death experience that occurs in deep relaxation.

What Kerry discovered as he looked within was not the terribly flawed self he had feared, but a man who had heroically survived a traumatic family environment; a resilient man who had learned from his parents' experience and had never become addicted to alcohol. He saw that he had carried a heavy burden of anxiety and shame into adulthood and that it was time to lay it down—to leave home and explore who he was in the world.

Kerry began to face his life anxiety. He realized that he had not yet fully accepted the adult responsibility of defining his own identity in the world. As he healed his childhood wounds and began to have compassion for himself, he found that he was growing up psychologically in a way that enabled him to accept both the anxiety and the excitement of being an independent self. Accepting the unguaranteed life, he decided to focus his energy on opening a sporting goods store with his friend Lorenzo. Previously, he had been caught in an either/or struggle between a corporate career in communications and the dream of owning his own store. Now his more-integrated self began to see the possibility for a both/and solution. Kerry realized that he could combine his love of sports and his fascination with electronics and specialize in selling hi-tech sports equipment through a retail store and via the Internet.

Kerry now began the hard work of making his dream into a reality. He was not free from anxiety, but now he knew how to transform it appropriately into either relaxation or excitement. He was ready to live life on its own terms—in between life and death.

EMBRACING THE GREAT POLARITY

Otto Rank wrote that between the twin poles of life anxiety and death anxiety, "the individual is thrown back and forth all his life."[2] This is the ultimate paradox for human beings—we are self and non-self, we have an independent existence and yet we do not. We are both earthly creatures and heavenly beings, and the tug of war between our dual natures can create tremendous anxiety in daily life. Even the smallest incidents, such as someone brusquely bumping into us on the sidewalk, can evoke this dual pull: should we assert ourselves, push back, express our irritation, or should we gracefully let it go, forgive, flow with it?

We have explored our dread of the ultimate states of Non-Being and Being and we have seen how we can become paralyzed by trying to avoid them. But we also crave these states. We crave any stimulation that accentuates our sense of aliveness—sex, caffeine, power, thrilling movies, and roller coaster rides. We also have an overwhelming desire to lose our self. We try to lose our self in a movie, in a cause, in alcohol, and in sex. We desire the sweet release of oblivion—to be free of the burden of the self for even a few moments is bliss! At these times we desperately want to give up the same precious self that we defend so vehemently at other times. Given that we so deeply dread and crave these two polar opposites, it is easy to understand how we can be tossed back and forth by them from the moment we are born until the day we die.

Yet there is a state that may make us even more anxious than both Being and Non-Being, and that is the state we are in right now: the in-between state. At certain times, we may become oppressed, tortured, and paralyzed by an excruciating sense that we are trapped between the Scylla of Being and the Charybdis of Non-Being. For example, after the unexpected death of a close friend, St. Augustine poignantly described the great anxiety he felt as he was forced to confront the transitory and unpredictable nature of human life: "I was at once utterly weary of life and in great fear of death."

This is the ultimate existential double bind: When we turn and run from life anxiety, we run smack into the gaping abyss of death anxiety, then when we flee from death anxiety, we run straight into the blazing fire of life anxiety. While animals enjoy their simple, instinctive life and the angels enjoy their transcendent existence, we are caught between heaven and earth, continually trying to find a balance between our dual natures.

Life and death is the great polarity of human existence. If we accept this and relax with this paradoxical anxiety then we can be nourished and supported by both poles. What a glorious position to be in! Animals lack consciousness and angels lack bodies. We have both. The Greek gods were constantly coming down from Mount Olympus to earth, taking on bodies, and mingling with mortals because it was so much more interesting down here! As Kierkegaard noted:

> If a human being were a beast or an angel, he could not be in anxiety. Because he is a synthesis, he can be in anxiety; and the more profoundly he is in anxiety, the greater is the man.[3]

If the universe could speak to us it might say, "You are where it's at. You are the meeting place of opposites. You are the point at which the circle completes itself. You are the channel through which possibility becomes actuality. You are the universe evolving. You are the incarnation of God. You are the living mystery."

We human beings hold one great trump card: freedom of choice. We can choose to live in harmony with the great polarity. As we learn to live more consciously with life and death, instead of being tortured and trampled by them, we can be nourished and massaged by them. F. Scott Fitzgerald was referring to this ability to live gracefully with paradox when he observed:

> The test of a first-rate intelligence is the ability to hold two opposed ideas in the mind at the same time, and still retain the ability to function.[4]

Of course this is virtually impossible without a well-developed sense of humor. One of the most powerful ways to liberate ourselves from our most dreaded anxiety is to laugh at it. Anxiety hates being laughed at and begins to shrivel up with the very first glimmer of a smile. The more we accept the paradoxical nature of life, the more we develop a sublime sense of humor about the human predicament.

The capacity to smile in the face of adversity or disappointment is an outward sign of inner wisdom—the healthy detachment that Buddha said is essential to mental equilibrium. A sense of humor helps us to live gracefully with the paradoxes. A smile affirms that we are safe and gives us the courage to take that next step. Working with the great polarity of life means opening ourselves more fully to the ecstasy of Being—to power, individuation, pleasure, aliveness, joy, freedom, self-expression, giving, growth, light, consciousness. It also means simultaneously opening ourselves to the ecstasy of Non-Being—to surrendering, relaxing, receiving, letting go, following the Way, being nothing, and being one with everything.

We can develop our ability to venture voluntarily into the divine realms of Being and Non-Being and then return to the domain of the self, carrying blessings from beyond back to our world. As we learn to dance with the great polarity, we begin to feel safer in the world and to apprehend our true vastness and our eternal nature. In the Gospel of Thomas, Jesus said, "When you make the two into one, you will become true human beings and have the power to move mountains."[5] Beyond the great polarity lies the oneness from which it sprang into being.

BRINGING ACCEPTANCE AND AWARENESS TO THE GREAT POLARITY

We may become paralyzed between polarities as we seek to somehow reconcile them. When we can perceive nothing concrete to fight against or to flee from, we often freeze; when we feel that there is nowhere to run and nowhere to hide, we panic and become paralyzed by confusion. Our breathing becomes shallow and rapid, our heart thumps rapidly, our muscular system becomes immobilized, and our mind races—dysfunctional responses that simply enable anxiety to torture us mercilessly.

Fortunately, we can avoid becoming paralyzed and panicked by the polarities of life and death. By choosing to sit with anxiety, using acceptance and awareness (the first two steps of the A$^+$ Formula), we avoid the twin traps of fighting anxiety or trying to run from it. Instead of letting the twin poles of anxiety paralyze us, we voluntarily acknowledge that, in an existential sense, we are always caught between them.

A revered rabbi was once asked how he managed to live with such serenity amid life's existential paradoxes and ever-changing circumstances. He replied, "I have two pockets into which I can reach at any time according to my needs. In my right pocket I keep the words: For my sake the world was created. In my left pocket I keep the words: I am dust and ashes."

The following is a simple exercise for learning to sit with life and death.

When I enter this process myself, I let go of trying to find my security in temporal circumstances. I resign from playing God and pretending that the fate of the world hangs upon my every move. Gradually, I find myself being connected to a larger reality. As soon as I let go of whatever I was hanging on to for dear life, I notice that in its place I am now connected to something far greater. Sometimes, I feel myself expanding into the universe and becoming part of this endless creation. I notice that the ups and downs of my little life are not so important. I observe that the universe is working, evolution is happening, and God is everywhere. In this meditative state I disappear into the sea of Non-Being for a while. Later, I return, better able to see things in their proper perspective, and to accept my state of not knowing.

We can learn a lot about ourselves by identifying what we have attached ourselves to. If we cling to life's changing circumstances we are in for a bumpy ride. But when we stop demanding that life be a certain way and accept all the possibilities inherent in life, we can align ourselves with the universal force. When our whole world is falling apart, we will fall apart with it if we try to hold on. If we let go, we stand a very good chance of discovering our true self—it's the part of us that's left after everything has fallen apart.

SITTING WITH LIFE AND DEATH

When you experience a vague anxiety, sit with it. Notice that life anxiety towers in front of you and death anxiety looms behind you. Have these dual anxieties begun to squeeze you into a claustrophobic little comfort zone? Choose to expand your awareness. Remind yourself that you are safe. Breathe deeply and fully to remind your body that it is safe.

Now volunteer to look at life anxiety. Bring your awareness into the present moment and express gratitude for your aliveness in this moment. Allow yourself to simply sit with pure Being for a while. Ask yourself if there is some way that you are avoiding becoming more alive. Is there something you need to do, something you could allow yourself to feel more fully, something you need to express? Let yourself feel what you need to feel. Visualize yourself doing what you need to do. Volunteering to move into your personal growth zone enables you to take the amorphous cloud of life anxiety and focus it into taking your next step in life.

Now volunteer to contemplate the death anxiety lurking behind you. Relax and allow the present moment to be perfect just the way it is. Sit with Non-Being and imagine your own nonexistence.

Remind yourself that if God and the universe can accept things the way they are right now, then maybe you can too. Notice how you have been trying to have it your way. What are the conditions you are placing on life? What is it that you are making wrong, bad, or unfair? Imagine the worst that can happen and try to get a sense of what you have been holding on to.

After you have identified your preconceptions, demands, or conditions, imagine letting them go, knowing that you can take them back again if you want to. Let go (as best you can) of whatever you have been pinning your hopes on, and accept that your life is unfolding in a way you can never fully comprehend. Sometimes, to experience peace of mind, we may be required to let go of the very things to which we are most deeply attached. Accept not knowing how things will turn out.

In this way, we can use any experience of anxiety to practice facing Being and Non-Being, transforming them from dreaded unknowns into the great polarity of existence that nourishes and guides us as we follow our path in life. The more effortlessly we can move between the polarities of our life, the less anxiety and stress we feel. To be able to fully develop and express our individual selfhood (our radiant Being) and the next moment to dissolve into our non-self nature (our empty Non-Being) enables us to live harmoniously with others and to enjoy living in between heaven and earth.

TRANSFORMING LIFE AND DEATH ANXIETY INTO SERENITY

Death is the great mystery of life. The big question, the most unfathomable one for all of us is, What happens when I die? There is a part of me that can't wait to find out how the story ends—what happens after death? The meaning we give life is inseparable from the meaning we give death. A universal essence within me knows that, when the body and brain cease functioning, the adventure of consciousness continues in some other form. Even our daily need to visit the dark realm of sleep reminds us of the presence of death—the "big sleep"—in the midst of life. Our desire for relaxation is evidence of our need to "die" regularly, and of death's rejuvenating powers.

Our anxiety about death keeps us from recognizing our own true and healthy love of death. When we accept the reality and the mystery of death, we can begin to love death in a positive way, as a part of the perpetually renewing cycle of life, as liberation and reunion with our Source. Far from signifying any morbid desire to die, loving death simply means accepting death as a natural and sacred part of life.

When we deny or ignore both our death anxiety and our death love, the death urge turns toxic and we are doomed to act it out destructively as self-sabotage or as injurious behavior toward others. Freud called this repressed attraction to death *thanatos* and described how it turns into aggression and self-destruction. But if we embrace the Grim Reaper, we find that its terrifying appearance is nothing but the embodiment of our own fears. Wise men and women throughout the ages spent their lives preparing for and becoming friends with death, so that when it came it neither took them by surprise nor made them anxious. Once accepted, it is transformed into the Angel who guides us on our eternal journey. Our death anxiety dies and is reborn as a sacred love of death.

Just as embracing death anxiety allows us to experience a healthy love and acceptance of death, choosing to face the life anxiety of selfhood will usher us into the sacred realm of abundant and eternal life. Then we can finally allow life energy (what Freud called *eros*) to course through us, free and unfettered. Our life anxiety becomes a sacred love of life that experiences the miracle of aliveness with wonder and gratitude. When we love both life and death there is nothing left to fear.

Chapter Sixteen

SACRED ANXIETY:
A PATHWAY
TO OUR SOURCE

LESSONS IN SACRED ANXIETY FROM THE
LIVES OF SPIRITUAL TEACHERS

What would happen if we really let anxiety work on us and take us past the boundaries of our limited self and into the realms of spirit? The founders of the world's major religions, Moses, Mohammed, Jesus, and Buddha, have much to teach us in this regard. It may seem surprising at first to contemplate such luminous figures as these in terms of anxiety, yet each of them was actually led to his spiritual understanding by Sacred Anxiety.

Contrary to the popular impression left by later legends and stories, none of these revered masters was born blessed by serenity and security. Each was afflicted by an anxiety so intense that it demanded his total attention and took him to the very brink of madness. Each suffered a traumatic childhood and deep emotional wounds, yet found a way to use his suffering as an opportunity for the profoundest level of healing. Each transformed the Toxic Anxiety left by the wounds of his childhood and the

Natural Anxiety of challenging social conditions into Sacred Anxiety. Each found the courage to face the ultimate terror of Sacred Anxiety and underwent a transformative experience in which the wall separating the self from God came tumbling down. Now possessing a direct connection to the deepest source of love, each was able to return to the world, bringing with him a fresh revelation concerning the true nature of human life.

Buddha's life, the story of one who had it all and yet felt a strange emptiness, has a special resonance today for many modern men and women whose relative success and material security still leave them vaguely unsatisfied. We saw in Chapter 9 how Buddha encountered Natural Anxiety outside the castle walls. The larger story of Buddha's life dramatically illustrates anxiety's role as a guiding Angel who leads us to serenity.[1]

BUDDHA: THE AWAKENED ONE

Prince Siddhartha was born about 2,500 years ago to Queen Maya and King Suddhodana, who ruled one of India's wealthiest feudal kingdoms. As was the custom in those times, Queen Maya left the palace with her retinue to journey to her parents' castle to give birth. Unfortunately, the queen began to experience birth pains before she had reached her parents' home. A prolonged labor, difficult and painful for both mother and child, took place in the middle of the forest, and they returned as quickly as possible to Suddhodana's castle. The baby boy was healthy, but Maya was unable to recover her strength; she died a few days after reaching the castle.

Suddhodana was devout, but he was also strong-willed. The court astrologers predicted that his newborn son would become a great man, either a powerful worldly ruler like his father or a renowned spiritual leader. Because Prince Siddhartha was his only child, Suddhodana was determined that the boy would follow in his own footsteps and rule the kingdom. His will hardened even more after the death of his beloved wife. "The gods have taken my wife, but they will not take my son away from me to become a wandering monk," he vowed.

Prajapati, Maya's sister, cared for the young prince as if he were her own son. Suddhodana decided that the best way to ensure that Siddhartha would become a king rather than a monk would be to shield him from all suffering. He knew that suffering led to questioning, and that questions about life and death led men to spirituality. So Suddhodana decreed that no effort be spared in providing his son with a happy and carefree life. Most important, no one could ever tell Siddhartha about his mother's tragic and painful death; the child grew up assuming that his aunt Prajapati was his mother. He lived a life of luxury within the confines of the castle and its spacious grounds, tutored by the most intelligent and learned teachers in the kingdom—with, of course, as little mention of philosophy and religion as possible.

Siddhartha was a happy child, but as he grew older he became moody and introspective. Why did he sense such a dark undercurrent, such a vague sense of unease, in the midst of this earthly paradise? He did not have a name for it, nor a reason for it, which only made it more disturbing. He was expected to be a strong and confident leader and take over his father's throne when he was older. Thousands of boys would be thrilled to have such a glorious opportunity. Yet Prince Siddhartha did not feel enthusiastic when he contemplated his royal future.

His powerful, domineering father was always busy with affairs of state. Though Suddhodana loved Siddhartha, he was a distant figure in the boy's life. Occasionally, Suddhodana would ask his moody son, "What is wrong with you? I have given you everything you need and more!" And indeed, Siddhartha had every material possession he desired, the finest food, the most exquisite entertainment, and every sensual delight imaginable. His strange ambivalence about his good fortune made him feel confused and guilty.

As he approached manhood, Siddhartha's anxiety and curiosity propelled him out beyond the confines of the royal compound in which he had spent his young life. One morning, slipping out of the castle before dawn, he ventured into the outside world and, for the first time, encountered life's insecurities, raw and unvarnished. We have seen earlier how Prince Siddhartha learned about sickness, old age, poverty, and death and was plunged into the deepest level of Sacred Anxiety. After this he could no longer enjoy the privileged life of a wealthy prince. Even he, with all his riches, was subject to the anxiety inherent in human life; all the knowledge of the wisest people, all the vast material resources, and all the love of his family could not protect him from life's precariousness and death's certainty.

At first Siddhartha tried to distract himself from this disquieting revelation by throwing himself into his royal duties. As his father's only son, he knew that he must uphold the family tradition. He knew that he should be grateful for all his father had given him and he did not wish to disappoint him. Yet anxiety dogged his every step, giving him no peace as he went about his princely tasks. "What do they matter, any of these things that I do for my parents or for my subjects, when all must suffer and die in the end? There is no meaning in anything that I do!"

Then he remembered the holy man, the saddhu he had seen, meditating serenely in the midst of the marketplace. Siddhartha craved his simple life and his peace of mind. That is what he wanted to do: to be free from worldly demands and to seek the truth of existence. Yet how could he desert his family and his station in life? Which path demonstrated courage and which cowardice?

Tortured by this conflict day and night, Siddhartha tried everything he could to suppress and deny it. He worked longer and more compulsively, trying to surpass his father's success in amassing riches. He could not sleep at night until he had drunk several bottles of wine. He sought relief in the momentary release of sexual activity with the many willing young women available to him. Siddhartha became short-tempered and found his moods swinging wildly from one day to the next. At times he withdrew from all social interactions, anxious that he might fall apart or that someone might look into his eyes and see the hollowness inside. At other times he sought out companions, drinking and talking non-stop into the night.

Suddhodana and his advisers pressured Siddhartha into getting married, hoping that having a family of his own would make him curb his wild behavior, settle down, and carry out his royal responsibilities with dignity. Soon Siddhartha wedded a beautiful, loving woman named Yasodhara in a sumptuous and spectacular celebration. The months following his wedding were some of the happiest Siddhartha had ever experienced, and his troubling moods, though not gone entirely, were far less frequent.

Within the year, Yasodhara became pregnant and the couple's joy grew deeper. Before the baby was due she journeyed to her parents' home to give birth. Siddhartha became very anxious in her absence and worried constantly that some misfortune would befall her while she was gone. When she returned with a healthy baby boy, he was greatly relieved. But when he gazed upon his radiant wife and newborn child, the joy he felt was mixed with a strange melancholy and a vague anxiety. He became increasingly upset with himself—could he not enjoy even this innocent bliss without the intrusion of dark and unsettling thoughts?

One afternoon, in the midst of a busy day, Siddhartha's head began to spin. His heart was racing and his breath came rapidly. He felt dizzy and faint. Catastrophic thoughts rushed through his mind, "I am dying! I am dying!" Then everything went black.

When he regained consciousness, Prajapati was at his side. "Mother," he pleaded desperately, "can you not help me? I feel I am going crazy. Even the sight of my wife and newborn son fill me with dread!"

Out of compassion for Siddhartha's excruciating turmoil, Prajapati finally broke her promise to Suddhodana, and told Siddhartha the story of his traumatic birth, his mother's tragic death, and the court astrologers' prophecy. Siddhartha realized that the birth of his son had awakened deeply buried memories of his own anxiety-filled entrance into the world and the loss of his mother. All the feelings he had felt during his entire life made sense at last. He understood why, in the midst of the beautiful façade his father had created for him, he had always sensed the existence of suffering.

Then Siddhartha's lifelong anxiety turned to anger. He stormed into his father's royal chamber, "Why did you deceive me? Why did you contrive to control my destiny?" After a tempestuous confrontation, father and son wept and reconciled. Siddhartha understood that, although his father's willful deception had caused him much emotional suffering, it had not been done out of malice, but out of Suddhodana's own unresolved anxiety about loss and death. Suddhodana finally realized that all his kingly power could not stop his son from following his own path *in life. Siddhartha forgave his father, feeling even more committed to un-raveling the source of human suffering.*

Next Siddhartha went to his wife. They began to talk, painfully, truthfully. Siddhartha felt his wife's love for him. It made it even more difficult for him to tell her what he knew he needed to do—to be free to seek the truth of his existence.

Siddhartha realized that no one could really understand what he was doing; he did not even understand it himself. Yet when the decision to leave was made and announced, along with a searing pain in his heart, Siddhartha began to feel a sense of peace and freedom deeper than any he had known before. He felt like a boat, previously tethered to the shore, now untied and moving swiftly, caught for the first time by the current of his own life.

The next day Siddhartha left the castle before the sun was up. But the peace he had felt was short-lived. Now anxiety pursued him even more fiercely. He had seen through the veils of his childhood condition-ing and was free at last. Now what would he do with his freedom?

Knowing that he craved the serenity of the holy monk he had seen sitting in the marketplace, Siddhartha donned the traditional robes and joined a group of holy men who lived in the forest. He listened to their wise discourse and began to practice the yogic science of self-discipline and spiritual development. Anxiety became something he could conquer and control through austerity and self-discipline. He became adept at meditation, at knowledge of esoteric scriptures. His ability to maintain ascetic practices longer than any other monk won him a revered reputa-tion.

Yet after seven years of this disciplined practice, Siddhartha still felt troubled by anxiety. He could control it, but it always came back to per-turb his hard-won equanimity. He decided it was time to wage all-out war upon this terrible foe. He vowed to fast until he had conquered anx-iety and attained enlightenment. The other monks marveled at his courage and holy ardor.

After several weeks without food, sipping only a few drops of water a day, Siddhartha plunged into a deep depression. He looked at his body, once healthy and supple, now a skin-covered skeleton. He felt like an old man near death; weak and emaciated, he could no longer walk or even crawl. What had he done? He had devastated his family and destroyed his body—and for what? His meditations, his austerities, and his hours of reading holy scriptures and listening to wise gurus all had changed nothing. He still had a body, and now he was in pain and near death. He still had not found any answers to life's ultimate questions. He realized with a shock that his craving for peace of mind, his compulsion to find serenity, amounted to little more than a sophisticated spiritual version of the ordinary human propensity to escape from anxiety.

At that moment Siddhartha gave up—he surrendered to the Sacred Anxiety he had struggled against for so long. He lay in the forest, helpless, no longer able to move. Just then, a young woman from a nearby village, going to fetch water from the stream, spied his body lying on the ground. She saved his life by bringing water to his parched lips and feeding him a few grains of rice. Gradually, Siddhartha's strength returned, and he thanked the young woman.

When his fellow monks heard what had happened—that Siddhartha, instead of achieving enlightenment, had given up and succumbed to temptation—they lost their faith in him and deserted him. Abandoned by everyone and having failed in his supreme effort to conquer the anxiety of life and death, Siddhartha felt he no longer had anything left to lose. Finding a quiet spot under a spreading bodhi tree, he gave up trying to control his anxiety and decided to simply sit with it.

He sat under the bodhi tree. All his long-suppressed worldly desires returned to tempt him as visions of beautiful women, royal wealth, and power. And he sat with them and breathed. Then all his fears and anxieties assaulted him in the form of demons and attacked him mercilessly from all sides. And Siddhartha sat with them and breathed. Then he felt himself disappearing into a cold, black, bottomless abyss of infinite nothingness. Still he sat with nothingness and breathed it in. Suddenly, a blazing light, brighter and hotter than a thousand suns, appeared before him and he felt himself being consumed by it. Yet he continued to sit and breathe. Siddhartha had become one who, in Kierkegaard's words:

remains with anxiety; he does not permit himself to be
deceived by its countless falsifications . . . Then the assaults of

anxiety, even though they be terrifying, will not be such that
he flees from them. For him anxiety becomes a serving spirit
that against its will leads him where he wishes to go.[2]

What happened next is called enlightenment and must remain a mystery for each of us until we join Siddhartha and sit with our anxiety as he did. Siddhartha suddenly felt as though a veil were lifted, as though he had awakened from a sleep of a thousand lifetimes. He saw that Siddhartha did not exist, and yet that he had always existed. He saw that Siddhartha was nothing, and yet that he was everything. The walls that had always separated self from God, and life from death, collapsed into the stunning oneness of eternal life.

Siddhartha had found the courage to let the fire of anxiety rage until it burned itself out. Anxiety had consumed everything mortal, everything transitory in his being. What rose from the ashes of anxiety was the only thing in Prince Siddhartha that could not be destroyed: his eternal Buddha nature.

For the first time he was completely free from the underlying anxiety of existence and he felt an abiding sense of serenity and sublime happiness. He knew now that it was the illusion of being a separate self that created anxiety—he no longer experienced anxiety because there was no longer a separated self to experience it. Buddha had penetrated the wisdom of anxiety, and he smiled an eternal smile.

For many years Buddha shared what he had learned by teaching the Four Truths, the Eightfold Path, and the Middle Way to all who would listen. When his wife and son joined his spiritual community, a deep wound in his heart was finally healed. One day an admiring disciple asked him if he were a man or a god. The Buddha replied simply, "I am awake."

Buddha taught that all who were willing to practice awareness
could become enlightened. (The word *buddha* means, "one who
is awake.") If we listen to our anxiety in the right way, it will
wake us up. What we will awaken from is the illusion of suffering, separation, and death; what we will awaken to is eternal life.

SACRED ANXIETY AS A GUIDING ANGEL
WHO LEADS US TO SERENITY

In the extraordinary life of Buddha, we witness a living testament to the power of anxiety when rightly used. Jesus, too, did not become a spiritual teacher because he was blessed at birth with wisdom and serenity, but because he was blessed with anxiety, struggled with it, and finally surrendered to it as a guiding Angel who could lead him to God. His life, and the lives of Mohammed, Moses, and other spiritual luminaries, become far more relevant to us when we understand that they were human beings like us. They were formed in God's divine image, yet made of earthly flesh and blood. They struggled with anxiety, self-doubt, and the challenge of living in between heaven and earth. They courageously penetrated to the very nucleus of existence, triggering an explosion of light in the world's consciousness that continues to illuminate our world today.

There are many such examples in every culture. Black Elk, the great medicine man of the Sioux tribe, recalled the role of Sacred Anxiety in summoning him to his life's work:

> . . . And if the great fear had not come upon me, as it did, and
> forced me to do my duty, I might have been less good to the
> people than some man who had never dreamed at all, even
> with the memory of so great a vision in me. But the fear
> came, and if I had not obeyed it, I am sure it would have
> killed me in a little while.[3]

The lives of those who have gone before us teach us that no one is exempt from anxiety. Even for these great spiritual leaders, anxiety returned again and again, and each time they transformed it into serenity. They encourage us by their examples to take the time to sit with our anxiety when it comes and to offer it up to growth and to life. Their lives give our bruised hearts and wounded souls comfort. Our wounds are not signs that we are bad or guilty. Our wounds are the sacred openings through which grace can enter our lives.

MAKING THE TWO INTO ONE

We can begin to live with serenity in the Age of Anxiety when we accept that we live a double life every day, an outer life and an inner life. We live our outer life as a unique individual personality in a material world. Yet we also live as a soul, a non-self spiritual being who is universal and divine. We need to honor both lives, and to remember that each nurtures the other. In Siddhartha's life, we saw how the individual self could not become actualized until it was connected to the soul self. Only when we honor both can we make the two into one and become truly human.

We can honor our dual nature in daily life by practicing the Golden Rule: Do unto others as you would have others do unto you. The essence of the Golden Rule is that you and I are one. This is why it makes sense for me to relate to you and for you to relate to me with kindness, compassion, and love. Love is our natural tendency, though all too often Toxic Anxiety blocks its expression.

After we understand that taking responsibility for our own anxiety is the surest route to spiritual growth, our life path becomes much more clearly defined. We learn to recognize anxiety far more quickly and accurately than we have done in the past and then transform it into energy for evolution.

Understanding the crucial role anxiety plays helps us to grapple productively with the existence of evil. We have seen that existential evil is the refusal to face our own anxiety and that social evil is projecting our anxiety onto others. With this understanding, we bring the concept of evil, the antilife force, out of the exotic realm of terrorists and mass murderers and into our own hearts and minds. We begin to recognize its presence in our daily life—which is the only place we ever can battle against the forces of ignorance, unawareness, and willful arrogance. Facing and transforming one's own anxiety is the path of the spiritual warrior, the path of peace.

BOTH ANXIETY AND LOVE CALL US HOME

We have seen how anxiety, especially its sacred aspect, plays a vital role in guiding us to serenity. There are two reasons why we require its sometimes painful prodding: First, without misfortune and anxiety, we could easily become too entranced by what the Hindus call *maya,* the highly entertaining material world of the senses, and forever skim along the surface of life. Second, we need anxiety because we often feel too unworthy—or too proud—to allow divine love to enter our heart. George Herbert, the seventeenth-century metaphysical poet, evoked this strange resistance in his poem, "Love":

> *Love bade me welcome; yet my soul drew back,*
> *Guilty of dust and sin.*[4]

In his poem, "The Pulley," George Herbert explores the mysterious role anxiety plays in the divine plan for human salvation. God decided to allow humanity all his many treasures, but to withhold the jewel of inner peace. Human beings could have "beauty . . . honour, wisdom, pleasure," but they would also know restlessness, anxiety, yearning, and weariness.[5] In this way, if goodness and love did not lead people to God, then anxiety would guide them unerringly back to their source.

Anxiety is the back door to God's house. Love is the front door, but most of us feel too unworthy of love or too proud to admit we need it and we pass by that imposing and majestic entrance. But in his infinite compassion, God made a back door, so that if we missed the main entrance we could always find our way in.

Both love and anxiety search out everything in us and claim it for themselves. In the heat of passion, lovers seek out every inch of each other's body, demanding surrender to the power of love. God, too, is a lover who cries, "I want all of you," who keeps asking for more and more until there is nothing left of the separated self. What if we recognized anxiety as a passionate lover? God calls to us through anxiety as well as love. What would happen if we allowed the fires of anxiety to consume the house we call our personality and burn it completely to the ground? Kierkegaard reminds us that when a person surrenders to anxiety in the right way:

> Then anxiety enters into his soul and searches out everything and anxiously torments everything finite and petty out of him, and then it leads him where he wants to go . . . [Thus] the individual through anxiety is educated into faith.[6]

We can surrender to divine love and let it penetrate us; as in lovemaking, the pain of letting go of the self is compensated for by the joy of union. Or we can resist love and feel separate, which permits anxiety to gnaw at us—which eventually leads to seeking love's embrace. Throughout our lives anxiety and love work together, like the two hands of God, to draw us closer.

God wisely made a back door called anxiety so that, missing love we would find anxiety and enter in. Anxiety is God's gift to us, the universe's fail-safe plan for salvation.

NAIVE HOPE OR MATURE FAITH?

We began this adventure into anxiety with a glance backward at our origins in the Garden of Eden myth. We saw that eating the apple and receiving the divine gift of human consciousness was not our original sin against God, but God's original blessing upon us. We conclude our journey with a forward look, a vision of our destiny, our future.

Perhaps the most important question we have about our own life—and the one at the heart of every story—is, Will it have a happy ending?

Most of us struggle to have faith in the future. If we are to live with a joyful spirit in an Age of Anxiety, it is important to understand the difference between hope and faith. Although they appear to refer to similar attitudes, in reality they represent very different approaches to life.

To hope is to wish for a particular outcome; it is often contrasted with despair or cynicism. Although it is considered a positive emotion, hope suffers from the same limitations from which all versions of "having it our way" suffer: We hope that things will turn out a certain way. We wait anxiously and either are relieved when they do or devastated when they don't. This cycle, being hopeful that somehow things will be different this time, actually can serve to keep us trapped in our comfort zone. It represents a naive mode of thinking that requires the denial of realistic possibilities and, therefore, is doomed to alternate continually with anxiety, despair, and cynicism. This repetitive hope/despair cycle is a sad and ultimately self-defeating misuse of our capacity for true faith.

Faith, unlike hope, does not attach its positive spirit to particular outcomes. Faith is more than an emotion: It is an enduring attitude toward life. Faith may project a desired outcome, but it does not attach its inner serenity to that outcome. Ultimately, faith is trust in life itself. Hope is wishing that the results of a medical test will be favorable. Faith includes this hope but goes much deeper; faith consists in knowing that we will continue to love life and be one with life no matter what the circumstances.

Faith teaches that the universe of which we are each an integral part is ultimately an amazingly wonderful Being that is evolving toward some unimaginable state of conscious wholeness and harmony. Mature faith embraces the ebullient spirit of hope and the clear-eyed realism of despair and merges them into an unconditional trust in life.

Erik Erikson, in his study of human development, found that a sense of basic trust was the foundation for all other levels of human growth. Our sense of faith is too precious to be entrusted to the transitory and uncertain. Faith goes deeper and includes our sense of being part of something larger. Our small story and the universal story are one and the same. Each of us is helping to write that larger story. Faith is trusting that this great story has a happy never-ending ending.

LIVING WITH SERENITY IN THE AGE OF ANXIETY

In this Age of Anxiety, we frequently lack faith in the future and do not feel safe in the present. One of the most basic questions at all times in life is, Can I trust life? Am I safe? Anxious people in particular ask themselves this question constantly.

This question has a sacred dimension that is reflected in the revival camp preacher's searing question: "Brothers and sisters, are you saved?" Safety is the secular version; salvation is its spiritual counterpart. As we have seen in the stories of Janet, Bill, Carla, Kerry, Rachel, and others, underneath their temporal concerns lay a terrifying sense of living in an uncaring, mechanical universe or one presided over by a harsh, judgmental God.

Salvation, feeling safe in the world, depends upon feeling one with the wholeness of life. It goes to the core question, "Who am I?" Ultimately, am I this separated "I" who feels constant anxiety?

To be saved, we need to be made whole. We need to be reborn, first from discordant, conflicting parts into a mindbody wholeness and then from a whole, separate self into communion with others and reunion with God. Salvation is knowing we are safe forever: free to create and play, to work and love with the understanding that we are safe at all times. The poet Rainer Maria Rilke wrote about this intimate relationship between anxiety and feeling safe in the world:

> We have no reason to harbor any mistrust against our world,
> for it is not against *us*. If it has terrors, they are *our* terrors; if
> it has abysses, these abysses belong to us; if there are dangers,
> we must try to love them . . . Perhaps all the dragons in our
> lives are princesses who are only waiting to see us act, just
> once, with beauty and courage . . . You must realize . . . that
> life has not forgotten you, that it holds you in its hand and
> will not let you fall.[7]

We allow the earthly competition for position and resources to pit us against each other, but the quest for salvation does not bring us into competition with anyone. The true purpose of human community is to create a world in which we can all feel safe. If even one person feels threatened, then not one of us is truly safe. Salvation, though an individual responsibility, is also a collective endeavor. The reason world saviors such as Buddha and Christ come back to us is because they know that true salvation is universal salvation. Water cannot boil until every drop is heated.

To love life unconditionally is our greatest challenge. Serenity does not arise from the permanent absence of anxiety, but from the divine task of continuously transmuting our human anxieties into greater love. Love is the nature and essence of our universe, and "perfect love casts out fear."[8] Love is the secret to mastering anxiety and guides us unerringly to serenity.

Each time we transform our anxiety into love it furthers our spiritual growth and enables us to see life more clearly. Jesus, like Buddha, continually reminded his listeners that if only we would shed our illusions and become aware, we would realize that we already are saved, that we already are living within the kingdom of God:

> If the priests tell you that the kingdom of God is in heaven,
> then the birds will get there before you . . . Truly, the kingdom
> is within you, and all around you . . . [it] is spread out upon
> the earth, and people do not see it.[9]

From Jesus and Buddha to Moses and Mohammed, the world's spiritual teachers all direct our attention to the paradise of the present moment. We seldom see this heaven on earth because we gaze at the world through anxious eyes. Yet if we can embrace this anxiety, we will pass through it and into a new and resplendent realm where waking up in the morning is to be present at the dawn of creation and meeting another human being is to encounter God. Every age, even this Age of Anxiety, can become a Golden Age if we open our eyes and perceive life's invitation to evolution.

Writing this book has been my own next step in mastering my anxiety and, predictably, it has brought me new and more interesting forms of anxiety. But it has also brought me a sense of joy and serenity far deeper than I have ever experienced before. Not yet a resident, I am becoming a more frequent visitor to that blissful realm Jesus called the kingdom of God. On certain spring days I have breathed the sweet air of Eden. In the stillness of the night I have sometimes heard celestial music. I have glimpsed the radiance of the kingdom in a young child's face. I am not alone in this. You have seen it too. Perhaps one reason we share this earth is simply to remind each other of the sacredness of existence.

When we are willing to give up both our grandiosity and our escapism and work with the very real daily challenges of being human, we will find that we already have a paradise on earth— not a heavenly paradise free of problems, but an earthly paradise, where problems become opportunities for love and growth.

We can create a far happier home for ourselves on our planet if we become willing to take our crucial place in the universe. We are the meeting place, the connecting link between heaven and earth. Humanity is the tension between the finite and infinite; prayer, meditation, and meaningful community rituals enable us to live with awareness of our unique position in the cosmos. We embody the wholeness of the universe. The more Sacred Anxiety we can bear, the more wisdom and vitality we can bring to the task that Judaism calls *tikkun*—healing ourselves and our world into wholeness. The individual dimension of serenity can be experienced in solitude, but achieving serenity as a community, whether local or global, is something we can only do together.

We are living at the end of an era and before the beginning of another. Such times of transition are ideal opportunities, both in our personal lives and our lives as communities and nations, to embrace the anxiety of the unknown and go deeper, beyond the cultural forms and ideologies that divide us, deeper than ever before, to the source of life. Can we admit to each other that we are anxious and confused and that we don't have the answers to today's unprecedented challenges? Can we humbly open ourselves to each other and to spiritual guidance? Only then can the new age we are waiting for begin.

May you follow your anxiety and your bliss to find the serenity of living the life you were born to live. The universe is so wonderfully constructed that all paths lead home. Both love and anxiety stand ready to wake us from our troubled dream of strife and separation so that we may live in the paradise of the present moment.

Endnotes

Introduction

1. The case studies, clinical vignettes, and examples used in the book are based on the experiences of my clients and workshop participants. In all such instances, the names and identifying characteristics have been altered to protect confidentiality. The only exceptions to this are when I relate my own experiences or the documented experiences of public figures.

2. Throughout this book I use the word "God" to represent the ultimate reality which remains inaccessible to the intellect—the unfathomable, inexpressible mystery that encompasses the universe and the Higher Power that we human beings are often able to connect with through prayer and meditation. It is not used in any specific religious context, and readers are encouraged to interpret it in terms of their own belief systems.

Chapter One

1. Statistics derived from results of the National Comorbidity Survey, reported in "Lifetime and 12-Month Prevalence of Psychiatric Disorders in the United States," *Arch. Gen. Psych.*, 51 (1994): 8–19.

2. Dorothy P. Rice, Ph.D., and Leonard S. Miller, Ph.D., *Update of the Costs of Mental Illness in the United States,* (1997). Figures for the year 1994.

3. Ralph Waldo Emerson, "Self-Reliance," *Essays, First Series,* 1841.

Chapter Two

1. Shakespeare, *Hamlet.*

2. Sigmund Freud, "Twenty-fifth Lecture: Anxiety," trans. Joan Riviere, *General Introduction to Psychoanalysis* (New York: Pocket, 1953): 401.

3. Duke University study published in June 1996 *Journal of the American Medical Association.* This study was reported in an article entitled "Mental Stress Tests May Outdo Treadmill at Predicting Heart Trouble" that appeared in the *Boston Globe,* 5 June 1996, p. 6.

4. Alfred Adler, *Problems of Neurosis* (New York: Harper, 1929): 145.

5. Paul Tillich, *The Courage To Be* (New Haven: Yale University Press, 1952): 39.

6. Gen. 32:26.

CHAPTER THREE

1. This study was reported in an article entitled "People Long on Neuroticism Appear To Be Short on a Gene" that appeared in the *New York Times,* 29 November 1996, p. 1.

2. Gen. 3:6.

3. Gen. 3:7.

4. Gen. 3:5.

5. Ralph Waldo Emerson, "Experience," *Essays, Second Series,* 1844.

6. Gen. 3:10.

7. Paul Tillich, *The Courage To Be* (New Haven: Yale University Press, 1952).

8. Gen. 3:18–19.

9. Gen. 3:21.

10. Leonard Shengold, *Soul Murder: The Effects of Childhood Abuse and Deprivation* (New Haven: Yale, 1989): 2.

11. Gen. 4:8.

12. Gen. 4:7.

13. Exodus 20:4.

14. Exodus 20:3.

15. M. Scott Peck, *People of the Lie: The Hope for Healing Human Evil* (New York: Simon & Schuster, 1983).

16. Viktor E. Frankl, *Man's Search for Meaning* (New York: Simon & Schuster/Touchstone, 1984): 147.

CHAPTER FOUR

1. Several of the quotations and scientific studies cited in this section are referred to in an article, "What To Do About Stress," by John Carpi, which appeared in *Psychology Today,* January/February 1996.

2. Quoted in "Targeting the Brain," Judith Hooper, *TIME's Frontiers of Medicine Special Issue* 148.14, Fall 1996, p. 49–50.

3. Jon Kabat-Zinn, *Full Catastrophe Living: Using the Wisdom of Your Body and Mind to Face Stress, Pain and Illness* (New York: Delta, 1990).

4. There are many excellent self-help books available to individuals suffering from anxiety symptoms. Here is a small sampling of some of the best: Edmund J. Bourne, *Anxiety and Phobia Workbook,* 2nd ed. (Oakland: New Harbinger, 1995); R. Reid Wilson, *Don't Panic: Taking Control of Anxiety Attacks* (New York: Harper & Row, 1986); Reneau Z. Peurifoy, *Anxiety, Phobias and Panic: Taking Charge and Conquering Fear* (Citrus Heights, CA: Lifeskills, 1992); David Barlow and Michelle Craske, *Mastery of Your Anxiety and Panic* (Albany: Graywind, 1989); Jerilyn Ross, *Triumph Over Fear* (New York: Bantam, 1994); Susan Jeffers, *Feel the Fear and Do It Anyway* (New York: Ballantine, 1987).

In addition to conventional medical and psychological approaches, you also may want to explore alternative therapies such as acupuncture, hypnosis, neurolinguistic programming (NLP), Alexander technique, Feldenkrais method, mindbody counseling, homoeopathy, naturopathy, nutrition, herbal therapy, eye movement desensitization and reprocessing (EMDR), and others. As in any field, the quality of holistic practitioners varies tremendously, and consumers need to be informed and exercise good judgment.

The Anxiety Disorders Association of America (ADAA) is an excellent self-help organization and information resource [11900 Parklawn Drive, Suite 100, Rockville, MD 20852. Phone: (301) 231-9350]. The National Institute of Mental Health (NIMH) offers a free anxiety information packet to those who call (888) 8-ANXIETY.

5. See Daniel Goleman's highly readable and well-researched overview, *Emotional Intelligence* (New York: Bantam, 1995).

6. Daniel Goleman, *Emotional Literacy: A Field Report* (Kalamazoo, MI: Fetzer Institute, 1994): 2.

7. Howard Gardner, *Frames of Mind: The Theory of Multiple Intelligences* (New York: Basic, 1983).

CHAPTER FIVE

1. Rollo May, *Man's Search for Himself* (New York: Norton, 1953).

2. Rollo May, *Meaning of Anxiety* (New York: Norton, 1977): 256.

CHAPTER SEVEN

1. Sheldon Kopp, *If You Meet the Buddha on the Road, Kill Him* (New York: Bantam, 1976): 223–24.

2. Herbert Benson, *Timeless Healing* (New York: Scribner/Touchstone, 1996).

CHAPTER EIGHT

1. Some excellent books on meditation: David Harp, *New Three-Minute Meditator* (Oakland, CA: New Harbinger, 1990); David Fontana, *Elements of Meditation* (New York: Element, 1991); Daniel Goleman, *Meditative Mind: The Varieties of Meditative Experience* (Los Angeles: Tarcher, 1988); Joseph Goldstein and Jack Kornfeld, *Seeking the Heart of Wisdom: The Path of Insight Meditation* (Boston: Shambala, 1987); Jon Kabat-Zinn, *Full Catastrophe Living: Using the Wisdom of Your Body and Mind to Face Stress, Pain and Illness* (New York: Delta, 1990); Thich Nhat Hanh, *The Miracle of Mindfulness: A Manual on Meditation* (Boston: Beacon, 1976).

CHAPTER NINE

1. This fable was adapted from a traditional tale about Buddha.

2. Søren Kierkegaard, *The Concept of Anxiety,* ed. and trans. Reidar Thomte (Princeton: Princeton University Press, 1844/1980): 155–59.

3. Ralph Waldo Emerson, "Compensation," *Essays, First Series,* 1841.

4. Ralph Waldo Emerson, *Journals.*

5. Andrew Marvell, "The Definition of Love," in *Concise Treasury of Great Poems,* ed. Louis J. Untermeyer (New York: Pocket, 1958): 151.

6. Gretchen Reynolds, "Oprah Grows Up," *TV Guide,* 7 January 1995.

7. Ibid.

CHAPTER TEN

1. Ralph Waldo Emerson, "Compensation," in *Emerson's Essays* (New York: Harper & Row, 1926): 76.

2. Many years ago, I encountered the writings of Sheldon Kopp. Reading his books was like taking a cold shower; the sharp spray of his Zen-like wisdom helped wake me up and sent many of my illusions down the drain. The "Least Favorite Laws of Life" was inspired by his "Eschatological Laundry List." I recommend Sheldon Kopp, *If You Meet the Buddha on the Road, Kill Him* (New York: Bantam, 1976): 223–24.

CHAPTER ELEVEN

1. Helen Keller, *The Open Door* (Garden City, N.Y.: Doubleday, 1957).

2. Viktor E. Frankl, *Man's Search for Meaning* (New York: Simon & Schuster/Touchstone, 1984): 48.

3. "It Took a Mighty Big Jolt to Open My Eyes," *Parade,* 29 October 1995.

4. Ernest Becker, *Denial of Death* (New York: Free Press, 1973): 5.

5. Joseph Campbell, *Hero with a Thousand Faces* (Princeton: Princeton University Press, 1968): 19–20.

6. Ibid.

CHAPTER TWELVE

1. See such popular and helpful books as: Harriet Goldhorn Lerner's *Dance of Intimacy* (New York: Harper, 1989); Harville Hendrix's *Getting the Love You Want* (New York: Harper, 1990); Jordon and Margaret Paul's *From Conflict to Caring* (Minneapolis: CompCare, 1989); Gay and Kathlyn Hendrick's *Conscious Loving* (New York: Bantam, 1990); John Gray's *Men Are from Mars, Women Are from Venus* (New York: Harper-Collins, 1992).

CHAPTER THIRTEEN

1. From a Louis Harris poll conducted in February 1996. Reported in *Business Week,* 11 March 1996.

2. From a CNBC/Gallup Poll, "The American Dream," June 1993.

3. Michael Sandel, "America's Search for a New Public Philosophy," *Atlantic Monthly,* March 1996, p. 57–58. See his insightful book, *Democracy's Discontent: America in Search of a Public Philosophy* (Cambridge: Harvard University Press, 1996).

4. See Larry Dossey's *Space, Time and Medicine* (Boulder: Shambala, 1982) and Stephan Rechtschaffen's *Timeshifting: Creating More Time to Enjoy Your Life* (New York: Doubleday, 1996).

5. Psalm 118:24.

6. Joseph Campbell, *Primitive Mythology* (New York: Penguin, 1976).

7. Kurt Goldstein, *Human Nature: In the Light of Psychopathology* (Cambridge: Harvard University Press, 1940): 118.

CHAPTER FOURTEEN

1. Psalm 112:10, Prov. 9:10.

2. This is my adaptation of verse 2 of *The Gospel of Thomas*. Most translations use the word "troubled" in place of anxious, but the latter is a more psychologically accurate term. Two of the better translations are: Marvin Meyer's *The Gospel of Thomas* (New York: HarperSanFrancisco, 1992) and Thomas O. Lambdin's translation in *The Nag Hammadi Library,* ed. James M. Robinson (New York: HarperSanFrancisco, 1990).

3. Søren Kierkegaard, *The Concept of Anxiety,* ed. and trans. Reidar Thomte (Princeton: Princeton University Press, 1980): 155.

4. Poem 1323, *Complete Poems of Emily Dickinson,* ed. Thomas H. Johnson (New York: Little, Brown, 1960): 574.

5. Rudolf Otto, *The Idea of the Holy* (London: Oxford University Press, 1950): 15.

6. Plato, cited in Huston Smith, *The World's Religions* (New York: HarperSanFrancisco, 1991): 301.

7. Rudolf Otto, *The Idea of the Holy* (London: Oxford University Press, 1950): 16.

8. Bill Gates, quoted in Walter Isaacson's "In Search of the Real Bill Gates," *Time,* 13 January 1997, p. 57.

9. Adapted from James Legge's translation of the *Tao Te Ching of Lao Tzu* (New York: Dover, 1962), Chapter 15.

10. C. S. Lewis, *Miracles,* (New York: Macmillan, 1955): 114.

11. *National Catholic Reporter* 6 September 1996. Excerpted in "Monks in Overdrive," *Utne Reader,* February 1997, p. 32.

12. Matt. 5:45.

13. Matt. 7:1–2.

14. See the *Tao Te Ching* (also known as *The Book of the Way*). Various excellent translations are available including Stephen Mitchell's *Tao Te Ching* (New York: Harper Perennial, 1988).

15. Acts 9:2, 19:23, 22:4.

Chapter Fifteen

1. Eric Hoffler, *The Passionate State of Mind and Other Aphorisms* (New York: Harper, 1955).

2. Otto Rank, *Will Therapy* (New York: Knopf, 1936): 175.

3. Søren Kierkegaard, *The Concept of Anxiety,* ed. and trans. Reidar Thomte (Princeton: Princeton University Press, 1980): 155.

4. F. Scott Fitzgerald, *The Crack-Up* (New York: New Direction, 1956).

5. *Gospel of Thomas,* verse 106. My interpretation is based on the aforementioned translations.

Chapter Sixteen

1. In this retelling of Buddha's life, I have drawn upon traditional Buddhist tales, viewing them through a psychospiritual perspective.

2. Søren Kierkegaard, *The Concept of Anxiety,* ed. and trans. Reidar Thomte (Princeton: Princeton University Press, 1980): 159.

3. John G. Neihardt, *Black Elk Speaks* (Lincoln: University of Nebraska Press, 1961).

4. George Herbert, "Love," in *Immortal Poems of the English Language,* ed. Oscar Williams (New York: Pocket, 1952): 101.

5. Ibid, p. 100.

6. Søren Kierkegaard, *The Concept of Anxiety,* ed. and trans. Reidar Thomte (Princeton: Princeton University Press, 1980): 155–59.

7. Rainer Maria Rilke, *Letters to a Young Poet,* trans. Stephen Mitchell (New York: Random, 1984): 91–93.

8. John 4:18.

9. *Gospel of Thomas,* verses 3 and 113. My interpretation is based on the aforementioned translations. See also a similar verse in Luke 17:20–21.

To the Reader

Dear Reader,

I believe we all possess a portion of the collective wisdom of humanity, so please share your adventures in finding serenity. Share them with your friends, family, and co-workers. You may find it helpful to start a Serenity Circle to support each other in transforming anxiety into personal and spiritual growth. If you feel moved to do so, please write about your experiences and send them to me.

An audiocassette version of *Finding Serenity in the Age of Anxiety* is available at your local bookstore or from HighBridge Company (1-800-755-8532).

If you would like more information about lectures, workshops, consultations, and meditation tapes, contact me at the address below. Please include a large, self-addressed, stamped envelope with all correspondence.

May life bless you.
Robert Gerzon
P.O. Box 434
Concord, MA 01742-0434

Acknowledgments

This book would never have been written without the love and support of my wife, Christine. She has always been my "first reader" and the source of my inspiration. Her faith in me never wavered and she nourished my creative spirit with her own.

The process of transforming ideas into a book is one that cannot be done alone and I have many others to thank.

My father, Koert, read my first draft enthusiastically and perceptively, making many helpful comments and suggestions. He has taught me some valuable lessons over the years, among them: Life is an adventure and we are each the hero (or heroine) of our own life story. Always love life, even in the midst of the greatest anxiety.

My mother, Ina, taught me to have faith in things unseen, which has encouraged me to look beyond the visible and to listen to the silence. My siblings and my children have all contributed in unique ways to my understanding of both anxiety and love. My brother Mark, an author of many insightful books, gave generously of his support and experience.

A great deal of what I have written about in this book I have learned from counseling people who recognized the disturbing presence of anxiety in their lives; they journeyed with me to the realm of psyche and soul where our lives are truly lived. The participants of my Mastering Anxiety workshops at Harvard Community Health Plan and at Interface helped me to clarify and refine the concepts and techniques in this book. They inspired me with their willingness to face anxiety and provided living proof that using it in the right way could transform lives.

My agent, Nina Ryan, guided me through every stage of the book-making process; for her heartfelt commitment and magnificent support at crucial times I am very grateful.

My book, benefiting from a rare confluence of events, passed through the hands of three skilled editors. My original editor, Emily Heckman, was the first to grasp the vision of this book and was instrumental in giving it shape; I have greatly appreciated her continuing enthusiasm and support. John Michel not only edited the chapters, but also skillfully shepherded the book through the publication process. Sara Blackburn, an insightful freelance editor, helped to polish the manuscript.

Without the dedicated staff at Macmillan this book would not have found its way into your hands. Natalie Chapman, Jennifer Feldman, Kristin Sampson, and many others all contributed their skilled professional abilities in publishing, production, and marketing.

The ideas in this book owe much to the many men and women, today and throughout history, who have had the courage to ask, and offer answers to, life's most anxiety-provoking questions.

To everyone who played a role in making *Finding Serenity in the Age of Anxiety* a reality, my sincere thanks.

Index

About the Author

———————

ROBERT GERZON is a psychotherapist, writer, and lecturer with a background in psychology, holistic medicine, philosophy, and spiritual studies. His "Mastering Anxiety" program offered at Harvard Community Health Plan and other medical and educational centers has helped hundreds of people learn to transform anxiety into personal growth. He lives in the Boston area with his wife and children.